*The
Wind
in the
Oak*

The Wind in the Oak

MARTIN MUNCASTER

The Life, Work and Philosophy
of the Marine and Landscape Artist
Claude Muncaster

Robin Garton

LONDON · MCMLXXVIII

First published 1978 by Robin Garton Ltd.
9 Lancashire Court, New Bond Street, London, W1
Tel. 01-493 2820

Produced by
Richmond-Davies & Associates Ltd., London, WC2
and printed in England by
Gem Graphic Services, Didcot, Oxfordshire

I would particularly like to record my gratitude to H.R.H. Prince Philip, Duke of Edinburgh for his foreword to this book. My thanks are also due to Rear Admiral P. W. Brock, CB, DSO for his painstaking care in checking wartime information; Admiral Sir William Davis for his assistance in providing wartime illustrations; Captain John Williams and Alex Hurst for their helpful advice on the Horn chapter. No less important are all those who were kind enough to write to me with helpful corroboration of this saga.

CLAUDE MUNCASTER

Grahame Hall, son of Oliver Hall, R.A., changed his name to Claude Muncaster in 1922 when he was 18. This was to sidestep innuendoes that his father was helping with his paintings. As a child Claude Muncaster was known as "Gray" and he is referred to by this name in the first three chapters. When signing on for the Royal Naval Volunteer Reserve (Chapter 9) he had not then changed his name by deed poll which he did in 1945, and a number of paintings during the War are signed Lt. Cdr. Grahame Hall R.N.V.R., sometimes followed by Claude Muncaster.

When I refer then to my grandfather it is to Oliver Hall and when I refer to my father it is to Claude Muncaster.

M.M.

For Iona

CONTENTS

ILLUSTRATIONS

Talent seems to be one of the few human qualities which still defy scientific or statistical explanation. The talent of an artist is the most mysterious of all. The coordination of hand and eye and brain required to create an illusion on paper or canvas would appear to be such a normal human ability, yet the fortunate few can produce results which are unmistakably more pleasurable and impressive.

I do not think this quality will ever be explained satisfactorily, but for anyone interested in the creation of pictures there is a fascination in reading about the lives of artists. There is always the hope that somewhere a small clue may be discovered to explain their success.

All I can say is that I look at Claude Muncaster's landscape watercolours at Sandringham and Balmoral and the one big landscape in oils and I wonder in hopeless mystification just how he managed to do it. It is not that he just had a talent for applying paint, he had an unerring instinct for a subject and with some sort of secret antenna he was able to sense the atmosphere and then to incorporate it into the picture in a way which was uniquely his. Technique and observation obviously played their parts, but there is more to it than that. Attitude, experience, application; certainly, but in the end there is no other word for it than sheer talent.

1978

Chapter 1

Heir to a Vision

"The most important gift is the power of the mind to think and feel the beauty underlying all natural objects. We do not ponder sufficiently over things.

"The second part of our gift is the power through constant practice and hard work to be able to draw and paint the objects which most appeal to us. Having had all my life a great love of nature, and especially of trees, it has been my habit to study them at all times and at all seasons of the year.

"Nothing to me is more fascinating and enjoyable than to stroll out into the byways of an old forest, ruminating on and analysing the beauty of trees, noting their characteristics of form and colour and lines of composition. The play of sunlight and shadow, swept on a day of west wind in March, is very beautiful."

Oliver Hall, R.A., R.W.S., R.E.

My grandfather, Oliver Hall, was born in 1869, the son of a well-to-do Scottish business man. His early life was spent in a luxurious home at Tulse Hill, London. But in 1899 his father died leaving behind nothing of the family fortune, and it befell my grandfather to support his mother until she died at the age of ninety-eight. She had parked herself for a number of years on him and his young family. My father wrote in his diaries that he remembered his paternal grandmother as a helpless, complaining old lady, and that the remnants of the family's ugly Victorian furniture which she had brought with her were the bane of his mother's life.

Curiously enough, for one so artistic, my grandfather was not much concerned about the tastefulness of his immediate surroundings so long as they were simple. "Simplicity is the greatest art," he used to say, and both his work and way of life personified this maxim.

He was an honourable man, and an individualist of great integrity; remarkably humble before nature and the Almighty. I remember him as a tall, thin, slightly stooping old gentleman with a droopy, walrus moustache, the ends of which got wet when he drank soup – which he loved. My brother Clive and I were rather frightened of him and were on our best behaviour when he was about. His presence was well advertised because he smoked a dreadfully pungent pipe, using his own mixture which, to save money, included a twist of raspberry leaves from the kitchen garden.

His frankness could be devastating. One day, my brother gave us a concert of his own compositions in the sitting room. Clive played the violin, while a friend accompanied him on the piano. My parents beamed; Clive was only twelve. The concert ended and there was a hush while we awaited grandfather's verdict. He had been listening intently, standing and warming himself by the fire with his hands linked behind his back. "Prefer Brahms, m'self," he grunted. He could also be frighteningly severe. But he was capable, too, of deep emotion which balanced the sterner side of his nature. My father had the greatest respect for him both as a man and as a painter.

Strangely, my grandfather's parents seem to have been completely inartistic, and actually discouraged him from becoming an artist. Fortunately he did have one great ally and art adviser in D. A. Williamson, an uncle by marriage, who lived in the Lake District. It was almost certainly Williamson who was responsible for Oliver Hall's intense love of the North Country, and who instilled in him a reverence for nature and the old masters, which was in turn transmitted in full measure to Claude Muncaster.

As a family we always felt there was a link between my father's character and his birthday. He was born on July 4th, 1903, and of all the traits which made up his character, independence was one of the strongest. He would rather have it that he was just obstinate, and would remind us that obstinacy was not a particularly desirable quality. Nevertheless, in his own defence, I think he felt that being obstinate helped him to stick to his own unshakable convictions.

My grandfather believed completely in the power of beauty. He wanted his son to carry on the best traditions of British painting. My father told me that very soon after setting out as a professional painter, he had come to understand that beauty is a positive power for good. It was the responsibility of an artist to create beauty with every means in his power. "My one fear", he wrote shortly before his death, "is that I have failed to make the best of my inheritance, for it must be on this consideration that one is finally judged."

He had arrived in the world on that July day at the turn of the century, in a tiny house in Gay Street, West Chiltington, Sussex – in bad physical shape. He was born a cripple with feet twisted round the wrong way. This was a source of suffering and concern for his mother, and a considerable financial worry for his father, at that time a struggling artist who could ill afford the treatment needed to cure his new-born son's deformity.

With patience and determination my grandmother bandaged and massaged her son's misshapen feet and legs three times a day. She also had to make exhausting trips to London, and to save the expense of a pony and trap she would carry her young son across the fields to the station, three miles away. With persistence and the skill of the orthopaedic surgeon, the boy was walking more or less normally by the age of seven, and was able to throw away his leg-irons and surgical boots.

My grandmother was born Sarah Stephenson. Her mother had been a Miss Muncaster who had lived at Oxen Park, near Coniston, and married Willie Stephenson, a yeoman farmer in the fells south of Coniston Water. Willie was an open-hearted and generous fellow, but also a hard drinker and gambler which no doubt contributed to the parlous state of his bank balance. When he died, he left his wife penniless. The former Miss Muncaster had a heart of gold and, according to my father, a tenacity which carried her through all but insuperable difficulties. The young Sarah clearly inherited the best of these qualities, together with a poetry of soul and depth of understanding which surpassed even that of the sensitive artist she was to marry.

In later years, my father wrote of his closeness to his mother and of his gratitude to her. "Perhaps it was my disability which endeared me so much to her," he said. "She never failed me. I owe her much."

Soon after my father was born the family moved from West Chiltington to Woodruff, an ancient Sussex farmhouse in a hollow at Egdean, near Petworth. The only approach was down a narrow lane which was frequently ankle deep in mud. People thought twice before visiting the Halls, but these wild country surroundings provided my father's happiest childhood memories.

At Egdean with his brother Leslie, and later his younger brother Philip, he was part of a family in which art was a natural part of everyday life. There was nothing special about their father's work. It was a job just like any other. The fact that Oliver Hall, Royal Academician, was held in high regard by the art world generally quite passed them by. But the great man was now becoming renowned as an etcher, lithographer and painter on both sides of the Atlantic. He held several successful one-man exhibitions in London, and at the Leicester Galleries in 1917 sales amounted to over £635, a considerable sum in those days.

In 1914, my grandfather and his family moved from Woodruff to a house on the Leconfield estate in the charming little downland village of Sutton. With her husband frequently away on sketching trips it was far less lonely and more convenient for my grandmother, who had been ill largely as a result of bringing my uncle, Philip, into the world. My father painted the view overlooking woodlands and marshes to distant Chanctonbury many times in every kind of mood and weather. He wrote of that view: "It was a classical landscape with not a house in sight, and one which Claude Lorraine might have thought worthy of his genius."

Winter closed in on the family at Sutton even more icily than it had at Woodruff. Father slept in a tiny L-shaped room at the end of which stood a washstand supporting a basin and jug of cold water. Although the house was so cold he slept with his bedhead against the window sill so that he could watch the dawns and the sunrises, never twice the same.

Grandfather apparently was generous about keeping a good fire going in the dining room which doubled as a living room. But he stoked up the fire himself in case anyone else should be too liberal with the logs, and would light his pipe from it with spills made of twisted paper by the boys. It was their job to keep him supplied. He kept these lighters on the mantelpiece, together with his oil brushes which he stuck into an old brass shell case after he had cleaned them.

The house at Sutton, built originally in the early sixteen-hundreds, was primitive; lack of any up to date method of heating was only one of its deficiencies. It had to be lit by oil lamps, and the only water came from an eighty-foot-deep well outside the back door. My grandmother was terrified of it: she would not even lift the lid. One of my father's regular chores was to wind up a fresh supply of water from the well and transfer it to pails which then had to be humped to the kitchen.

In fact, the water from that antique well was cool, beautifully clear and good to drink, but so hard that to wash in it was like trying to use sea water. In hot weather the well shaft was used as a kind of fridge. One day the bucket inadvertently overbalanced, tipping out a whole week's supply of meat and butter. What happened to the water's purity after that isn't recorded.

As boys, Leslie and Grahame – or Gray, as my father was called – loved the life of the neighbouring farm. For the time being, it was halcyon days at home, and a happy innocence of the harsh realities of a world which would soon be going to war. They spent hours with the animals and with Puttick and his shaggy cart horses; riding on the waggons and bouncing on the stacked sheaves of corn as they were pulled over the stubble fields to the barn with the horse brasses glinting and jingling to the motion. There was also the threshing machine, which would come trundling down the lane to the farmyard with a hum of its spinning governor and fly-wheel.

"Don't worry, Mrs. 'all, we'll keep 'em away from tha' there drive belt!" Old Francis's Sussex drawl was re-assuring, but Mrs. Hall worried just the same. "That wheel thing's dangerous!", she'd warn. Mothers have a visionary way of foreseeing accidents.

But Francis, the driver, did allow the lads on to the footplate. He had enjoyed the threshing machine since boyhood. Its summer hum blended with the smell of warm oil, with the whirr of the long, undulating drive belt and the sound of the shooting steam. "Hiss, chuff. Hiss, chuff" it sounded in rhythm as the great iron fly-wheel whirred round and the stream of grain poured into the waiting sacks.

In those dusty summer days the sun seemed always to be shining.

Fly-fishing was one of my grandfather's passions, and although his son never approved he did not actually say so. He told me that my grandfather was so keen on fly-fishing in his younger days that when eventually it began to interfere with his work he broke his fishing rod across his knees.

Muncaster later confessed that as a boy he had tried to catch dace in the local stream with a bent pin on the end of a bit of string. But he didn't persevere. "I preferred," he said, "to lie on the grass to look down into the water and watch the fish swimming slowly around at the foot of the shrubs. But I could quite understand why my father loved fly-fishing in a fast flowing river like the Duddon in Cumberland where he also loved to paint."

He spoke vividly of these childhood memories. As is often the case, early memories move into sharper focus with the onset of age.

When he was nine Gray joined his brother, Leslie, at a preparatory school at Herne Bay in Kent, and began the long, hard years of being educated. He found himself at a school where the headmaster, a sadist who ruled by fear, took every opportunity, often quite inexcusably, to inflict pain on his pupils.

In this unhappy environment the young Grahame Hall was spared at least some misery because he was good at games and also had a fine singing voice. Unfortunately, when he was selected as soloist for the end of term concerts he was sick with nerves. This fear of appearing in public never left him. In fact, in later life it got worse.

It was a happy chance that saved him from the headmaster's uncontrollable temper. The headmaster had the same name as one of the great old masters and was convinced that his own talent for painting was of equal stature. His subjects consisted of lurid sunsets over strawberry-jam moors. Gray, with commendable vision, asked to be allowed to try and copy some of these works. Not only was the man flattered by the boy's interest but pleased with the copies he produced. Thus Gray tended to escape the punishment meted out to others even though they were far better scholars than he. At the end of one term he was singled out for a good conduct medal, which could not have endeared him to his colleagues.

But the copying arrangement came to an abrupt end. After a few terms the headmaster's promising artist pupil proudly showed some of his handiwork to his father who was absolutely horrified. Grandfather must have written to the headmaster forthwith, as his son was not asked to do any more copies.

During the holidays it was back to a happy life of family and of long carefree hours on the farm. The Hall breakfast always began by my grandfather reading from some favourite anthology of verse or prose; then grace, before the boys could attack their cooling porridge. They were permitted a small portion of golden syrup with it and a careful ration of one spoonful of milk.

"Don't take more than your share!" he would comment fiercely. Economy was always the watchword with my grandfather. In fact, he would have seemed mean to anyone who did not know his circumstances. When he did indulge in a bottle of ale or stout he rationed himself to one glass. When the remainder came back flat the next day he fizzed it up with a spoonful of salt.

Religion in the Hall home was strict. Grandfather was a Swedenborgian and my grandmother Church of England with a strong Chapel background. The two faiths seemed to rub along together all right and never caused friction. The boys attended Matins at Fittleworth Church every Sunday, and the Children's Service at Egdean on Sunday afternoons. Leslie and Gray liked the Vicar, the Reverend Lyne and his pretty, gay wife. She was kind to the two boys, taking them for drives in her pony trap, wrapping a warm fur rug around their knees. Leslie fell helplessly in love with her, and when she caught scarlet fever and had to go away, he made up a rhyme and drove the family mad by repeating it over and over again.

Although the boys liked the Vicar and his wife they were frightened of the Rector. He shouted when he preached and gesticulated violently, one day catching his surplice alight with the pulpit candle. This seemed to aggravate his tempestuous manner rather than moderate it. Life had its excitements.

Gray had no particular ambition to become a painter. He had rather set his mind on being a sailor. On the odd occasion he tried his hand at drawing in a small way, but with no more success than any other child of similar age. Once he tried to copy a part of a farmhouse which his father had painted, finding it quite beyond him. He began to see that to draw and paint as Oliver Hall did was truly remarkable.

On a rare outing to Littlehampton, Gray had his first sight of a sailing ship. The impression it made on him is recorded in his diary.

"I will never forget standing on the pier and watching a sailing ship going to sea in the wake of a tug. She passed very close and we could hear the seamen singing out at the ropes. Many feet were up aloft and men were lying out on the yard-arm unfurling the sails. I watched spellbound. At length her sails were set, the wind filled them, and she sailed away over the horizon for distant lands. I vowed I would sail in a ship like that, right away round to the other side of the world just to see what it looks like. In the meantime, I was content to climb the struts of the barn door, imagining them to be the yards of a sailing ship."

It was probably because of his early disability that Gray tended to be something of a recluse. He was teased about this and called Little Professor because he was often to be seen with a large picture-book under his arm, trotting off to a secluded corner where he could be alone to study it. "I really preferred to study the blue heavens", he wrote. "I lay on my back on the lawn and wondered whether it was the puffy white clouds which moved, or our Elizabethan farmhouse. I was too young to realise at what speed the world was in fact revolving."

One of the better things about his preparatory school was the half-term outings. It was during one of these, when he was eleven, that we find a clue to his innate eye for a picture. It also demonstrates his feeling for romance and poetry which was the source of much of his inspiration. Later he recorded this outing to Chatham Dockyard and Rochester Castle.

"We arrived at the Castle in the late evening and immediately climbed to the top whence there was a magnificent view over the river. I withdrew from my companions for a few moments and quietly contemplated the scene. Dusk was upon us and the Medway reflected the golden light of the western sky. A sailing barge, her brown sails dark against it and her green starboard light burning brightly in her shrouds, drifted lazily down on the tide. Lights flickered on the water. A London-bound train rumbled over the bridge and as the fireman opened the fire-box to refuel, the red glow illuminated the white smoke. A slight mist hung over the distance shrouding the river and landscape and city in a romantic world of make-believe. What I beheld so fired my imagination that I determined that one day I would be a painter and paint pictures of scenes just like this." But it was not to be until the later stages of his public school days at Cranbrook that he began to draw and paint to any degree.

The rigours of the First World War were reflected in attitudes to education. At my father's school, for instance, it was considered important that academic advance should be regular, and any drop in form order at the end of the week was met with corporal punishment. Even though he earned precious few marks for mathematics or science, and feared for the weekly form-order results, artistic gifts came once again to the rescue. Some of the boys began to take quite an interest in the drawings young Hall was producing. It occurred to him that he might, after all, make use of the gifts he did have. An agreement was struck. He would get his maths done in return for maps and copies of well known pictures such as Landseer's "Monarch of the Glen", or even beautiful Indian maidens. The scheme worked quite well up to the time of his Junior Cambridge exams. These he managed except for the maths papers in which he was unable to answer a single question. But worse, he only just scraped through the drawing examination. He had been given the outline of a kettle to draw but thought he could produce a much better picture of a kettle than the one represented on the question paper, and proceeded to embellish his creation with all manner of subtle lights and shades. Alas, it bore little resemblance to the one he was supposed to be copying.

Grahame Hall had to admit that his heart was just not in it when it came to school and paper-work. As he reported in his memoirs, "I was neither a good nor keen scholar, and preferred watching the trees waving in the wind and the changing skies above them to giving any concentration to the blackboard or exercise book. I adored the sunlight and shadow and the whirling snowflakes in winter. I wanted desperately to be out among nature, observing her and painting her."

At last, my grandfather got the message. He decided it was uneconomical to throw away more of his hard-earned money after bad, and took Gray away from the school at the age of fifteen. Since he clearly had some propensity for drawing, he launched his son into a career as a landscape painter. He insisted on doing this himself at the outset, saying that art schools were a waste of time. Nature was to be the model and he would be the professor. My father accepted this arrangement with equanimity and conscientiously submitted everything he did to his father for criticism. But it was to prove a tremendous strain on the relationship between them. Grandfather was a stern and uncompromising critic, and did nothing to spare his young pupil's feelings. Indeed, my father spoke of this to me time and again so it must have made a deep impression. "I dreaded my father's criticisms", he said, "and when he pulled to pieces some study into which I had put my all, often I was reduced to tears and left his studio convinced that I would never excel as a painter."

In the neighbourhood at around the time Grahame Hall was setting out on his career there lived a little coterie of artists including Estall, Edward Stott, Arthur Rackham, Charles Sims, P. H. Padwick, Vicat Cole, Stratton and Clarkson. Oliver Hall seemed to be the leader of this group, and his family thought him quite the best painter. Padwick was the most prolific. He saved himself much time by refusing to draw. I gather my grandfather often used to remark, "if that chap Padwick would only draw, what a master he would be."

Several of the group were most helpful and interested in the progress of young Grahame Hall. The conversation at home usually centred round the affairs of the art world, so a great deal of general knowledge could be picked up on the subject just by being a good listener. There was, on the whole, dislike of the Post Impressionists and the Moderns, and "those two chaps Cezanne and Van Gogh" did not go unscathed. The Royal Academy was upbraided or esteemed, according to whether an artist's work had been rejected or hung. My father listened intently to it all, weighing up his own opinions.

But he had no doubts when it came to discussion about the great traditions of the early English painters, and was fully in sympathy with unadulterated praise of the Norwich School, the Barbizon School and the Spanish and Italian painters. During holidays from school, he had been set to copying works by Cotman, Cox, de Wint, Constable, Turner and Crome and felt that he was thus becoming equipped for his own ideal, "to carry on the best traditions of English painting".

He did, of course, have a great deal to learn and, clearly, my grandfather thought so too. He decided he should give his son a few lessons to teach him something about the craft of watercolour painting. Father was absolutely delighted; and during lesson one, a demonstration of how to tackle a piece of foliage and sky, he watched the old man with awe. Indeed, as the lesson progressed and the paint started to flow with such mastery from the brush, he was deeply moved. But soon his feelings got the better of him and he found himself having somehow to release the emotion. Should he laugh, or cry? In the event, the noise that came out sounded very much like a laugh and my grandfather completely misunderstood its meaning. How could his son take the important business of learning so lightly? Furious, he snapped his colourbox shut and threatened, "all right my boy, if you can't take this thing seriously, I'll have to apprentice you to some machine shop."

The lesson had lasted barely ten minutes, and there was never to be another.

* * *

The first Grahame Hall studio was just ten feet by six, a conversion from the old playroom. It had been good for trains, but scarcely served for a serious landscape artist. The small west window was partially obscured by trees, and the few struggling shafts of daylight only just sufficed for painting even on the brightest day.

The room had a brick floor with some coconut matting for covering. Through the long winter days a little warmth shimmered reluctantly from a well-used paraffin Valor stove. At least the studio was small, so the temperature reached the tolerable a good deal earlier than in the other rooms of the gaunt, perishing cold homestead.

In the evenings, an Aladdin lamp served for lighting, but often through a blackening haze. The artist, off into one of his reveries or absorbed in writing, was usually lazy about tending the wick of the stove. The half-burnt paraffin smelt strongly. There were things my father noticed and others that seemed not to bother him. So the Valor just smoked. It clearly didn't sicken him as his father's pipe did. Perhaps the lack of raspberry leaves had something to do with it.

Although his studio was inconvenient in every way, father became quite attached to it and painted busily there for more than a year. Then he began to work on larger canvases and found himself badly in need of storage space for equipment. He looked around, and came upon what he wanted in the Rectory just up the road. With a bit of persuasion, he got the Rector's wife, Mrs. Newman, to agree to let him rent an attic room she was not using.

Daylight was again at a premium. The room faced north, which admittedly was an improvement, but the tall chestnut and copper beech trees nearby overshadowed the window and very little of the precious light actually penetrated into the studio. Indeed, the artist often found himself having to work on the window-sill to catch what illumination there was. But at least he was alone – happy, too, to have put some distance between himself and his father.

Though my grandfather's strictures on his artist son had included insistence on hard work, he did make it clear from the beginning that for a balanced life he should play hard too. It had been sound advice, but play came rather more easily than work. He also swung in and out of love as easily as he drove a golf ball off a tee. It was always platonic, he assured us. It started at about the age of twelve, when he fell violently for the post girl who had a lovely smile. He longed to prove to her how clever he was by showing her some of his sketches.

Some while later, when staying at Bardsea, he became captivated by his grandmother's daily, a fisherman's daughter who was tall, blonde and really very pretty. "Unknown to me, she had a certain reputation. But I would not have understood this, nor would I have believed it had I been told."

Then destiny pulled a few fresh strings and the lovesick artist transferred his affections to a local private secretary five years his senior. It was no longer love at a distance. This was the real thing, or so he thought; when she suggested marriage he readily agreed. Thus, he had a fiancée while he was still only seventeen. They kept it to themselves for nearly two years, after which it became official.

He was also a fair hand at golf and later became a scratch player, but before he reached such heights he was to be thankful simply for the game itself. While staying at Bardsea, he was invited to join in a mixed foursome. "By the end of the round, my partner had set my heart a-fluttering, and I realised that I was not nearly as deeply in love with my fiancée as I had imagined. I broke off the engagement and was sensible enough not to repeat such folly."

* * *

The Rectory studio, in all its gloom, seemed however to be having the desired effect. Work of noticeable calibre began to emerge from it, and suddenly Grahame Hall had his first sale. A friend of his father's in the village bought a little pencil study of an ash tree and ivy. "He paid me half a guinea, and I felt a millionaire."

This first sale was effected on the third of July 1919, the day before his sixteenth birthday. By the end of the year, several other Grahame Hall works had been sold for a total of six pounds and thirteen shillings.

The next year he was to have two works accepted by the Royal Academy which in those days, to a young beginner, was the summit of success. His father sent him a telegram: "Congratulations. Two watercolours on the line."

The financial record of the first few years' sales is of some interest:

1920	£44 – 2 – 0
1921	£30 – 9 – 0
1922	£31 – 10 – 0
1923	£122 – 7 – 0
1924	£132 – 5 – 0
1925	£226 – 13 – 0

These figures were scarcely world shattering, even for those days when money had such a very different value. But the graph was looking hopeful. His work was becoming quite well known and the income from sales allowed for travel. But there was one major cause of friction. With success, he became increasingly aware that his painting was being judged against that of his father. Artist acquaintances who had been most friendly and helpful while in his teens now began to drop hints that they knew who was doing Grahame Hall's homework for him. Indeed, one day he was told it to his face.

He was infuriated by this as it was totally untrue. He had always striven to be independent, and was determined to establish his own identity. Early in 1922 he therefore decided to adopt a *nom-de-plume*. He chose the family name of Muncaster and added to it the name of one of the old masters whose work he so much admired and respected. Thus Grahame Hall became Claude Muncaster, and comparisons with his father's work magically faded.

With his new name, he went off in the summer of 1922 on a painting visit to Portsmouth. Although he was so much in love with nature, my father also had an urge to record contemporary life. He felt strongly that this was very much part of a representational artist's work. Smoky industrial subjects and ships fascinated him – especially ships, which were to become a lifelong interest.

Being essentially a naval port, not many merchant ships of any size docked in Portsmouth. But there was a wealth of interest in the assortment of vessels in the Camber or berthed at the Hard, sailing craft, coastal steamers, barges, all of which provided subjects.

One sunny morning, well before the dockyard 'maties' were swarming on to the quays, he was delighted to come upon the Norwegian barquentine *Roma* discharging a cargo of pulpwood. Immediately he set about making a careful pen and colour-wash drawing of her from astern. "I had nearly completed the picture" he wrote "when her Scandinavian mate who had been looking over my shoulder for some time volunteered a suggestion. 'Dat's good', he said, 'but you not paint de whole sheep dat vay. You go for'ard now and see de sheep from dere, and feenish her so'. I laughed. 'I can't paint the ship from both sides at once.' 'Why not?', said the mate. 'It make good picture so. Everything in'. But modern abstract painting was unknown to me then."

Some delightful work survives from his spell at Portsmouth which gives an idea of the days when commercial sail was still much in evidence. Even though at that time he knew very little about the workings of ships' rigging, he found it fascinating to draw. A note exists about the *Emmanuel* which he drew alongside in the Camber: "She was a challenge. I enjoyed dissecting her, as it were, and tracing out where each rope led from and to; trying to see its significance, for I was sure that no rope would be without a purpose." He later made a delightful etching of the subject; as he did of the barquentine *Roma*.

The Scandinavian mate remained oblivious of the fact that the painter who had caught his eye hated being watched while he was at work. It upset him completely, so much so that, as children, Clive and I were barred from the studio – I was really quite frightened even to knock on the door when I was bearing some urgent message from my mother. There were, though, special occasions like Christmas Eve when the barrier came down. Then father used to paint a picture specially for the boys and he would talk his way through as he worked. It was always something out of his head. One year he painted us a romantic night harbour scene, an old sailing ship being escorted out past the pier by a tug, with the lighthouse and beacon at the harbour entrance winking their warning lights seaward. We were enchanted. It certainly added to the magical anticipation and excitement of Christmas. It became even more evocative when he cut out the ship's navigation lights with his mounting knife, made windows in the lighthouse lanterns, and punched holes in the sky for stars and in the water for the reflections. Then he backed the holes he had made with different coloured crêpe paper; red and green for the navigation lights, and yellow for the sky and harbour lights. When the finished picture was held in front of the table lamp it came to life.

During the winter months which followed he set himself the task of painting a really difficult dockland subject which included an overhead crane. It was tricky enough to draw, but to carry it out in detail in oil meant a huge effort. The 22 by 28 inch canvas was larger than he usually tackled at that time, but he completed it and sold the picture to Mrs. Kerr, the local doctor's wife, for seventeen guineas.

The Portsmouth experience had been useful. It was the first time he had been away on his own and it helped him to stand on his own feet. It also brought some badly needed artistic development which prepared him for big industrial subjects which were to come later.

Meantime it was back to the country and nature. It was always his practice to paint in watercolour as far as possible on the spot. In the early days he walked many miles to his subjects carrying his gear. Then he acquired a bicycle and went about with his equipment strapped to the handlebars as his father had done. This had the advantage of allowing him to pass the time of day with other people as he journeyed the by-ways, and brought him into closer contact with the landscape that surrounded him. He loved too the poetry of natural sound, undisturbed by the explosions of the internal combustion engine.

On one of these quiet excursions he had a strange experience. It happened that while he was painting the outside view of the tiny and isolated Barlavington Church in West Sussex, while he heard some beautiful organ music, which continued. Wanting a break, he went into the church to listen and was astounded when he got inside to find that there was no music, no organ playing. The place, in fact, was deserted and the organ console well and truly locked.

above: Practising golf at Sutton, mid-1920s: Oliver Hall (right) and Claude Muncaster.

below: Making an etching. Muncaster watching Oliver Hall at work in the studio at Sutton.

Two views of Hardham Mill at Pulborough in 1919, when the artist was sixteen: *watercolours*.

Oliver Hall had bought himself a Zenith motor-cycle and sidecar. Surprisingly, considering their sometimes strained relationship, father and son began to set out together on sketching trips.

These excursions were not without dangers. Oliver was entirely lacking in road sense and would fly round corners and across 'T' junctions without slackening speed or so much as a glance to right or left. That he did not meet with an accident, even in those days, was something of a miracle, or due to the considerable skill of other road users.

A Zenith was fitted with what was termed a "gradual gear". This consisted of an adjustable flanged pulley around which rode a rubber belt attached to the back axle. As the gear handle was moved across to the right, so the flange narrowed, the belt rode higher, and greater speed was achieved. If the belt got wet, however, the device was useless.

At Sutton End, down the road from the family home, there used to be a ford. Returning from Petworth with his mother aboard one rainy morning, Hall observed that the water had risen considerably since going through it on his way out. So small a detail as water in full spate deterred him not in the least. He tore on at speed and drove into the ford, with spectacular displacement of the floodwaters. The belt was instantly affected and the machine came to a bumpy halt in midstream. His mother had far more confidence in horses and carts anyway, and in recounting the incident afterwards described how "some water got into the engine and put the fire out."

Eventually my grandfather graduated to a baby Austin and my father took on the Zenith. He had a number of spills when driving solo because the balance was wrong, but he came to no serious harm. However, when he came off on a frosty road and sprained his wrist, his doctor advised that the hands of an artist should be carefully preserved and that he should buy a car. Out went my father, like Toad of Toad Hall, and proudly bounced home in a second-hand Salmson sports car. He never was good at judging a bargain. In no time the thing had cost him much more than its price in repairs.

He traded it in for a little MG, one of the first of its type on the road, so he said. His bank balance never levelled up again. But to the outside world the car gave him status.

On the first visit to London in 1923 he stayed at Campden Hill with Mr. and Mrs. Rex Vicat Cole, who were great friends of his parents. Vicat Cole, with Byam Shaw, had founded the Byam Shaw School of Art which still flourishes today. Father thought it one of the best in London. Although Oliver Hall made plain his view that art school for a landscape painter was a sheer waste of time, Rex Vicat Cole, understandably, had other ideas. At last young Muncaster was prevailed upon to attend a life class where he admitted to setting his eyes for the very first time on a nude female. He swore that it made no impression on him at all other than a purely artistic one, and that as a subject the nude was quite beyond his abilities. By tea time he had packed up and set off for the Pool of London.

As an artist, Claude Muncaster might have benefited from a closer study of the make-up of the human figure. He never did any portraiture, but often introduced figures into his works, mostly in a rather free way, suggesting form rather than giving them any detail. Usually this worked well, particularly in watercolour, as the dockers, sailors or bystanders were really incidental and placed there to give scale or balance. But when he was forced to introduce people into a picture because of a particular commission or because figures were important to the nature of the subject, I felt they did not always ring quite true. On the positive side, however, I think it was surprising that he painted crowd scenes as well as he did. Sometimes, they really 'came off', to use his own expression. The packed tiers of the glittering congregation at the Queen's coronation in 1953, for instance, which he sketched in the Abbey and later painted in oil, portrayed the essence of that unique occasion well.

But in those early days in London he found working outside a considerable strain. Not only was he constantly the focus of attention wherever he set down his sketching stool, but he had to cope with the frustrating business of overcoming bureaucratic red tape. To get to the vantage points on piers and wharves that interested him, he had to have the requisite passes. These sometimes took some getting. He recorded his first such attempt when he had to present himself at the Port of London Authority offices on Tower Hill. Quite apart from feeling daunted by the immensity of that massive building, he was not in the least put at ease by the smartly polished commissionaire on the door who eyed with suspicion this young intruder in sports jacket, baggy grey flannels and brown brogues, with a haversack over his shoulder and carrying a package something like a camping kit. He placed his assortment of equipment on the floor beside him and diffidently came to the matter of a permit.

The commissionaire, ruddy faced, issued an order. "Wait here, if you please. Mr. . . . er . . .?" "Muncaster. Claude Muncaster."

With as casual an air as he could muster, Mr. Muncaster settled himself into a black, horse-hair chair to await events.

By now, a busy office staff behind a hundred desks had become staringly aware of the new arrival who was feeling conspicuous in that starched, high-collared community. A few minutes more of the treatment and he would have fled, and damn the permit. A voice broke the tension. "Ah. There you are, Sir. I think you'll find that's all in order. But perhaps you'd like to glance through it, just in case."

A quick inspection revealed, however, that the form was made out to Mr. Lancaster. The artist hesitantly pointed out that his name was, in fact, Muncaster. Immediate apologies from the clerk, and an invitation to wait just a few moments. More embarrassing stares – for five, ten minutes. Back came the permit, this time made out in the name of – Mr. Manchester. More profuse apologies and an even longer period to endure scrutiny by the staff. To an extremely shy artist, as he most certainly was as a

The clerk came hurrying back at last, a trifle pink and puffed, and presented the form for the final time. 'Newcastle' had now been substituted for the name 'Manchester'! At that point he accepted defeat.

So, through all that summer, 'Mr. Newcastle' sketched the Port of London Authority Docks and its colourful river traffic.

Chapter 2

Ladders and Galleries

Claude Muncaster, complete with his permit, soon found that Campden Hill was quite a march from the subjects he had really come to London to paint and decided to stay somewhere closer to dockland. Being a lover of Dickens he elected to book himself in to the 'George' in the Borough which is so famously associated with that classic author. The charges for the 'George' were beyond the means of a struggling student artist but he reckoned he could manage somehow on half rations. He'd had good training in frugal living after all, and money would come from somewhere. He was as much a born optimist as his father was an inveterate pessimist.

One morning because the weather was so foul that it was useless to try to work on any subject outside, he decided to paint a picture of his bedroom. He was rather proud of the result and went downstairs to show it off to his landlady. But she threw up her hands in dismay. "Lawks" she cried, "are my curtains as dirty as that?" The artist considered his masterpiece for a moment and replied that he thought he'd painted them as he'd seen them.

The weather cleared and out he went. When he returned that evening to look through his folio in the bedroom he noticed that beautifully clean curtains now hung at the windows. There was a brand new coverlet on the bed and even a mat on the floor. True representation clearly had its rewards.

There is no doubt that Bankside and Hays Wharf on the south bank of the river provided the greatest wealth of subjects. He had been there once before as a boy when his parents had visited a nephew, Samuel Teed, who was taking up painting professionally and had a studio there. He wrote, "the view from the window overlooking the river fascinated me. The tide was high at the time and Thames traffic was thronging by, lighters, sailing barges with their masts un-stepped for shooting the bridges, and tugs with smoke belching from their gaily marked funnels. Immediately opposite rose St. Paul's. One could hear the tug sirens, the shouts of the bargees and longshoremen, the whistles of the trains, the clopping of hooves and the clamour of drays."

Certainly the painted record that Claude Muncaster made keeps alive something of the atmosphere of the period. Time, the ravages of War and a completely new concept in architecture have wiped away the character of a river life that inspired so much fine painting.

It was from that same spot on Bankside, which he had visited as a boy, that he worked a detailed pen and wash drawing introducing the warehouses opposite and the majestic edifice of St. Paul's. The dome of St. Paul's is difficult to draw, but in that case he considered he had mastered it. Henry Rushbury, R.A., who was staying near Sutton at the time, thought otherwise. He remarked that it was quite obvious that the artist had been "holding on to his back teeth when he was drawing that dome", and advised him to go back and have a look at it again to see where he had gone wrong. My father sold the picture, nevertheless. Forty years later he bought it back in a sale and, remembering Henry Rushbury's criticism, studied the dome critically. But he could find very little amiss. Later on, the picture was purchased by Alistair McAlpine who had his office on the very spot from which the drawing had been worked all those years before.

After dark the river had a most romantic appeal for an artist. Father frequently went down to Murrel's Wharf on Bankside and tried to do watercolours by the light of street lamps, where any stood more or less in the right place. He worked in the early dawn, too, sometimes finding refreshment with a cup of tea and a sandwich at some street stall along with night workers and wharfingers. They were a friendly crowd, some real characters among them. One he named The Lyrical Night Watchman who replied in rhyme to everything said to him. A simple "good evening" drew this remarkable reply:

"Good evening to you, Sir,
Good evening to you.
The sun is a-shining
The ships are on view.
There's a barge in the offing,
I hear her mate coughing,
His wife's down below cooking vegetable stew."

This kind of thing came spontaneously and was entertaining – for a time. But a sensible question never provoked a straightforward answer. This was a pity as the man possessed a fund of local knowledge which could have been invaluable to an artist looking for subjects.

One evening a crane driver, who had been watching from a distance for some time, came up to the painter, looked over his shoulder and remarked, "That's a nice view you've got there, Guv. But I can show you a better." "Oh. Where?" "From the end of my jib up there. I'm just goin' up to grease 'er. Like to come?"

This invitation to view the panorama of the surrounding scenery was reluctantly declined. The artist explained that he had no head for heights.

"All right, Guv. What abaht the roof o' the ware'ouse? Easy climb, wonderful view!"

This suggestion seemed fair enough. There would be stairs of some sort inside the warehouse. Not so. The way to the roof was by way of a rather rusty, outside ladder. The view was well worth the climb. It was tremendous, and the crane driver was promised that it would make the subject for a big picture some day. "Well, it's all yours, Guv. Any time. But all good things 'ave to come to an end, as they say. We'd best get down on deck again."

He returned to the wharf the following evening after dark, to get some more slants on dockland scenery at night. But it was not long before he was thinking again of that view from the top of the warehouse. It must be even more exciting by night. Why not have a look? He climbed up. The ladder shook a little, but that was to be expected. He relaxed on the roof and drank in one of the most thrilling and romantic sights he had ever seen. Inspiration began to flow. Just go down to collect some painting things and he could come back and do a sketch. But the ladder, with a single hand? He would be gripping his gear with the other.

The more he dwelt on the precariousness of the situation, the more apprehensive he became. Suddenly he was overcome by a nauseating terror, accompanied by a cold sweat and violent trembling. It was no longer the thought of struggling back up that was troubling him. First he had to get down. Paralysis set in. The very idea of having to climb over that parapet and get a foothold on the rungs of the ladder sticking up thinly in the dimness froze him. Reason vanished. He would be up here for ever. Stuck. Alone. Nobody missing him, perhaps for days.

This agony of anticipation lasted quite some time until, with a huge effort of will, he regained enough self-control to make a move. He got down on to his hands and knees and crawled gradually along the gutter alongside the parapet. At least he could not fall over while he kept low and had the parapet's protection. Reaching the ladder at last he groped for the iron supports, his hands gripping the rough iron so that his trembling set the ladder shaking in its bolts.

Eventually he forced himself to put a leg over the edge of the parapet and got a foothold on the topmost rung of the ladder. Then, summoning a last fragment of will power, he worked over the other foot to the rung below. Slowly, slowly, the ladder rattling with every movement, he lowered himself down from the heights to the ground with an overwhelming sense of relief.

It is fascinating to look at those studies and sketches of the London of the early 1920's. They show the determination of the artist. He would attempt anything and everything; every angle, every aspect of ships, barges, tugs, sails, rigging, yards, masts, funnels, warehouses, horses, wagons, cranes, docks, water, bridges, and in all states of weather and conditions of light. He was always active, eager to learn, interpret and to perfect techniques.

A good example is the drawing 'Under Murrel's Wharf'. It isn't known where he originally sold it, but in 1969 it was discovered in a barn in Yorkshire with a number of other Muncaster watercolours. The scene is below Murrel's Wharf where the wagons and carts were stored overnight and the horses stabled. He was so interested in the problems of draughtsmanship which that subject had set him that he bought the picture back. I found a note about it which he wrote after he had gone nearly blind and could no longer paint, "I rather wonder on studying this work whether, even if I could now see to paint, I could draw the wheels as well as I did in 1923 when I was barely twenty years of age."

* * *

In 1924, the Society of Sussex Painters, Sculptors and Engravers was formed in Worthing and Claude Muncaster was elected a member. His father was made President, but only held office for a year as he could not bear to appear, far less speak, in public. He handed over to Bertram Nicholls who was for many years also President of the Royal Society of British Artists (R.B.A.). Muncaster made his first public speech at the opening of the Society of Sussex Painters' inaugural exhibition: "I said what I thought to be a few important things, but Nicholls remarked after I had sat down, 'It doesn't much matter what this young man has to say, it is always a pleasure to listen to his voice.' This made me mad. I never thought about my voice. But I had thought a very great deal about what I was going to say and had rehearsed it for hours, suffering agonies of nervous anticipation. I always do before a speech, sometimes for weeks ahead."

In later years when he was broadcasting in the 'Thought for the Day' series on B.B.C. Radio 4, one of the producers had said a similar thing about his voice and it evoked a similar reaction.

With a few years' concentrated study behind him, and having built up quite a selection of works, in 1925 Claude Muncaster held his first one-man exhibition. It was hung in no less a place than the Women's Institute hut at Sutton but he sold eleven watercolours and two oils. This exciting success brought in some £117 and raised his spirits considerably. He refused to remind himself that it was only a local affair and unimportant.

By 1926, the ambition began to set in. It was clearly time to go for a one-man show in London. He mounted a collection of watercolours and set off foot-slogging round the London galleries. Predictably he met with disappointment after disappointment. The regard which had been so warmly shown for his work in the wooden hut in his home village, clearly was not shared by the censorious agents of the sophisticated city galleries. But he comforted himself with a story of how badly Oliver Hall had done on similar errands. There is a note in my grandfather's book of *Exhibitions and Sales* for the year 1896.

"Wherever I went", he wrote, "my work was much admired. But all the dealers said the same thing: 'too artistic; too good for our public'." While my grandfather was not especially known for his modesty the remark was probably true, but may be considered as one of the more polite ways in which a dealer still manages to give an artist the 'brush off.'

Muncaster's description of his own plodding sales trips is revealing: "This business of carting around under one's arm a large parcel of watercolours and arriving at some lush gallery with the request that somebody should look at one's work, can be a soul-destroying exercise. When someone does at last consent to look, the carefully wrapped parcel is undone nervously under the eye of some aloof personage. His condescending glance at the works, which look their very worst, brings negative reactions, and any remarks are quickly terminated as some likely looking client enters the gallery. The drawings now have to be wrapped up again. The crackling paper trespasses noisily on the gallery hush, and the result is an untidy parcel bunched up with string and some very unsailor-like knots. Naturally, one endeavours to put up a brave front and smiles at the third-in-command seated at his desk by the glass door which leads to the street. Here parcel and person contrive to get jammed, before finally winning through and leaving the door behind to slam with a resounding crash."

But as the proverb has it, as one door closes another opens. At last, after many weeks of trial and rejection, success came. The Fine Art Society in New Bond Street agreed to hold an exhibition of Claude Muncaster watercolours and etchings. They offered him the small gallery at the top of the stairs. Commission on sales would be at the rate of thirty-three and a third per cent, and he had to promise not to sell any of his work during the six months prior to the exhibition. For the six months following, too, any sales would be subject to the gallery's percentage. The same would apply to any commissions that came his way. His share of the expenses included the cost of a flag to be flown in the street outside the gallery. "I agreed to the flag, since I thought it would be grand to have my name in large letters for all the world to see from Piccadilly or Oxford Street. That my name was virtually unknown mattered little. My vanity knew no bounds. A first London one-man exhibition is always exciting. Hopes run high and imagination runs wild. Already, I was forecasting headlines in the national newspapers: 'Discovery of young genius of watercolour painting. Fantastic success of first exhibition. All pictures sell in first hour."

Several critics were mildly approving, and the show did, in fact, do fairly well. Certainly, it established my father's name. But at the age of twenty-two this had its disadvantages. As father said: "I had set a standard for myself which would always have to be bettered in the future. This was a formidable challenge. But at least it taught me some humility."

In fact, in some ways, it almost taught him too much humility. He was never any good at selling his own work. He always knocked it down. On returning from one of his sketching trips, his longing to show the family what he had created was mingled with an agony of concern about its quality and what we would all think. He used to stand in front of his easel, hiding each picture with his body fiddling with the mount to get it straight and ready for view. Then, rather diffidently, he would stand back and await the family verdict. Thank goodness, we could nearly always be honestly complimentary. But he never really took it well if my mother had some critical comment to make. Perhaps it was her direct way of expressing it. Perhaps it was the deeply ingrained fear which had grown from having to show all his works to his father, only to have them torn to shreds.

One picture which hung in the 1926 exhibition, 'Demolition on Hay's Wharf,' was purchased by the Trustees of the Tate Gallery. Mr. Dawbarn, the Director of the Fine Art Society, when writing to inform him of the purchase, said: "I am sure you will be gratified with this early and valuable recognition of your services." Certainly, he was very pleased at the time, and felt it was something of a feather in his cap: "though I hope I took it in proper perspective."

There came a thrilling development late one afternoon towards the end of the exhibition. A youngish, well-dressed gentleman appeared in the gallery and began to show an unusual interest in the paintings, making notes of certain works. The artist approached him, and rather bashfully made himself known. The man explained that he was making a collection of watercolours and would very much like to include in it some examples of Claude Muncaster's work. He enquired the price of one small water-colour and said he would like to buy it. He examined another larger one, and said he would like to purchase that too. The artist, naturally, became very excited and got busy sticking on the red spots. By closing time the client had bought all the unsold watercolours, some fifteen of them. Father was beside himself.

"Well now", said the collector, "I would like to pay for these, but have not my cheque book with me. But I will be coming in tomorrow, and we'll fix up then. Will that be all right?" All right, did the man say?

"Er, what time would be convenient?", he went on. The painter assured him that absolutely any time would be convenient. He would have been there at four o'clock in the morning if the buyer had requested it. They eventually arranged the meeting for ten-thirty.

Next day, ten-thirty came and passed; then coffee time, and finally lunchtime, and still the buyer had not appeared. In fact, he was never seen again. "Of course, he may have been run over by a tram, but I could only assume that the deal was, after all, not on, and I had the sad task of removing all the red spots. This was an unpleasant experience, but it taught me to be more wary in the future."

Chapter 3

A Rolls-Royce for Ballast

The picture he was working on was a difficult one and every reserve of experience, craftsmanship and artistic proficiency was being stretched. The detail. That was the thing. If he could only get the detail right, the rest would fall into place. Then, surely, this major and taxing canvas would be the picture of pictures.

The artist stood back and surveyed progress. Yes, it was going well. Here at last, on this grey, winter's morning he was realising all the poetry which had formed in his mind during that sketching trip to Rochester.

He had found her lying asleep at her berth in a turn of the River – the Finnish barque *Plus*. What a beauty she had looked, her yards angling darkly against the easterly light; the shapely contours of her hull, her network of rigging, so delicately outlined in contrast to the stiff, straight structure of the wharves. He had filled half a sketchbook with her; every beautiful foot of her he had studied and carefully re-formed with his pencil. Now, at last, all the heartfelt work, the loving attention, was coming together.

The click of the latch on the studio door broke the spell. Unannounced, Oliver Hall strode into the studio to borrow a tube of cobalt blue. He had just run out and needed some while the paint was still wet on his own morning's work.

His eye was taken by his son's present endeavours. Just a quick, critical glance. "Why all that detail? You're detracting from the main interest which I assume is the ship. Cut out that fussy distance and make it simpler, boy. Detail doesn't make a masterpiece." He scrabbled amongst a box of colour tubes, found what he wanted, and was gone.

Meanwhile, his son was left to ruminate, nearly mad with fury. "What the hell does he know about ships and poetry and Rochester? He's all bound up with tedious technique and old-fashioned ideas about vignetting the corners; leaving things to the imagination. He says colour must be suggested, not realised; that realism is only for the cheapjacks, the commercialists. Simplicity is the greatest art. All right, I'll show him how to simplify!"

In his fury, Muncaster grabbed a one pound tube of flake white and squeezed the lot on to his palette. Then taking handfuls of the sticky paint he threw it at the canvas until it was nothing but a splutter of white. After which he crashed out of the studio, slamming the door behind him with so much force that it rocked on its foundations.

While the studio settled, the artist was searching out six balls from his golf bag and setting them down on the lawn. Then, deliberately, one by one, he swiped them with all his might out into the field below the garden, far from sight in muddy depressions in the grass. The star of this remarkable performance then followed them over the fence to find as many as he could, in order to come back and repeat the exercise. Before long, there were only a couple of golf balls left. The others had hidden themselves in disgust; and anyway, the steam had gone out of things. With his driver and the two remaining, rather dirty white rounds of ammunition, the artist plodded back to the studio.

He beheld the mess. "You stupid idiot", he breathed to himself.

Where was the palette knife? Better scrape some of the white off. Awful waste to leave it like that. Working carefully, he gradually transferred it from the canvas back to the palette, and as the white came away, so did a good deal of the detail. He stepped back to survey at a distance the result of this 'doctoring'. An improvement. No doubt about it: a very measurable improvement. "Damn it! The Old Man's right again."

His new studio was to become a wonderful refuge. "I spent much time in it, not only painting, but reading and trying to work out a philosophy of life. I wrote quite a lot, and since I was always in love, also composed poems to my current girl friend". It was an 18ft. by 14ft. room with a window to the east and much lighter than the one at the old Rectory. Father had also taken the precaution of having it built in a part of the garden as far as possible from grandfather's studio. Actually, his father had lent him the sixty-six pounds and five shillings for the construction of the studio. Percy Penfold, the village carpenter and wheelwright was a friendly fellow. He had kept the price down and charged no extras. But he did have to be paid. The borrower with a tottering bank balance, was rather slower at returning the funds than the lender would have wished, and my grandfather made that fact plain on a number of occasions.

It was clearly necessary to get some more saleable work done. So a series of painting trips to provincial cities was decided on which would build up experience, allow him to be alone for a bit, and, hopefully, bring in some money. He decided to search out industrial and shipping subjects, in particular, as these he could not find near home.

Within two years he had made extended visits to Newcastle upon Tyne, Edinburgh, Glasgow, Liverpool and Manchester, and much of his work of that period had a quality and sensitivity which retains its freshness today. In fact, many people look especially for it. His earlier work inevitably had the influence of his father, but by now he was standing firmly on his own and creating in his own style. He noted in his diaries: "during these provincial wanderings, I gained a greater experience of watercolour painting and at last some confidence in myself which had been in very short supply."

At just about this time he was invited to stay with Sir Edmund and Lady Davies at their villa on Lake Maggiore in Northern Italy. He did some memorable work there too, and must have remained in favour, because he was later asked to be one of a house party at Chilham Castle for Canterbury Cricket Week. Sir Edmund was a millionaire financier with an interest in diamonds in South Africa. He had bought Chilham Castle and restored it to a perfect period piece, both inside and out. The old masters were superb and every piece of furniture equally so, and priceless.

In 1929 my father was painting in Norfolk. He had forsaken the grimy chimneys and drifting smoke of industry and returned to his real love, the countryside. During the autumn of 1928, a dealer living near Norwich, invited him to send some work on sale or return to an exhibition he was holding during the winter. Several of the works were sold and the dealer suggested that Muncaster might visit Norwich to paint some local scenes both in oil and watercolour, then hold a one-man exhibition. He did not at that time know Norwich, or indeed Norfolk, but being steeped in the traditions of the Norwich School found the idea instantly appealing.

So it was that on a bitter day in March 1929, with deep drifts from the long cold spell still heaped in the ditches, artist and painting gear set off for Norfolk. The ancient Salmson Sports still served him then, and its bright blue contrasted with the white patches of snow as it bounced and slithered along the ice-encrusted highway.

With the light fading, and a long and exhausting journey behind him, Claude Muncaster pulled up outside the house at Norwich. Soon he was introducing himself to the gallery owner. Then, in a room behind the gallery, more introductions, to the owner's wife and three wagging spaniels. This back room was utter confusion; as indeed was the whole place; chaotic and primitive. The artist had a private ponder. Could such disorder ever possibly be cleared and a well organised exhibition mounted? The dealer's wife matched her surroundings, with her mop of raggle-taggle grey hair and florid complexion. She wore a thick woollen jersey, an ill-fitting tweed skirt, stockings that were in urgent need of a hitch-up, and sloppy, brown shoes. Her husband clearly suffered from an insatiable thirst. A whisky bottle was easily to hand and spent much of its time on the move towards a nearby glass.

The evening struggled on and the visitor grew hungrier and hungrier. By ten o'clock he was famished, tired and cold. He had discovered by then that no provision had been made for his lodgings and that he was expected to stay with these two at their cottage about eight miles to the north. Some time after ten, came a faint suggestion that they were considering making for home. Not to miss the moment, the visitor unseated himself from the upturned box which had served him as a chair, and made purposefully to the door. Yes, he had interpreted the mumblings aright; they were off, and within a quarter of an hour he was bumping his way through the arctic dark towards some sustenance.

But arrival at the cottage brought little comfort. The disarray here was worse, if anything, than that at the gallery. And no suggestion of a meal.

Eventually, at around midnight, some kind of a meat mixture came steaming to the table and was dished up without haste. There were other guests as well. A couple of Shetland ponies were led round the table, allowed a sniff or three and given a mouthful of this and that, while the dogs, too, were generously provided for. By now a daughter had arrived from somewhere and was very soon taking sides with her mother against her father, who appeared to be very much in his family's bad books. But, eventually, everyone was fed.

In these salubrious surroundings, Muncaster was entertained for several months while he worked in the fields and fens and marshes of Norfolk. He was caught by the atmosphere of that lovely county; "I soon fell victim to its charms. The Norfolk landscape, its wide open spaces, its particular light, cloud formations and effects, the windmills, the wherries, the Norfolk architecture with its Dutch influence, and the colour of the marshlands and reed banks in their winter colouring, proved extremely attractive to me.

"Unfortunately, the Spring of 1929 produced much misty weather and often the only hope was a close subject. I found many in Norwich itself and the Market Place provided a wonderful spectacle. There were also many Norwich streets which interested me pictorially. The cobble streets are still a feature. In my search for subjects I found Ludham Mills most attractive and it became a favourite subject. Alas, all those draining mills have now disappeared. Just the shells of some remain, bereft of their sweeps and the fascinating wheels which turned the mill towards the direction of the wind."

Once again his love of ships and shipping found satisfaction in Norfolk. The wherries particularly attracted him and he made many sketches of them as they moved quietly along the Broads. "The trading wherries intrigued me almost as much as the old barges had done on the Thames. Sadly, many of them have now been converted into house boats and never leave their moorings. They were truly wonderful craft, and to see them tacking in narrow Broadland rivers was a quite magical sight. I was constantly taking notes of them from various angles so that I had studies to introduce into watercolours when I felt the need of their added interest. The motor cruisers and noisy beer-drinking, bottle-throwing crowd upset me badly. They discomposed the tranquillity of the scene, disturbed the reflections and introduced an element of materialism which went ill with the surroundings. But a wherry, quietly tacking up against a headwind; that was a joy to behold. I once took passage in one from Wroxham to Great Yarmouth, and it has the pleasantest of memories."

During the stay in Norfolk, his host told him of a young fellow who was painting horses in the manner of A. J. Munnings, and that his work was quite brilliant. Muncaster was asked if he would go and visit this promising young painter, who was only 19, and give him some advice about his artistic career. Being intrigued by this story, although not feeling in any way equipped to tell someone else how to paint, he agreed to try and help. After all, there might at least be painters' yarns to swap.

In due course, having followed the dealer's rather scanty directions, he was knocking at the imposing front door of an elegant mansion. A fresh-faced young man, flamboyantly dressed, came to the door and was most welcoming. Muncaster explained his mission. Before long, he had persuaded his new acquaintance to bring down some canvases from his studio above the cow stalls. "There, sure enough, were some oils of horses so much in the style of Munnings and executed with such amazing skill that I was at a loss to know what advice I could possibly offer. This artist, it seemed, had already arrived. However, I did mention that this kind of work had been seen before, and asked whether he had ever tried his hand at painting landscape in watercolours. The artist said he had not but would very much like to try, so I suggested that after lunch we might go out and seek some subject. I would try and paint it and he could look over my shoulder as I worked, while I explained at the same time why I did this or that. After lunch, as agreed, we set off and found an old water mill which seemed suitable. I started work and he watched. After a very short time, he sat down himself, and having all the necessary equipment at hand, started to make a picture of the water mill. In a short while he had completed a sketch in which there was very obvious merit. I suggested he took it to Norwich to have it hung in the show. To his surprise and mortification it did not sell, and he was even more annoyed when mine did.

"That was Edward Seago. Very soon he was selling his works in oils and watercolour at Colnaghi's in Bond Street like hot cakes, and at very high prices.

"There was certainly a great charm about his works, based rather on the Impressionists. But there was to my mind a certain degree of facility about them which was slightly superficial, although at first glance they were very easy on the eye. But I have no hesitation in considering him an artist of more than usual stature and also, incidentally, a good writer."

Meanwhile, the show in Norwich was going well, and Claude Muncaster wrote home to say that he was "fast becoming a Broadland pot-boiler". As gaps appeared on the gallery walls, out he went to paint another Norfolk scene which, in its turn, found a purchaser.

He made a number of studies of mills including the post mill on Mousehole Heath which John Crome had introduced into several of his works. There were very few post mills left in Norfolk even in 1929. Great Yarmouth, too, provided good sketching material. Once he went there and found that the Scottish herring fleet had come into harbour in their hundreds. "On Sundays when there was no fishing, the river was tightly packed with boats and one could walk from one side of the river to the other without getting one's feet wet. Very early on another summer morning at Yarmouth, I witnessed an extraordinary sight. A fleet of barges was discharging a cargo of Chinese rice for Colman's starch. I did a large watercolour of the subject which my father bought. Getting up so early, I was naturally more than ready for breakfast by eight o'clock when I'd finished that watercolour, and I remember the smell of fried eggs and bacon which came wafting up the companionways of the barges was tantalising!"

These excursions to keep the gallery walls filled also led to some good studies of Norfolk churches: "Another feature of the Norfolk architecture was the round flint towers and thatched roofs of a number of the churches. There was one at Potter Heigham, and another at Haddiscoe which I drew. Arnesby Brown, R.A., renowned for his paintings of cows in shadowy pastures and dappled sunlight, lived in this village. He became so successful at this subject that he vowed he would never paint another cow, which was a courageous decision and one to which he adhered. Nevertheless, he was so well acquainted with nature's beauty that there were plenty of other subjects for him to paint, which he did well. Sadly, he gradually lost his sight and had to give up painting. Since this has happened to me, I have every sympathy."

The Norwich exhibition came to an end and the matter of the final monetary settlement had to be dealt with. There was not, apparently, much organisation on this front, either. The dealer would not pay up and Muncaster eventually threatened to take him to court. The situation certainly must have been serious for it to have come to that. He hated rows. However, after this threat, the money dribbled in "though I was never sure whether he paid me my rightful dues. This was purely bad business on my part. I should have kept a far more rigid record. I did not see him again and gather that his addiction to drink was his undoing. I very much doubt whether he died solvent."

* * *

By now, Claude Muncaster had stayed out of love for a long time. But within weeks of getting home he was struck down by another "merciless attack of love-sickness. She was tall, blonde, athletic and vivacious. She was everything. I was overtaken by a series of delicious hopes and fancies which were constantly dashed, and I would encounter times of the most bitter despair. Indeed, my life became so ruled by this gorgeous girl with her gay demeanour and *joie de vivre* that I would go subject hunting near her home in the hope of getting a glimpse of her in the garden; or I would choose a subject by the road along which I felt she might travel. I imagined myself flagging her down as she approached in her yellow Armstrong-Siddeley and having a few words with her. Actually, I had a rival. He was a good friend of mine and we quite accepted that we felt the same way about her, content to share her company as we squashed down into the MG, or his old bull-nosed Morris. And thus we did the rounds; Wimbledon, the Hendon Air Display, the Military Tattoo, motor racing at Brooklands. There were, too, tennis parties, golf foursomes, treasure hunts, dances and private dinner parties which my friend and I arranged for her. Afterwards we would often sit and eulogise on her charms until the early hours of the morning. The extraordinary thing was, looking back on it, that we never fell out. But we must have been the laughing stock of the neighbourhood."

It had to end, of course. One day she asked Muncaster to take her to a dance at a fine Georgian house at Chiddingfold, and the prospect, naturally, filled him with excitement and anticipation. Alas, she condescended to dance with him only once. He drove her home afterwards in a fury, and in a moment of madness suddenly proposed to her. The answer was "no", but that did nothing to abate his emotions. Rather, it exacerbated his rage. "All right", I said to myself, "I'm sick of all this frustration and mucking about. I'm off to sea!"

Never one to make an idle threat, he booked a passage in a 2,000 tonner of the MacAndrews Line – *Pizzaro*. "She was rather tanker-like in construction with engines aft, a flying bridge for'ard and accommodation for just two passengers. She ran down to Portugal, Spain and Gibraltar with general cargo, then returned home stuffed with tomatoes and sardines. My fellow passenger, Mr. McClure, who shared my cabin, was an author. He wrote novels with a Spanish flavour and spoke Spanish fluently.

"We sailed on the morning of 18 January, 1930. As usual, I was hugely excited by the passage down river and was busy with my pencil taking notes of ships and dockland scenes. At Gravesend, a beautiful four-masted barque, *Olivebank*, lay at anchor; and although I was content enough with *Pizzaro*, I felt a longing to beg a passage in a sailing ship like that.

"As we chugged on down Channel I stood in the bows and felt the first lift to the Atlantic swell as our little ship bowed gracefully to it. Then, as we turned south, we began to roll slowly but heavily since we were light in cargo and carried below nothing more than a little ballast and a Rolls-Royce for the King of Spain."

He came back from this trip with plenty of material. It had provided a variety of fascinating subjects including, for instance, the shipbuilding yards and steelworks at Bilbao. "I was absolutely thrilled by the effects of the steelworks and shipyards as we proceeded slowly up river in the early hours of the morning before daylight, and sketched away frantically in an effort to get everything down. I always found night effects amongst ships and docks and industry appealing and a great challenge to artistic abilities. When we got to sea again I made a large watercolour from memory of the lighting effects caused by the steelworks, and I believe it was this work which was largely responsible for my election as an Associate of the Royal Society of Painters in Watercolour. Founded in 1804, it is the oldest watercolour society in the kingdom, and I think is still the most revered. I was elected in 1931 at the age of twenty-seven and I suppose this was something of a feather in my cap. In any case, I felt it a great honour to be elected."

Nothing which he brought home from that passage, however, had the slightest effect on the current girl of his dreams.

above: Under Murrel's Wharf, 1923: *watercolour*.

below: Etching of a tramp steamer, c.1920

above: Study of trees in a Sussex wood, 1922: *pen and ink*.

below: Study of an ash tree, 1920: *pen and ink*.

Pen Study of Ash Tree.
Aug. 10th 1920.

Chapter 4

Forty Days to Finland

A black, thundery day it was, as the bus bumped its way to the docks at Barrow-in-Furness. Amongst the collection of tanned country passengers who had joined the old open-topped double-decker on its route via the farms, sat one who had boarded it in the little village of Bardsea. On the top deck now, he gazed out over the broad fell scenery. The browning bracken of the fells, the mossy grey stone walls winding across the fields, the bluish hazy hues of the distant mountains were all being recorded in the artist's mind. This marvellous landscape was at least some compensation for unrequited love. Bardsea was the provider of balm for emotional sores. He recalled the hours spent studying trees in Bardsea Park, which his father had painted so many times. The nearby estuary and the surrounding Lakeland helped to lessen the dragging loneliness. This time, though, there was an extra motive for the trip to the old family home. He was in search of another restorative, that of masts, spars and rigging.

As the bus came near to the docks, he spotted amidst the industrial murk something which to him stood alone. There lay a white painted, three-masted barque. On the instant, he made up his mind that wherever that ship was bound he would be sailing with her. When the bus stopped by the dockyard he got out, slipped in behind the back of a policeman on the gate, scrambled between the buffers of a couple of goods trucks and made along the wharves towards the ship. A few strides up the gangway and he was on board. He learned that the Captain was ashore and was told he would have to go below and see the Mate. A tall, thin, angular man, the Mate sat typing in the Captain's day room. The young visitor explained his mission.

"Vell", not the slightest indication of surprise in the voice, "dat may be possible, but de Captain – he ashore. Ven he return you ask him. You vait, huh?" And the mate went back to checking out the ship's accounts.

Soon, though, they got talking – about ships, and it was not long before the Mate had the photographs out. They told their own story – of the time they had been through a terrific gale near the Horn. Some of the sails were in tatters and the lifeboat smashed to pieces. "Ah, but de vind-jammer life not alvays so hard. See here!" It was a photograph of the cabin they stood in filled with lovely Australian girls and a plentiful supply of liquor on the table. "You should try it sometime", said the Mate with an experienced smile.

But this ship was not bound for Australia. She had come from there with a cargo of grain; had now discharged her load and was heading for home – Helsinki in a couple of days' time. As they talked the Captain returned. He seemed a young man to skipper such a ship, but as it turned out was an excellent seaman and the youngest captain in the Erikson fleet. He was quiet spoken and friendly and seemed quite happy to have an artist passenger aboard for the final leg to Finland. Officialdom needed to be satisfied, however, and the new recruit had to be signed on as a proper member of the crew. This formality was fixed up the following morning, and at the stroke of a company pen Mr. C. Muncaster became ship's painter aboard the Finnish barque, *Favell*.

There was, however, a problem. Most of the gear and materials needed for such a painting passage were down at Sutton in Sussex. Arrangements had to be made for a quick journey there and back in time to catch *Favell* before she sailed. Fortunately, all the train connections worked. He was home by evening, and spent the next day packing and preparing for sea. Then it was "goodbyes" and the night sleeper back to Barrow.

He arrived at half-past-five in the morning, and *Favell* presented a more beautiful picture than ever. "Her white masts, spars and hull gleamed in the early sunlight, and her rigging formed delicate and intricate patterns across the sky." A sleepy nightwatchman eyed him suspiciously as he made his way below and into the Captain's day cabin. There, weary after the night's noisy train journey, he settled himself on the settee to wait, and fell asleep.

An astonished steward was hovering over him when he eventually opened his eyes around breakfast time. Evidently, the poor fellow had not been told he would have a passenger on his hands. But he was resourceful. Before long, he had set up the ship's painter in a space off the day cabin which, until that moment, had served as a locker for vegetables. The steward produced a box for a wash-stand, a basin and a jug, strapped up a bunk to the bulkhead, covered it with blankets, and there was instant passenger accommodation, with even a small porthole. The artist felt at home. It still smelt like a grocer's shop, but he was in a sailing ship and his dreams were coming true.

Conversation at breakfast was scant. He got the impression that the officers were not on the best of terms with each other. But by the end of a protracted and testing voyage, no doubt all the small talk had long since been spent. If the conversation at the Captain's table was not exactly lively, work out on deck certainly was as the ship prepared for sea. The shouted commands in a foreign language, the scurryings of the crew, the continual "thrupp, thrupp" of coiled ropes being thrown down on to the deck all made for manifest chaos.

It had been a life's ambition to go up the mast of a sailing ship. Here at last was his chance. All he had to do was climb. Surreptitiously he started out on to the pin-rail, took hold of the rungs of the rope ladders, or shrouds as they are known, and began gingerly to make his way aloft. He had selected the mainmast for this personal trial, so the first goal was the main-top, some forty feet up and about a third of the total height of the mast. By about thirty feet he found himself looking down the dockside chimneys. At this point, he had reached the futtock shrouds which are a continuation of the first set of shrouds attached to the mast just below the main-top platform. They lead on upwards and outwards to the edge of the platform to join the next set of shrouds which in their turn lead to the topmast. Thus, on the futtock shrouds the climber is making his way aloft with his back at a steep angle to the deck before he gets high enough to grasp the upper shrouds and haul himself over the edge of the platform. It was here, on the futtock shrouds that Muncaster, artist and self-appointed seaman, found his resolve slipping. Above him he beheld the massive overhanging structure of the main-top platform and he began to feel giddy and shake almost uncontrollably. It was Hay's Wharf all over again. He wanted to yell out for help. With a great effort of self-control, however, he managed to regain enough composure to begin, very cautiously, the descent to the deck. As he lowered himself, he gripped the shrouds with the same intensity as he had that iron ladder up the dockshed wall. He arrived below, white, trembling and completely humiliated. Looking around him, expecting peals of derision, he realised that other people were far too occupied to have noticed his predicament. After all preparing a sailing ship for sea, is a complicated and all absorbing business. But how in heaven's name was he going to do paintings of a ship like this properly if he could not work from the rigging? He had had visions of climbing about like a monkey, and making sketches anywhere he wanted. They sailed that afternoon.

Some two miles out at sea, the Tug Master blew a series of blasts on the siren, shouted some parting good wishes through a greasy old megaphone, and *Favell* was 'let go'. The tug was put about, and away she went back to port, with a cloud of black smoke issuing from her tall, thin stack. A little later, the Pilot, suitably refreshed from the Captain's bar specially reserved for such V.I.P.s was returned to his waiting launch, and *Favell* was on her own.

The ship had now been transformed into a wealth of brilliant white canvas, the sails casting fascinating shadows. But they hung listlessly up and down: there was not a breath of wind to fill them. The only progress came from the drift of the tide flowing out of Morecambe Bay. The helmsman stood idle, one elbow on the wheel, a hand picking his teeth without need to turn a spoke. "How different from the kick of that great wheel in the wild waters of the southern ocean, where it required all a man's strength, perhaps even two men, to keep it under control." Around the ship were the wheeling, mewing gulls, eyes alert for any offal or gash which might be thrown overboard from the galley. Sometimes they would alight on the water and their whiteness would be reflected in the surface of the sea.

Later in the afternoon, the Captain moved in and out of the charthouse tapping the barometer. Back on deck he would stare out, searching for a wind. "De glass, she drop a leetle", he said at last. "I tink vee get vint tonight."

Meanwhile, the ship's painter, very much a passenger painter at this moment, could not keep his eyes off those shrouds. "Surely I couldn't be such a damned cissy as to be defeated by a height which even at the summit was not much more than a hundred-and-twenty feet. Besides, the sails were now set, and I would be generally hidden from prying eyes. If I disgraced myself again, who was to know? I told the Captain of my intention. His only comment was to remind me she was an old ship and that much of the gear had seen its best days. 'Take care,' he said, 'and be sure to grip de sides of de shrouds – not de rungs. Some of dem might be made of rotten rope.'"

So once again, with infinite caution, the artist began the long climb skywards. "I managed the futtock shrouds and was delighted to find that there was no return of the giddiness. Up and up I went, hauled myself over the first platform and then on up the next set of ladders; even over the upper futtock shrouds, and so to the top where I stood on the royal yard. Astonishing! Why hadn't I suffered that terrible giddiness? I could only conclude that at sea there is no comparison of heights as there is in dock. Somehow, at sea, one did not get the same sense of scale looking down at the flat expanse of water.

"I felt proud of my achievement. But mostly because I knew that from now on I could go anywhere I wanted aloft and feel no anxiety. Though I must confess that the first attempt to get out on to the end of a yard-arm made me not a little bit anxious. There is no support for one's feet other than the footrope, and nothing to hold on to except the steel jack-stay running out on to the end of the yard, and to look down and see nothing but sea far below was a trifle daunting. But very soon I even overcame this fear, too. The greatest difficulty was climbing and carrying my gear at the same time, and to find a spot more or less comfortable and safe from which to paint."

That night they "got de vint". The artist was awakened in the early hours by the heavy tramping of feet on the poop deck above his locker cabin, the familiar "thrupp, thrupp" of ropes being thrown down on deck, the clatter of blocks and tackle, the singing of the men hauling on the braces and the demands of the Mate in his rasping Finnish. The ship was now moving around fairly violently and the heavy spray being lashed by the wind against the little cabin porthole. But this was the blow the crew had been praying for. The days of "more days, more dollars" were over and all they needed now was a fair wind and a quick passage home. If the weather held like this, they would be able to make the passage north-about in ten days or so. The weather did not, however, oblige. Headwinds and calms kept them drifting, and guessing, for very nearly six weeks. This suited the ship's painter admirably. For him, more days meant more pictures. But he began to get the uncomfortable feeling that his presence on board was not welcome. In fact, he became downright unpopular. "I was an artist, and artists are proverbially

Jonahs. I was getting the blame for the lack of wind."

Out on deck that first morning it was raining; the skies leaden grey and the wind straight down from the North, a dead muzzler. The ship was heading for the Irish coast and a grey-green sea with toppling white horses tumbled about her. The crew put *Favell* on the port tack, then the starboard, not once, but many times and the Calf of Man and the misty line of the Irish hills became all too familiar landmarks. Progress northwards was negligible.

Then the Captain suddenly changed his mind and decided to go south-about. So the ship was brought round to a southerly course and in minutes was racing down channel at a speed of some twelve knots. She steadied on her keel, the clamour aloft eased and became little more than a song in the rigging.

That evening, though, the capricious weather developed a new fancy. The wind died away and off the south-west corner of Cornwall they lay absolutely becalmed. The sea, what there had been of it, rolled itself out and with but the slightest of motion, only the sounds of the creaking spars and blocks, and the gentle swishing of the idle sails chaffing against the backstays, *Favell* became a lifeless model. But the artist was happy astride the royal yard, and peered through his binoculars at the toy people ashore, swimming or sunbathing, the sounds of their voices reaching out to the ship across the summer stillness. Looking down into the blue sea below, he could study the shadow of the ship in the water.

To seaward, he could see steamers appearing on the horizon, and watch the paths made by their wakes across the ocean. Several of them approached close for a better look at the old windbag and perhaps get a photo or two. A couple of them even dipped their ensigns in salute to the glorious days of sail, and *Favell* responded. In fact, she would not have looked quite so elegant as the pencil sketch of her suggests, as at that time she had only a little ballast in her holds and was high out of the water. He never thought a ship looked her best until she was fully laden and down to her Plimsoll marks.

The Captain had generously put his day cabin at the disposal of his artist passenger. "For this I was deeply grateful. It meant that I could have a firm table to work on when I needed it and more freedom than I had in my minute cabin. Also I could prop up my paintings and view them from a distance to see how far I had been able to achieve the pictorial effects I had been aiming for. To my way of thinking, a picture must look well at a distance but also be enjoyed at close range, so that one can see the detail which has made up the whole. *Favell* provided me with a mass of material for painting and always alongside and around was the sea, sometimes animated, sometimes subdued; sometimes sparkling and criss-crossed with sunlight and shadow, at others so calm that the skies were perfectly reflected in it. And when she was sailing there was always the sound of the water either being thrust aside in the wash or parted by the bows as she dipped into the seas.

"For me, there are few things more beautiful than to lie on one's back on the fo'c'sle head in warm weather and a light wind, and look up into the foremast when all the sails are set. Their curves are so subtle. With a slight breeze, the foot of each sail curves upwards and outwards revealing the sails and rigging of the other masts; and the pattern of the blue sky between seems all the bluer because of the contrast of the white canvas. There are also the shadows cast from staysails and jibs. Nowhere is there a straight line. All ships have this peculiarity. Even the ridges of rungs are streamlined and curved. The decks are curved to take away the water. The masts and funnels are round and the only straight lines in a windjammer are the backstays. Most of the running rigging, by its own weight, has a sag to it, and the stays cannot remain taut when the staysails and jibs are set and straining. And how splendid the curves of the bow where they meet the water. And how graceful the lines of the bow itself, surmounted usually by some finely carved figurehead. It is this constant presence of curves that makes ships so difficult to draw; but what a fascinating challenge."

Because of calms and light headwinds *Favell*'s progress up the English Channel on her way to the Baltic was maddeningly slow. Sometimes the only advance would be occasioned by the flow of the tide, until it ebbed. Then the lifeless ship would simply drift astern again. Once she got on the wrong side of the Longships Lighthouse and the crew saw the red danger signal flashed from the lighthouse. But they were helpless all the while there was no wind. An attractive little barquentine, *Hilda*, overhauled them, as did a Brixham trawler. This annoyed the Captain, but he consoled himself by saying that they must have had auxiliary engines. Skippers driving on to a lee shore had faith in their engines' power to haul them out of danger. Unhappily, they often didn't have enough power, and many ships were lost this way. But mostly *Favell*'s Captain kept his ship well out into the Channel, out of sight of land, so for him there was no trouble with lee shores. Claude Muncaster, meanwhile, made the best of the slow progress by a greater productivity of paintings.

During this time he made several notes of figures; men working aloft, men hauling on the braces, men heaving in sail. In the sketches the man in the long coat is the Mate. Only the officers wore long oilskins as they were not expected to go aloft. The crew wore short oilskin jackets and long leggings, in heavy weather lashed by yarn round wrists, ankles and waist – known as body and soul lashings. But in the raging weather that was so often experienced down south, nothing would prevent the icy waters seeping through.

These lashings were sometimes a great deal more trouble than help. They could cause sea boils which were most painful and difficult to get rid of. Men mostly got them on the wrists and they were created by the skin chaffing against the sleeves in salt water. On one occasion when sketching on the poop, the artist looked up and saw a hefty cadet come aft to see the Mate. He showed him his wrists. They were a mass of sea boils. The Mate looked at them without noticeable sympathy, and ordering the lad to sit down, took each wrist and squeezed out the pus from the boils one by one. The poor young lad turned pale under this treatment, but withstood it all manfully. The Mate seemed almost to be enjoying himself. The crew feared him, but he was an excellent seaman and quite used to such minor emergencies. He could be touchy, though, and one day the ship's painter fell foul of him. There was an attractive scene looking aft along the port deck, and he decided to make a watercolour of it. The shadows appeared blue across the white deck-house and, of course, he painted them such. But when the Mate saw the picture he was furious:"Vot use me paint de sheep vite and you paint her blue?" Father did his best to explain, but never convinced him.

When the ship arrived off Dover after four weeks at sea, the wind failed them completely once again, and since the vessel might be a danger to other shipping if left in those busy waters to drift about in the tide, the Captain decided to anchor, clew up the sails and 'whistle for a wind'.

It arrived the following afternoon from the best possible quarter, the south-west. "We set everything and sailed clean over the Goodwin Sands. It was a daring thing to do, but young Sten Lille was a daring Captain. Our fair wind took us up to Denmark and the skipper was naturally anxious to know exactly what landfall he had made. He disappeared into the charthouse and dragged out the appropriate chart – only to find that the rats had gnawed into the coast of Denmark so greedily that it was useless." Fortunately, the situation was not critical. All they had to do was put the ship on a northerly course with the land on the starboard side until they reached the Skagerrak Sea. The rats had found the charts for that area less appetising and they were still intact.

Gradually, through more calms, a gale, and yet more calms, *Favell* made her way up through the Baltic and into the Gulf of Finland. For a couple of days she was becalmed in thick fog. A storm at sea never worried Muncaster, but he often said how much he feared and hated fog. In this case, well up into the Baltic, they were stuck in the middle of a busy shipping lane with only the rather feeble bleat of a hand bellow fog horn to warn of their presence. He was worried that this would not be heard by the big steamers whose deep sirens seemed to be sounding off all around, and very close. Just how close, they found out when the fog cleared. They were lucky not to have been run down. We often forget just how skilled sailors were before radar. They had none of the modern aids which we now take so much for granted.

At last, after almost six weeks at sea, the ship was edging her way towards Helsinki. Suddenly, the cry went up, "The tug, the tug". Soon, they were in tow, and never was the order, "aloft and make fast" obeyed with greater alacrity. In no time, the sails were down on deck and much of the beauty of the sailing ship had vanished.

"I stayed three days in Helsinki and lodged at the 'Seamen's Home' which was kept by an old windjammer man who met me at the door very early one morning, bare-footed, carrying a lighted candle, and dressed in a long nightshirt and woollen cap with a tassel. He presented a somewhat Dickensian picture and reminded me of drawings by Cruickshank. I was returning from a krafter crab party given by two of *Favell's* officers. Krafter crabs are rather like large prawns. The custom is, or was with these officers, to drink a tot of pure alcohol with each male crab and two with each female crab. I ate quite a number, but stuck to the males and kept sober, well, more or less. At least I can remember quite plainly walking back to the 'Seaman's Home' alone and being greeted by that old candle-carrying manager."

"The next day presented problems. I had only picked up the odd few words of Finnish and nobody seemed to speak English. Nor did I understand the Finnish money. I had to get myself a mid-day meal and also a ticket home in some ship. Somehow, mostly by sign language, I managed to get myself a berth in a ship bound for Hull the following afternoon.

"As we sailed down the harbour we passed very close to *Favell*. I could see Captain Lille on the poopdeck with a small gathering of people. I waved to him, but evidently he didn't see me. We steamed on into the open sea, *Favell* becoming smaller and smaller astern. Then we changed course to round a headland and she was, in a moment, completely lost to view."

Chapter 5

No Flag for your Coffin

Full of hope and smug satisfaction, one of the first things the artist-turned-sailor did on his return home was to visit the girl friend who had been the cause of his trip in *Favell*. But again there was no change. She was not in the least impressed.

Work, and thoughts of another exhibition helped to smother the disappointment. As a result of his trips to Spain and Italy, and now the one in *Favell*, there was quite a stock of new watercolours in the studio. So he set about arranging another exhibition with the Fine Art Society. This show, too, went off reasonably well.

The year 1930 was drawing to its end; life at home was uncomplicated. Leslie was an insurance clerk in London; brother Philip was now at Cambridge; Mrs Hall was busy as the first President of Sutton and Bignor Mothers' Union and often away giving talks and demonstrations of hay-box cooking. Oliver Hall was as busy as ever in the studio, or off on sketching trips. His friend Ernest MacAndrew, the artist, who spoke Spanish perfectly, took him on several visits to Spain. He came back with many paintings and later produced some equally fine etchings and dry-points.

As for Claude Muncaster, he was playing golf, painting a bit, dreaming of the sea and scouring the papers for any titbit of news about Erikson's Grain Fleet, with a view to a deep sea voyage across the Southern Ocean. But by then most of the ships had arrived in Australia and were loading grain for the homeward run. If he was to get to Australia to come back with one of them there was little time to be lost, even though the turn round took weeks, sometimes months.*

Once again, Bardsea provided the solution. A Captain Hurst (no relation to Alex Hurst – see below) was at the time staying with his grandmother there, at Bay View. He was the Harbourmaster at Liverpool and a man who had sailed in square riggers. Not unnaturally, when he heard of Muncaster's project, he took a considerable personal interest and offered to help all he could. A couple of weeks later, a letter arrived from Liverpool with the news that a passage had been procured for him in the *Tasmania*, an ancient ex-German freighter. He'd be able to live with the officers, but would be expected to do a certain amount of work about the ship to pay his way. He would be signed on as a supernumerary at one shilling a day.

On a foggy forenoon in late November, just before the *Tasmania* sailed, Liverpool's bluff Harbourmaster came to say farewell. "If that hand isn't as hard as a crab's shell when you get back", he said, "I'll know you haven't worked before the mast, and so far as I'm concerned, that'll be the end of you for me."

Muncaster recorded that at his first meal in the saloon aboard *Tasmania*, he was struck by the appearance of those at the table. Very different from sailing ships, "here uniforms were smart, collars cleanly white and black ties neatly tied."

But it was not long before, once again, the artist found himself the brunt of everyone's wit. At dusk the following evening on the bridge, Mr Muncaster noticed a rather disturbing characteristic about the light flashing away to starboard. It was the Longships Light, off Cornwall, but showing red. He mentioned this to the Captain. "I hope it isn't red!" said the skipper. "But it *does* flash red, doesn't it?" "Only in the danger area," replied the skipper. "Anyway, when did you see it red, from the land?"

The artist explained that he had last seen it red when he had been becalmed between the Longships and the coast in a sailing ship. Then, ill advisedly, he went on to point out a bay on the chart, saying "the last time I was there, was in a little tramp steamer and we lost our steering gear."

"Now look here," returned the Captain in a menacing voice, "you seem to be a chap with odd experiences. You'd better keep them to yourself while you're in my ship, or we'll have you over the side, and we won't spare a flag for your coffin." With which sally he stalked from the bridge.

Two mornings later, when the ship was about seventy miles off Lisbon, the Captain came up and asked acidly: "Can you smell the land?" "No, Sir. I'm afraid I can't." "Well, I can. Distinctly. The same scent as we get off the Cape. If you'd like a walk to see it, you have my permission. But mind the water. It's only about two miles deep."

---

* Alex Hurst has been kind enough to give us the following information:
   The turn round in Australia was very variable and depended on a number of factors. Ships loading in, say, Melbourne or Adelaide, clearly loaded more quickly, with dockside facilities, than those in out-ports, at anchor and loaded by ketches. On the other hand, at an out-port like Port Germein, where there was a wharf of a sort, only one vessel could load at a time, so if the ship was first on-turn she would load in about three weeks, but if three ships arrived there in two days, the last on-turn would have to wait for the others to finish before she started. In 1938 to 1939, when I was out there, we were some two months swinging at anchor waiting to get a charter at all. Of course, ships first had to get orders for their loading port and then to discharge their ballast themselves before loading. Or they may have had an outward timber charter, which would need to be discharged first. This was usually at Melbourne. *Olivebank* had taken such a cargo in 1929 to 1930 but had such a bad passage, and taken so long, and being leaky on arrival, was kept out in Australia until the 1931 season grain came through, when she was one of the first away. Two months might be a fair average for being in Australia. In 1931 the *Olivebank* was 122 days home, and that was a normal run. Indeed, taking all complete passages from 1921 to 1939, and including those round the Cape, the average was 123.3.

The Captain was not sparing with his humour. There was more to come that same afternoon.

The terms of the passage had included doing duty at the helm. "I felt most anxious about taking my first trick at the wheel. I'd be on duty for about two hours, and as it was a day of heavy showers, I thought I should try out my oilskins. When the Captain saw me he remarked "you're far too smart for a helmsman, and you've forgotten your umbrella, haven't you!"

As always, the man at the wheel reported the course when he was relieved by the new helmsman. "South, 34 east," said the Able Seaman handing over. "South, 34 how much?" asked the newcomer in surprise. "Sorry mate. South, 34 west."

This apparent artifice did nothing to instil confidence. The 'relief' was already nervous. He had done very little steering before, and certainly not in a ship as large as this one. But he had at least been alert enough to realise that to steer east would have put them straight on to the coast.

There was quite a sea running that day, as it often does in that part of the Atlantic, and the trainee helmsman was finding it very difficult to hold the course. The ship was taking charge. The Third Officer obviously appreciated the problem and came over to see what the trouble was. He glanced at the compass, then at the pallid helmsman, now grimly sweating with the wheel held hard over in an effort to counteract his mistake. The Third smiled, pulled an apple out of his pocket, and cut it in two to share it. "It's not easy at first," he said. "But you'll learn quick enough. The secret is not to react too much. The less wheel you use the better, then you won't find yourself chasing the compass."

At the dinner table that evening, the painter of notices cum helmsman was the brunt of loaded comment in respect of his steering. "Ah, hullo," said the Captain, "here comes the cause of all this rolling. I suppose you know the Second's cabin was flooded while you were at the wheel this afternoon. The flowers had to be put in a safe place, and what the Chief Engineer and his staff are saying about you down there is quite unrepeatable. That valve they've been having trouble with – all your fault, you know. A proper Jonah they say you are!"

But as the days passed he gradually got the knack of steering, and gave back as good as he got.

Early on the seventh morning he awoke to a stream of orange sunlight flooding the alleyway outside the cabin. The brightly printed curtains over the Captain's door swung with the motion of the ship. and there was a merry tinkle of rings on the brass rod. It was Sunday. He could take his ease, listen to the sound of the wash chasing down the ship's side, and ponder over the vast expanse of blue tranquillity which now surrounded them. Almost impossible to believe that only seven days separated them from fogs and winter rawness, and the sight of the great elms he had so often studied and drawn at home, black and gaunt against the frosty sunrise. Here it was warm and blue. Instant summer.

During the morning a shout broke the quiet, "there she blows." Whales. Easy to see as their great humping backs broke the surface, glistening, shining; then the hissing spouts shooting up, curling over, drifting and vanishing into the air, like small clouds of passing dust.

The wind freshened from the north, flecking the blue with white. Flying fish glinted as they skimmed over the waves. So wonderfully carefree and happy they looked. But they were, in fact, literally flying for their lives as they were chased by hungry bonito, dolphin and shark. Nature, at once beautiful and cruel.

Again in his records, Muncaster spoke of the difficulty of finding privacy for painting. Always there seemed to be somebody looking over his shoulder. His cabin seemed to be a free-for-all, the Captain especially paying frequent visits; (he was by way of being something of an etcher himself). He came in one morning and started poking about amongst some signs Muncaster had painted for the mate. He pointed to one of them and said: "So you're not a real artist then."

"What do you mean, Sir?"

"We couldn't have a real artist painting signs and notices. Nobody could read them!"

He thrust forward the sign he was holding. It said: 'NO HAWKERS.' "We often have artists come aboard trying to hawk their pictures. So when we get to our first port of call, don't let me catch you with your pictures propped up against the bulkhead with a cap alongside."

The Chief Engineer had his little jokes, too. He often came into the cabin on some pretext or other, never leaving without his quota of remarks. He affected to blame the artist for everything that went wrong in the engine room, and there was plenty of engine trouble in that old ship. The ultimate thrust came one morning when he hurried past, obviously very aggravated:

"Now what do you think ye've gone and done?" he blurted out angrily. "Ye've set the bloody ship alight. There's a fire doon below."

The offer of help was, apparently, not appreciated: "Don't ye go doon theer," yelled the Chief over his shoulder. "I won't tell ye what they're saying aboot ye. They've got no use for artist Jonahs. Ye just keep oot, I'm telling ye."

However, there was reconciliation a day or two later. Muncaster painted the Chief a picture of his home town from a postcard photograph. After gazing at it for some time, the Chief remarked in his broad Glaswegian accent, "Noo, yon's my ideerr of a bonny picture, two pubs and a kirrk!"

Muncaster later also gave J. V. Williams, the Captain, two watercolours for his efforts to try to make the passage to Australia bearable in spite of the inevitable sarcasm. One of them was of the parish church at Sidmouth in Devon, the Captain's native town.

There was in fact on that trip much for an artist that was beautiful and exciting. "There was a new moon tonight, the merest thread of a thumbnail. The sun went down in a bank of blue mist. There was dew on the decks and the Southern Cross hung low but bright over the southern horizon. The beauty of nature saddens me. It makes me feel conscious of my own insignificance. It is so elusive. I long to capture it. If only I could stretch out a hand and gather it in as one can gather a bunch of flowers; and keep it, to help me to remember and render the beauty of it truthfully. This might be one reason for one's existence. The effects of sea and sky, storm and calm never cease to cause me to wonder. What an artist the Creator! If only I could get on to paper a little of what I see."

Muncaster had obviously become quite attached to the ship by the time she reached Fremantle and he felt little enthusiasm for going ashore. There were no windjammers in and he was quite content to sail on round the coast in *Tasmania*. When they reached Adelaide he saw one possible ship – the four-masted barque *Lawhill*. He went aboard her and even climbed aloft. But she carried no royals and he was told by the sailors that she was a "bald-headed bastard." He decided he certainly was not prepared to sign on in an ugly box of tricks like that, and sailed on to Melbourne. There were, of course, plenty of jibes about getting cold feet. His companions were quite convinced he would never sail in a windjammer, even if he did discover one to his liking. They were all wrong.

Chapter 6

Round the Horn before the Mast

It was a strange little mobile world, this *Olivebank*, with its handful of men, their distinctive characters, their likes and prejudices. Within that steel hull, at the mercy of wind and wave, went on from day to day a powerful drama of extraordinary simplicity; yet had we given consideration to the matter, what a minute and lonely spot this human habitation remained on that immeasurable Pacific Ocean! Out of touch with the rest of the world, its problems and political crises, our lives were full with the perpetual routine of keeping things going.

From *Rolling Round The Horn*

* * *

Tasmania arrived off Melbourne late one very dark, wet January night. As the anchor cable clattered into the blackness, a young man in oilskins screwed his eyes against the sheeting rain to search for the shoreline. It was hopeless. The night was soupy thick. Any lights would be winking to themselves, blotted out by the weather. And he went below to heave off his dripping oilskins and turn in to a welcoming bunk. *Tasmania* gently lifted to the swell and soon, in one cabin at least, the unyielding night was not even so much as a memory.

Early the following morning, the Chief Officer whisked aside the curtains at the cabin doorway. "Wakey, wakey, Muncaster. If you want to see a fine sight, you'd better get out on deck pretty quick!"

The rain had cleared; the sun was about to rise as the artist clumped up the companion ladder and emerged into the light. There, hardly two cables distant to starboard, silhouetted against the dawn sky lay a four-masted barque. He focused on the name unbelieving: *Olivebank*, the ship he had so much admired that day in the Thames exactly a year ago, with her beautiful sheer and graceful hull.

His heart suddenly went off on leaps of romantic excitement, logic turned somersaults, and he raced below to pack. But, of course, no amount of haste now would get him quicker ashore. *Tasmania* had not even picked up her pilot. Yet there was no time to be lost. The barque was well down in the water, obviously fully laden; her sails bent on ready for sailing.

When the Pilot came aboard to take *Tasmania* into dock, he was pressed for news of *Olivebank*. Whose ship? Where was she bound? When was she due to sail? The answer came that she was one of Erikson's grain carrying ships; 2,800 odd tons, and built on the Clyde by Mackie and Thomson in 1892. She had a full crew and was simply waiting for a fair wind.

Tasmania was conned into Melbourne Docks in careful, slow motion. And one Englishman aboard, desperate to get ashore and contact *Olivebank*'s agents found the delay interminable.

When the old freighter was safely berthed, he ran down the gangway and immediately set about asking for directions. He found an official who told him he thought that Erikson's agents had their offices in Little Flinders Street. But after an exhaustive search and many enquiries, he still had not found it. For God's sake, where was the place? Seeing a telephone box, he thought perhaps the directory would help. Perhaps he'd been given the wrong address. But the box was occupied, and the man inside was obviously talking to his girl friend, oblivious of the figure waiting impatiently outside. The delay was agonising, and precious minutes were clocking by. Even at this moment *Olivebank* might be weighing anchor. He was about to push in and reach for the directory, when the man came out at last, "Sorry mate, gettin' some rush copy through to my paper," and hurried away up the street.

Erikson? Erikson? His fingers flipped the pages. Epps; Erdis; Erett. Erik . . . Then it became clear. Flinders Lane. That was it. Odd that no one he had asked had thought of it. Another couple of hurried enquiries, a ten minute walk; and he was there.

The clerk behind the desk was bored. "You're about the thousandth man to make the same request. No hope, Sonny. She's got a full crew and the Captain's not taking on anybody. Sorry."

Tasmania's ex-painter tried arguing and pleading but without result. The man clearly had his instructions. So, that was that.

As he made to leave the office, a man in a rather baggy, ill-fitting suit came in and moved over to the desk. The agent called out:

"Hi, Sonny, here's the Captain of the *Olivebank*, you'd best have a word with him."

Perhaps the Gods were on his side after all. The thought flashed through his mind that if it had not been for the delay over the telephone directory, he might never have met the Captain.

Muncaster asked him at once about the possibility of a passage in his ship. The Captain was a Finn, stockily built, with an iron-grey moustache and crow's feet at the corners of his keen blue eyes. Assuming that he intended to be a passenger, a figure of ten shillings a day was named. Muncaster

above: Distant view of Canterbury Cathedral from Chilham park, 1928: *watercolour*.

below: Open landscape, 1922: *pen and ink*.

above: Italian brigantine passing St. Mark's Square, first painting-in: *oil*.

below: The Baptistery, Cathedral and Leaning Tower of Pisa: *oil*.

made a quick reckoning as he was told that the passage might take as much as six months. If that were so it would cost some £90. Such a figure was out of the question, so £40 was mooted.

"All right, den, I take you for £40. But you will haff to steer, go aloft, haul on de braces – tings like dat."

"Suppose you sign me on as a sailor – what then?" He pondered.

"Been to sea before?"

"Not actually as a sailor."

"You Inglishman?"

"Yes."

"How long you been in Australia?"

"Since last night."

He laughed, a deep, throaty sound.

"And you want to get to sea already. What you been up to?"

Muncaster explained his reason for being there, that he was an artist and wanted to serve in a sailing ship.

"All right," said the Captain, "I got a man go sick. I vill sign you on this afternoon. You meet me at de Finnish Consul at two o'clock. You earn £2 a month as deck-hand?"

Thus it was settled.

So began for Claude Muncaster an adventure which was to have a profound and lasting effect on his thinking, his character, his whole life's work.

He returned to *Tasmania*, to collect his luggage and painting gear and spill his story. Reactions, predictably, were unanimous. Everyone thought he had gone completely mad.

His 'home' for the past six weeks sailed the next morning, smoke blowing away from her tall, straight stack, her stiff lines standing off starkly from the gaunt buildings. He helped slip the headrope from a bollard and watched the last link with friends splash into the water; waved farewell as *Tasmania's* black length slid behind a high dockshed with the red duster fluttering at her stern. He found himself alone on the now quiet quayside surrounded by rubbish. In the loneliness of this new isolation, he wondered too now whether he was not quite mad.

But there was no time for self-pity. Much had to be done to prepare for sea as member of a sailing ship's crew. He needed a donkey's breakfast (a mattress stuffed with straw) for his bunk, some cutlery, food, medicine and not least Keatings powder to keep the bugs at bay. These simple purchases he packed into a large, black family trunk and thus equipped, found a man with a motor boat to take him out to *Olivebank* lying about three miles off. But the closer they came to *Olivebank*, the more his apprehension grew. Six weeks in *Favell* had been more than enough for an understanding of what was in store, never mind six months. Maybe the warnings of his friends in *Tasmania* had been well founded. As the little motor boat bumped alongside, dwarfed by the great ship, the new member of the crew peered up her tall side into the eyes of a row of swarthy looking ruffians staring down at him. This was the moment when his nerve needed a lot of encouraging. More than half of him wanted to order the boatman to turn and make back to the shore. But then a young fellow climbed down into the boat and taking hold of the trunk exclaimed: "Strike me pink, Guv! Wot you got in 'ere – fevvers?" Such unexpected expression of humour, and in a Cockney-sounding voice, gave him new heart. Following up after him, Muncaster climbed over the side, jumped down to the deck and was aboard his windjammer.

Immediately he was surrounded by the crew who plied him with questions: "Vot ship you in last?" "How much money you get?" "You Inglishman?" and so on. At last, one of them said: "Now den, ve show you ver you sleep. Up here – de for'ard fo'c'sle. Drier up here in bad vedder. Not so much vater on deck!"

So, he was led to the for'ard fo'c'sle – actually the for'ard deckhouse – and shown an empty top bunk where he could sleep, and another empty one below where he could stow his gear. He was enjoying an altogether friendly welcome. But he learned later that there was motive behind the manners. Every Finn going for his Master's Ticket had to learn English, and they saw in their new member of crew a captive instructor. Apart from that, Englishmen were not popular.

In her own way, neither was *Olivebank* popular. Originally, she'd been one of Andrew Weir's Bank Line fleet and was said to be an unlucky ship, though Muncaster didn't know this until it was too late and he was well on his way home in her. For like many a beautiful woman she had her caprices and waywardnesses. Having such a low freeboard amidships she was a very wet ship, and they used to say of her that she took a dive in the Channel and came up off Australia. She made such slow passages that she was sometimes posted overdue, or even missing. Then when she did arrive it was more than once with her ensign at half-mast betokening a death or deaths on board. In those days beriberi, a disease resulting from lack of vitamins, was still a curse at sea. In the old sailing ships any vegetables or meat were bad after only a few days out.

For a vessel carrying four-and-a-half thousand tons of grain in her holds; *Olivebank* was grossly under-manned. The crew, including the Captain, numbered only twenty-two, and many of the hands had never been to sea before. It was extraordinary how those great ships, so heavy to work during that arduous and dangerous passage round the Horn, ever reached their destinations safely.

The height of *Olivebank's* mainmast from deck to truck was about a hundred and fifty feet, and the sail area of the 'main' about two thousand square feet; so it takes little imagination to realise what a fight it must have been to make that massive sail fast in a gale when it was soaked and blowing out as hard as a board. Fingernails could be torn out if they were not kept short.

Three miles off Melbourne, Australia, in mid January 1931, Muncaster takes up the story:

"*Olivebank*'s Master, Captain Lindgren, had under him three Mates, a Cook and Steward. There were two Able Seamen, a Bosun, and a Carpenter (Timberman). Of the remainder, most had never served as seamen and certainly none of us in a sailing ship. The majority were Finns. There was one Swede, one Belgian, Jim a young Australian apprentice, and three Englishmen other than myself. One of the Englishmen was an ex-stoker in the Merchant Service; the second obviously had some kind of secret to keep as he would never tell us what he was other than that he came from Birmingham. The third, Frank, a Cornish farmer lad, was lethargic by nature but a most popular member of the crew. The First Mate was a disciplinarian, but a fine seaman; the Second Mate a little soft and timorous, but humane. The Third Mate, very young and inexperienced, was a nice enough chap and easy to get along with, but we didn't rate him very highly. The average age of the crew was twenty. I was one of the oldest hands at twenty-seven.

"A ship's crew is divided into two watches for working purposes – a port watch and a starboard watch. The system in British ships is four hours on and four off. In the evenings, between four o'clock and eight, there are two dog watches of two hours each by which the rota of work is changed each day. In *Olivebank* there were no dog watches; the system in Finnish ships at that time was arranged differently. A watch would come on at 7 p.m. and work through five hours until midnight. It was then below until 4 a.m. when it turned to again until 8 o'clock. It then went below till 1 p.m., when it came back on deck until 7 o'clock in the evening. Thus no watch worked the same hours on two consecutive days. The starboard watch was under the command of the Captain and the Second Mate; the port watch under the First and Third Mates. I was drawn for the starboard watch and was glad because I liked the Second Mate. Later on, he often chatted when I was at the wheel, and asked how a chap like me got on with the windjammer life.

"The orders were given either by whistle – one blast on the Mate's whistle called the 'Policeman'; two blasts called the whole watch – or shouts in Swedish, which made things difficult for us Englishmen. We received no instruction in Swedish and were never told the names of the ropes or their purpose. We just had to pick it all up as best we could, and there were many times when we felt very foolish and inadequate, without the slightest idea of what we had to do. But a rope was very soon shoved into your hand with a loud expletive and some sort of elementary guidance like, ''ere you, you haul! You bloody well haul, like you pull de guts out of de devil.'

"As to the food, or tucker, I'd had some experience of this in *Favell*. But it didn't take me long to discover that the food aboard her was infinitely superior to that which was doled out to us in *Olivebank*. One day when looking through our library, which was a large sea chest stuffed with old newspapers and the cheapest of cheap comics, I came across an advertisement in a tattered Melbourne newspaper which read: 'Ship's food for sale. Very low price. Excellent fodder for pigs'. We were sure that the Cook and Steward had seen the advert, and bought up the lot. The description certainly seemed to match what we were being fed on! We had to get used to black potatoes boiled in their skins; bread which the Cook made, but with such poor yeast that green mildew was growing on it by next morning; butter, strictly rationed, which would have served very well as cart grease, and a wishy washy concoction described as soup. Salt horse was a luxury, as was the half-pound of sugar allowed each man each week. Sometimes, when the Cook wasn't about, we'd nip into the galley and pinch a portion of sugar to swell this meagre ration. A sailor's belongings, however small or seemingly insignificant, were respected as his own, but no one had scruples about scrounging a morsel from the stingy owners.

"On Friday we had pea soup and pancakes. This was the real feast day of the week. Though, when the pigs were slaughtered and we had blood pancakes, they made us all sick. Our stomachs weren't used to such delicacies. Drinking water was rationed to about a mug each per day, and we were allowed two syrup-cans full for washing. In the tropics we were served out unsweetened lime juice. It was a pretty ghastly thirst-quencher, but it may have staved off beriberi.

"One of the first things I had to do when I got aboard *Olivebank* was to surrender my passport to the Captain. The moment I'd done so, it seemed somehow that I'd lost my identity, an uncomfortable feeling. But there was no question of looking after so important a document myself, and I really understood why when I found out how the crew lived in the for'ard fo'c'sle. Anything could have got lost there. I suppose the Captain's cabin was the only safe place in the ship.

"For a long time, the Old Man had been Mate in *Olivebank*. Now that he was Captain he was a quiet and remote individual to whom we scarcely ever spoke. He was getting on in years, and we considered him a timid seaman who would take in his pocket handkerchiefs at the first sign of a puff of wind. But then he knew his ship, and the limitations of his crew. With their scant experience, he realised that they could only handle so much sail, and for many weeks we kept our mizzen royal yard lashed on deck. It was not sent aloft until we were round the Horn and well up into the south-east trade winds.

"Once we were under way, I soon found out the vast difference between being a passenger in a sailing ship and being one of the crew. I thought I'd learned that from my time in *Favell*, but how wrong I was. Any idea that a deckhand remained on deck was soon dispelled. Indeed, he was always the first man to be sent aloft and probably the last to be allowed down. He really was a 'dogsbody' and got the worst and the dirtiest jobs. In better weather, he chipped and scraped the paintwork, but was never permitted the luxury of actually painting, not even to brush on a coat of red lead. It seemed strange to me that I, a painter by profession, should be thought unworthy to apply a coat of paint. I simply had to accept that for me it was bang, bang, chip, bang, scrape.

"It was the duty of the junior members of the watch, arranged by rota, to carry the tucker which had to be taken along the deck to our mess in the for'ard fo'c'sle and also to the apprentices' fo'c'sle aft. When the ship was rolling and pitching heavily and the seas were sluicing aboard, to arrive from the galley with the tucker intact was quite a feat. If you failed, there was hell to pay. Poor Frank, being rather slow footed, was caught several times; so was Jim, and the day's dinner went clanging into the scuppers. There would never be a second helping available and we just had to be content with what we could make of the mildewed bread. It seems incredible thinking back on it now. And for me, at least, such privations were to take their toll.

"In the beginning, though, I was pretty keen, and managed all the chores with a good heart. There were plenty. In addition to hauling on ropes and generally working ship, the deckhand often steered, acted as policeman to call the watch, and did any job that required one man only. He also took his turn as lookout man up in the fo'c'sle head during the hours of darkness; he soda-washed, and cleaned and scrubbed and generally ran errands. It was the deckhand's duty to supply the Cook with fresh water, a couple of pails a day, pumped up from the holds. He also had to replenish the Captain's store through a glass stopper in the deck. Even though the water for the fo'c'sle was so carefully rationed, in the tropics it got down to danger level. Then we were each allowed only one small can a day for washing. This, of course, coincided with conditions when a wash in fresh water was very badly needed. After chipping and scraping in that sticky heat, the flakes of paint and rusted metal would be well distributed and clinging inside one's open shirt! Bunkering the Cook on Saturday mornings was a pretty dirty business, too. The coal was stored in a small locker in the fore-peak, and doubling oneself up, shovelling it into buckets in the sweltering, dusty dark was irksome to say the least. I swore more roundly and consistently in that stifling black hole than I have ever sworn before or since.

"It was the deckhand's job also to clear up the mess after meals and wash-up. Many times I would be called out to haul on the braces or go aloft, only to return to find the washing-up water stone cold. It was no use asking the Cook for more.

"Perhaps some of these things don't sound so very awful, but being carried out in trying circumstances, and over quite a period of time, they all added up. Windjammer life was tough all right – calling on all a man's resources of self-discipline, sheer physical strength, ability to move quickly, and sense of humour; he had to be able to laugh when things went wrong. I felt, sometimes, that was the only thing that got us through. Every man had to remember, too, that he was one of a team and needed to pull his weight however he felt. Any 'shinaniking' or 'skiving' was treated with a heavy seaboot up the backside.

"In the trades, life was a bit easier and pleasanter; but in the southern latitudes we went through weeks of working and sleeping in cold, sodden clothes, for nothing was dry and the galley was forbidden ground. I suppose men didn't suffer colds because of the salt water and the very life itself toughened us up.

"Our work had to be carried out irrespective of the conditions and one always had to keep alert for danger and remember not to take unnecessary risks. But going aloft in heavy weather was the most daunting. In a roaring, bitter gale with stinging rain and spray – even sleet or snow, the task was absolutely exhausting. With the decks a raging swelter of water, which could totally submerge a man, to hear the Mate's two whistles summoning the watch to take in sail struck fear into the stoutest heart. By day it was bad enough. By night it was hell.

"We had to stagger out of the shelter of the fo'c'sle into the inky blackness, the only glimmer of light reflecting from the foaming white surf, to feel for the lifeline overhead, a wire stretched from one end of the ship to the other. As we groped our way to the foot of the mast which carried the sail to be taken in, sheets and buntlines were thrust into our hands and we began hauling with all our might. Gradually, the yard aloft was lowered, the sail bunching and slatting out with reports like heavy gunfire as the order was yelled out 'aloft and make fast.' We jumped for the weather pin-rail, where the force of the wind helped to blow us against the shrouds, and began the long, cumbersome climb. Up we went, up, up . . . out over the futtock shrouds with our backs hanging over the deck and on up the next set of ladders, holding fast to the sides of them. The higher we climbed, the heavier the going became from the weight of oilskins, seaboots and sweaty clothing. On up we went, feeling always with our feet for a false foothold which could so easily be fatal. At last we reached the sail, thrashing out in the shrieking wind, and stepped out on to the footrope below the yard. That shaking footrope was the only support between ourselves and the ocean far below. We clutched at the jackstay on top of the yard and worked out to the end, hand over hand. Here we began to fight the canvas, punching it with bare fists to crease it to help get a hold. Inches by inches we hauled it up on to the top of the yard to make it fast with a gasket rope. Now we had to work our way inwards towards the mast, cross out to the other side to tackle that too; all the while, trusting the helmsman to keep her away from the wind a bit. If she should turn into it, the sail would be shipped backwards and we would be knocked off the yard. At last, it was down to the deck some hundred feet below, only to be told that there was another sail to be taken in; and that we had to start the whole operation all over again.

"At least the job warmed us up. Although the maxim aloft is 'one hand for yourself and the other for the owners,' naturally one cannot work one-handed, so there is danger. But one learnt to look after oneself rather like a cat. Personally, I preferred the work up amongst the rigging to working in the seas on deck. You still had to be mighty careful aloft, but it was safer.

"I was standing my lookout one wild morning near latitude 60° South. We were 'running our easting down' and heading for the Horn. I watched the dawn break low. Ugly dun-grey clouds, their edges tinged with pink, were ominous harbingers of storm. It was already blowing hard and the seas were piling up in terrific grandeur, some of them forty to fifty feet high from trough to crest. All the morning we spent snugging her down, and the next watch carried on where we'd left off. Then the wind suddenly backed into the south-east, a 'dead muzzler,' and we were forced to square away to the nor'ard a point or two. The seas were now confused and the ship was a smother of foam, spray and solid waters. The crests of the waves were being whipped off and driven over the spumy surface like a snow storm. The noise was terrific, and any time we expected to see the deckhouses swept overboard, for surely they couldn't withstand the massive weight of water that constantly pounded them. It seemed miraculous that they did.

"At dusk, the Captain decided to take in the last of the square sails, namely, the foresail. Both watches were sent aloft to hand this sail, all two thousand square feet of it. You can imagine what a herculean task it was in such conditions to handle that sail, stiff with rain and spray and blown out taut as a drum by the force of the wind. For my part, it took every drop of strength I had to fight the canvas into enough of a crease to grab a hold and heave it up the yard. When we at last finished the job, we were carrying only a mizzen and fore staysail. Apart from that she was running under bare poles.

"When we got back to the deck, darkness was beginning to close around us, blocking out the tempestuous seas; though not the noise which seemed, if possible, intensified.

"Round about midnight we were called out to haul on the mizzen braces. We had struggled along the deck and just started heaving, when a giant sea thundered aboard, and as the ship pitched the whole mass of solid water came roaring down upon us. Several managed to leap for safety up the poop ladder, but I was caught, lifted off my feet, stretched out on my back and over the side. For a few moments my frozen fingers were jammed between the rope I held and *Olivebank*'s side. *I was overboard.* The storm had me in its grip. Then with the roll of the ship another great sea surged aboard, and I came with it. By the grace of God I had grabbed that brace and managed to cling on, literally for dear life.

"I was soaked to the skin and, I don't mind saying, very scared. But I was alive. In all the turmoil, that was the only thought that seeped through to my numbed, sodden mind.

"The First Mate also went over in that tremendous fury of water. It was quite some time before his desperate shouts carried to us above the din, and he was well nigh done for when we hauled him inboard. We considered ourselves extremely lucky. Usually, if somebody goes over in a gale it means 'goodbye.' A sailing ship cannot be stopped like a powered ship, though even then it can be dangerous enough. Nor would it be possible to launch a boat in such weather, it would be smashed to atoms. So this had undoubtedly been an escape from death.

"Some time after we'd rounded Cape Horn, death sat on my shoulder again. Fortunately, I was unable to see into the future and for the moment just got on with each day as it came. We had just a fleeting view of the Horn, dimly outlined against a low, streaky dawn, and I later painted an oil of the subject. Were we glad to see that hump of rock. But we were even gladder to have it astern of us with our nose pointing up north-east, and homewards. We'd now been at sea some two and a half months and had sighted, except for the Horn itself, neither ship nor land and were to endure many more gales before we neared the warmer climes.

"Even in that hard weather, a job I did enjoy was steering. I felt responsible and not just a number. In the efficacy of my steering lay the safety of the ship and all the souls aboard her, though I admit there were some nerve-racking moments when running before a large following sea. The pressure of the seas on the rudder when it was hard over made it immovable and gradually the compass card would swing too far. One feared that the wind would get round on to the wrong side of the sails, we'd be caught 'flat-a-back' and the ship dismasted. When the sails did begin to flutter and slap, the Old Man was out in a jiffy, 'vot de hell you do?' he would shout. But not even with his help and the Second Mate's could we get the great heavy wheel, nearly six feet across, to budge. Until suddenly it would free itself and spin back at furious speed. You daren't touch it with a hand then. If you grabbed at a spoke, you'd be dashed to the deck. The only brake for this spinning was a knee pressed against the wheel's rim, acting as a kind of 'skid pan.'

"Thus, in time, one learned the trick of the wheel. Actually, I couldn't help taking a little personal pride in the fact that I was never sent down from the wheel, and only once or twice had to have an extra hand to help me.

"But almost as bad as these Cape Horn gales were the Cape Horn calms, which came between the storms, when the ship would make no progress at all and just lay wallowing. At such times, it was said she 'rolled the sticks out of her.' The lower yard arms did all but touch the water, and the bell suspended from the wheelhouse which was struck to announce the hours and times for the watchkeepers to rise and shine, clanged like a sort of death knell each time she rolled. Meanwhile the din aloft was quite terrifying; the clattering of blocks and gear, the dragging of the drooping sails against the backstays. Added to which was the roaring of the swell when it broke onboard, sweeping across the decks as she rolled; and the storm gates on the sides of the ship banging-to like sledgehammers beaten on an empty tank. Such a calm could be quite as frightening as a gale.

"But the weather was not always against us, as at last we neared the south-east trades. How we'd looked forward to the drying sun and those steady trade winds which blew warmly for days, allowing some relaxation and a pleasanter life. Steering in the trade wind weather on a clear moonlight night was a joy. The wind was light but reliable, and *Olivebank* would proceed on her leisurely way. The wind aloft was a composition of tender melodies, a rhythmical accompaniment to the sound of the wash of the water along the ship's side. There would be peace about the ship. No strident chipping or scraping. The watch below would be asleep, and those on watch yarning quietly on the fo'c'sle head. Perhaps the Mate was guilty of a nap or two, and only occasionally did his rounds to see that I had the course right and the weather edge of the royal sail lightly flapping in the moonlight; whilst I fixed my eye on a star, keeping the yardarm lined up with it so that I knew we were not adrift from the course. The wheel only needed to be moved a spoke or two at such times, and the difficulty was to keep awake in the warm night air.

"Except for this shooting pain in my stomach.

"It had been bothering me for a couple of days, but had only been intermittent, so I imagined it was simply a bit of indigestion. Within a week, however, I was in a terrible state, suffering severe gastric pains, vomiting and headaches; all of which began to sap my strength and it was often, even on balmy nights, the greatest effort of will to get out on deck and work. Before long, I was unable to manage the usual tucker and had to resort, as a special favour, to granite-like ship's biscuit; though somehow I continued to drink the foul, black coffee.

"We carried no doctor, of course, to whom I could have reported, no radio, no engine and were hundreds of miles from land. I began to get very worried and to wonder what would become of me. There was no room for a 'passenger' in a short-handed sailing ship.

"I came on deck one morning to find a flat calm and only the gentlest of swells. The Mate put me to soda-washing, and chipping and scraping the lower shrouds and deadeyes of the mizzen mast. I looked along the row of them and they seemed to be marching off into eternity. Lines upon lines of them. My head ached violently, there was considerable pain in my stomach, and I kept vomiting. How could I ever possibly finish?

"This particular job entailed standing on the top edge of the side of the ship, or gunwale. As a safety measure, a line was lashed to shroud, a turn taken round the body, then the other end lashed to another shroud. Thus, one was prevented from slipping back and falling into the sea. I tried to start work, but every impact of the chipping hammer against the steel prodded my throbbing temples to a degree that nearly drove me crazy. I stopped for a moment and looked down into the water some eight feet below. It was clear, still and a lovely deep blue-green. How inviting it looked. A thought grew in my mind, 'how marvellous it would be to slip down quietly into that stillness. Nobody would miss me. It would put an end to all this ghastly suffering.' I began to work out a plan of action. I knew that the Mate, at present slowly pacing the poop deck, would soon go for'ard to see how the rest of the watch were progressing. If I moved just a few feet to the left along the gunwale, the chart room would mask me from the eyes of the helmsman. The Captain was below. The starboard watch was below. I would be alone and unobserved. I got on with the job as best I could, and waited. There was not a breath of wind. The only sound came from the chipping hammers of the watch for'ard and the creaking of cordage in the rigging as the ship gently rolled. The sails hung limply up and down.

"As I'd anticipated, the Mate eventually came down from the poop, casually inspected my work without comment, and passed on forrard. I unlashed one end of the line and edged along the gunwale, until the helmsman could no longer see me. Now, I let down the line over the side till it trailed in the water. Perfect. I stood up, got the line between my legs and was just about to lower myself down when a voice seemed to whisper quite plainly from my shoulder, 'Don't go into the water! Get down on deck and go and see the Captain.' I hesitated. This was ridiculous. Nobody was there! I looked around me – no one. Nonsense, and the pain gripped my guts again. God Almighty! Then I let go of the line and jumped.

"But I jumped down to the deck; staggered up to the poop and sought out the Captain. He gave me one look and said 'You stay here. I get you someting.' He returned with a draught of brown looking fluid in a glass. 'Here – take dis.' I swallowed it, grimacing with the taste of ether. 'Now den,' he said. 'You go and sleep. I tell de vatch not to vake you ven de vatches change. You feel better ven you vake.' The watch did his bidding, and I slept for twelve hours, an unheard of thing in a windjammer. I awoke feeling weak but very much better, and was soon able to resume work without a return of the attacks. I am pretty certain that the medicine the Captain gave me was Dr. Collis Browne's Chlorodyne. Now, I always have some with me when I travel.

"It will be said, of course, that the Captain and his dose saved my life. So it did, once I'd gone to the Captain. But that 'voice' to me was utterly real. It was one of those personal experiences which has meaning for the person to whom it happens but is impossible to prove to anyone else. You could call it a Guardian Angel; you could call it conscience. I wonder if others have such experiences but are afraid to talk about them? Even on a more accepted level one could term it the inner voice. Unhappily, we so seldom listen to its sure, positive guidance. I am convinced there is far more to man than the mere physical, and that at last, even amid all the negativity and scepticism of the modern scientific world, we are coming nearer to an understanding of the true spiritual dimension of our being.

"From now on in *Olivebank* the thought uppermost in our minds was the coming of the trade winds. We suffered many false alarms and disappointments before we really picked them up in latitude about 35° South. Then the storm canvas came down and we sent aloft our summer glad rags, light sails, patched and often almost transparent. But they caught the lighter airs of the tropics better than the heavier sails.

"Trade winds meant a more comfortable existence, but the work about the ship went on incessantly – soda-washing, chipping, scraping, red-leading and painting became monotonous tasks. There were repairs to the rigging to be done, too, which would have been impossible or a waste of time when the decks were under feet of water. During the trades, there was little need to go aloft to take in sail. With the steady wind only a sweating up of the braces was necessary at sundown, when the wind eased.

Otherwise, the braces were hardly touched for days on end.

"While we crept up towards the tropics, we also took the opportunity during our watch below to give our fo'c'sle a spring clean. Everything came out on deck, including our clothes and damp donkey's breakfasts, and we would sleep under the stars or the shadow of a sail. When we'd had the turn out, we found that in one corner of the fo'c'sle there was a hole where the bulkhead had rusted through. No wonder we'd so often been subjected to a foot or more of water slopping across our messdeck. Somebody had the idea, now we had a cleaner fo'c'sle, that a bit of decoration was needed. I was asked to paint a girl on the for'ard bulkhead. So, with some ship's paint I accordingly produced a lifesize blonde with a very full bust and a plunging neckline. I gave her a black mini-skirt and a green blouse, what there was of it. To me the result really looked pretty awful, but it seemed to meet with the general approval of the others. Anyway, when I visited *Olivebank* in the Thames some years later and went into the fo'c'sle, my girl was still there, in her pristine beauty, with a few deft strokes here and there to add to her attractions.

"When all was done, we felt our home was now much more habitable and less encumbered with heavy weather gear and oilskins. The wise ones oiled them. The less wise threw them into a corner, saying they would have no use for them again. They had forgotten, or perhaps did not realise, that the North Atlantic can be almost as wild as the Horn.

"At least for the time being my bunk was dry, and the calm allowed me to enjoy my free time in it without being thrown about relentlessly and all too often painfully. Most of all, more than any other privilege, I appreciated my bunk. In the community life of a ship's fo'c'sle one of the most trying features, in my case anyway, consisted in having virtually no privacy, nowhere to withdraw and enjoy one's own thoughts, with the sole exception of the place for sleeping. To me this bunk connoted not merely an opportunity for resting, dozing, or even reading; it was the means for getting apart and conjuring up the beauties of an English landscape, its lanes, its hedgerows, its flowers. This little private corner enabled me to forget, shut out even for an hour, the vast, open waste of sea with never a single object to break the monotonous horizon.

"The shadow of the ship on the water was almost as well defined as the ship herself in such dead calms. They were pretty general as we left the south-east trades, but an occasional Pampero could blow up suddenly from Pernambuco in Brazil, and did. When one came, it did so completely without warning and more than once caught us with everything set. When that happened it was all too easy to lose one or two of our trade wind glad rags. Once, something more sinister occurred. Our fore-royal yard split at the centre in a Pampero and it was very fortunate that the halliards and lifts had held the yard aloft, or it might have crashed down through the roof of our fo'c'sle immediately below. That would have been serious.

"As the wind died out on the Equator, we found ourselves in the Doldrums. There, if we sailed a dozen miles a day we considered ourselves lucky. In the Doldrums the humidity is stifling, while at the same time a sailing ship has to catch every breath of wind she can find. If the slightest puff came our way, we had to trim the braces to the direction of the wind. Then, almost immediately, the wind would come back in the opposite direction and we were at it again. It was a nerve-racking period and brought out the worst in men. It was a time of brawls and fights and nobody seemed to do anything right. I had some very uncomfortable moments myself; as when I came back to the fo'c'sle from a trick at the wheel one particularly sticky afternoon, thirsty and wanting a drink. I found my mug on the table, but with some water in it. I wondered who'd been drinking from my mug and took it to the side and threw the contents overboard. Suddenly, I found myself looking straight into the fiery eyes of the Captain of the fo'c'sle, Koskinnen, a hefty Finn whom I'd come to know as a fine seaman in bad weather, but a very tricky customer indeed in the tropics. He had a terrible temper. Now, his face was pallid with rage.

" 'Now den!' he yelled. 'You bloody Englishman, you put up your fists and fight!'

"I was astonished.

" 'Fight?' I said. 'What on earth about?'

" 'You know what about! You throw de gin we get for extra work overboard. De next time ve 'ave gin, you give to us, see. Now, you fight.'

" 'How was I to know that was gin?' I said. 'We've never been served with gin before. I was at the wheel remember. And do you seriously think I would throw gin over the side? No! I'm not going to fight you over a silly thing like that. You can put your fists down and think again.'

"Although I tried to put on a calm front, inside I was shaking like a jelly. I'd seen what he'd done to the Steward one day when they'd had an argument and it wasn't pretty. I had no wish to feel his great leather boots in my ribs, stomach or face, with perhaps his sheath knife into the bargain. It was stupid to fight, so I just stood up to him and waited for the crash. But gradually he brought his fists down, the colour returned to his cheeks and he strode off to the fo'c'sle. I was never so relieved in my life. He wouldn't speak to me for several days, but then he seemed to think better of it and after that couldn't do enough for me.

"He didn't, however, offer to do a job I was given which meant going right up to the truck of the jiggermast. It had carried away in one of the gales and the carpenter had to make a new one. But before he could do this, the site of the truck had to be measured exactly. The truck is a wooden cap on the top of the mast through which are rove the signal halliards; the jiggermast, the fourth mast, is situated on or just forward of the poop and carries no squaresails. In *Olivebank* it was about a hundred and twenty feet high. There were shrouds to a point about half way up which were, of course, simple to climb. Beyond this, however, there were no ladders and only if the gaff topsail was set could the cringles (rings to which the sail is attached so that it can slide up and down the mast) be used for footholds. The peak of the topsail did not extend to the top of the mast by some twenty feet, and having reached the peak of the sail, one had to swarm up the rest of the way by means of a thin, taut wire, or backstay.

"This was the hardest and most dreaded climb in the ship. But not only did I have to climb it, I had to take up with me a heavy block with rope attached which I had to fix at a point on the mast immediately below the truck. I was willing, though, and set to with a cheerful heart. After all, it was a bit of a challenge. It was an opportunity to prove myself. Up I went at a rattling pace.

"But the higher I climbed, the greater the length of rope trailing below me and, of course, the heavier it became. I found that by the time I'd reached the peak of the topsail I was feeling pretty well all in. Yet the toughest part of the climb was still to come. I looked down and could see the Mate watching me and waving me on upwards. Somehow, I climbed out on to the stay and drew myself with aching arms up the remaining distance. When I arrived I was completely exhausted and could only rest by lying with the flat top of the mast in my stomach. Even that, after a bit, winded me. There were moments when I really did wonder if I could cling on long enough without losing control and falling to the deck below. I had never felt quite so close to absolute physical defeat. But preservation is a very strong instinct. Agonisingly slowly, I managed to do the job, and came back down to the deck with the diameter of the mast measured and the block fixed. Only to be told by the Mate that I'd done the job wrong and would have to go up again.

"I said that this would be quite impossible. My arms were now so tired that I could hardly raise them from my sides.

" 'You not too tired,' he replied. 'You go into de fo'c'sle; have a drink and rest for ten minutes, den come back. You be all right.'

"So I did as he ordered.

" 'Now den, I tell you,' he said when I got back to him, 'you not go up too fast dis time. De last man dat do dis yob, he an Australian. He vent up too qvick. He get too tired and fall down and he vas kilt.'

"That was encouraging to a man who was just going to make the same climb. But it was, of course, very sound advice. This time I ascended slowly all the way and not only managed better, but did the job correctly. I was still mighty glad to be back on deck again, though.

"Another job fell to my lot which didn't exactly fill me with cheer. I had to clean out the pigsties. We started out from Melbourne with three pigs, but after we'd rounded the Horn they had been slaughtered one by one and turned into salt horse. The pigs had not been good sailors and to clean up their mess, scrub each deck board and wash down the bulkheads was, well, let's say there are more pleasant ways of passing the time; and we were in the heat of the tropics. I must have shown my distaste of the whole business as the Second Mate who'd been watching me, suddenly said:

" 'Many better men dan you have done far vorse vork dan dat and been none de vorse for it!'

"I took this little lesson in humility to heart and thereafter tried to work with a better will.

"There were certain fair weather jobs, though, and dirty ones, that I enjoyed. One was tarring down, which meant tarring with a rag all the standing rigging. At least I felt like a real sailor doing this, swinging up in the rigging in a Bosun's chair with my rag and pot of tar. This was what I'd signed on for. Such a task, however, was no respecter of hands. But by then, blisters, which had been the lot of all of us landlubbers at first, had been forgotten as the stinging salt water had healed and hardened the skin. My hands could now put up with just about anything.

"Still the calm stayed with us and the sun blazed down from a shimmering sky. But at least in that heat and humidity there came the tropical rainstorms. It was marvellous to stand out in the downpours and cool off. Moreover, we were able to collect the rain in sheets of canvas and renew our freshwater tanks which had practically run dry.

"We were some two weeks in the Doldrums and considered ourselves lucky. But that was quite long enough. I did not care at all for the oily seas or the lightning and thunder which reverberated around the heavens making them seem all the vaster. Neither could I bring myself to enjoy the lightning playing about in the rigging. It may have been a beautiful sight, but I found it quite frightening, nevertheless, and awaited eagerly the first puff of wind betokening the north-east trades. We felt them once, but they died away again.

"Meanwhile, with no deck games or other sports to turn to, we fished from the jiboom. With bobbing bits of white paper we caught a number of bonito. We got a shark, too, and had shark steaks for tea. They tasted strong and Frank said he found a thumbnail in his portion. The shark's fin we nailed to the end of the jiboom. Any ship coming into port without displaying a shark's fin was reckoned not to be a deep water sailor or to have been round the Horn.

"Jim, the Australian, also speared a dolphin. This made me feel sad, as they are such lovely and, I believe, intelligent creatures. Once we'd got it aboard, the Cook prepared it for us; as he did the flying fish we found on the deck, that didn't go very far amongst five hungry seamen. The dolphin had a very strong flavour which was not particularly appetising, but it did at least represent a change of menu from the one the Cook usually served up. Although it was on his concoctions that the happiness of the ship largely depended, it was not his fault that he served us with such foul fare; he had no alternative. But we respected him. He had to work in the most appalling conditions. In the tropics he was all but roasted alive working in those cramped conditions over his galley stove; down in the southerly latitudes he'd practically been washed away. His galley was situated amidships and because the freeboard at this point was at its lowest, the seas found their way aboard there more than anywhere else. It was not unusual for the crashing waters to sweep pots and pans from his galley and even extinguish his fire. We grumbled at his horrible food, naturally. But he never failed in all that time to serve us with something hot.

"While we waited for our wind, we also caught an albatross by trailing a chunk of salt horse on a large hook. I hated to see this beautiful bird killed, with its magnificent six-foot wingspan. In any case, I thought it was supposed to be unlucky. The Finns had no such superstitions; though it did seem to be common knowledge that if a man fell overboard, the albatross would peck out his eyes. One could only hope that by then he was dead. The Finns made tobacco pouches from the webbed feet of albatrosses which they sold as souvenirs, so I suppose they saw them as a source of revenue.

"Then it came. A slight freshening one leaden afternoon. Wind. *Olivebank's* sails flapped, filled a bit, soon curved out, and there was the sound of the wash again. We were on the move.

"We close hauled her to make to windward and as much northing as we could. They were days of flying fish and deep blue waters; of puffy white clouds which gave the sky some form, light and shadow. At sundown you could see the sun drop down clear behind the horizon. Then in the warm evening we would damp down the decks and wash in a barrel of sea water; thinking of home. The whole atmosphere of the ship had changed. We could really enjoy this trade wind weather.

"It was the last Sunday in March; we'd finished the early morning work about the ship that had to be done, Sabbath or not, and each of us could relax in whatever way he preferred. For me it was an opportunity to make a few more renderings in watercolour. But the conditions were none too helpful. To begin with, one missed the chance of steady painting from day to day; and there was an absence of privacy. Whilst one realised that these impressions must be set down in the shortest possible time without mistakes, yet my shipmates would stare in such wonder that they embarrassed me.

"This date, too, suggested comparisons, which in turn aroused memories. Here we were coming more or less parallel with the distant Brazilian coastline through tropical heat. In Sussex it would be springtime, with the yellow daffodils nodding in the woodlands; violets as well, peeping out their little dots of colour in the grass. The bold March clouds would be ranging across the sky, blue shadows chasing each other over Down and new-turned furrow, where the white gulls follow the plough from morn till dusk. At noon the sun would be shining so comfortingly that folks just now would be turning their glad hearts to meet it, convinced that Spring had come and Summer would presently follow.

"Meanwhile, our weather gradually began to cool off and there was no more washing or sleeping out on deck. As we got into the North Atlantic, we took down our summer glad rags and sent back aloft our stout storm canvas. Some of the crew grumbled. They thought this an unnecessary precaution. But the Old Man knew his job. The glass was falling and it was increasingly obvious that we were in for a 'blow'. And blow it did. So hard that we thought we were in the Cape Horn latitudes again. Up to now we'd carried no navigation lights as we'd been far from the shipping lanes. Even after the Horn we'd only just sighted the coast of Brazil in the far distance; one island, Trinidade, and the smoke of a single ship beyond the horizon. It was going to be a very different matter, though, in the busy waters near the Azores; the chance of collision would be ever present. But as we fitted the steaming lights, so we lost our kerosene in the fo'c'sle! On the night of this great storm, *Olivebank* was caught by a gigantic breaker which hurled itself aboard with such power that the great ship shuddered all through her old bones. She shook it off, but not before the force of the wave had smashed our lifeboat to matchwood; swept for'ard, shattered our skylight too and carried away our fo'c'sle lamp. We lived in darkness for several nights afterwards, until someone had the time to fix up another.

"The gale also shifted a whole lot of the cargo and we had to go below, meeting plenty of rats as we did so, and re-stow it. This meant heaving heavy grain bags from one side of the ship to the other, and I found it needed a superhuman effort to get a sack on to my back then stumble across and throw it down in its correct position. The job was made all the worse for me because, in the blackness of the night running out to haul on the braces, I'd scraped my shin badly on a taut wire halliard attached to a capstan. It was agony to touch. But now as the ship rolled I continually lost my balance and knocked my shin. I got no sympathy. They all just laughed at my attempts to get a sack on to my back. Then someone showed me the trick of shifting these great sacks. After that it was simple. As he said, so rightly, 'there's a trick to every trade.' This is, of course, what amateur painters have so often come to me for, to learn the short cuts. But I've had to tell them that to paint properly there are no short cuts; just practice, practice, practice. Only by this can one learn to produce something poetical which is not just a technical display.

"After the great gale, the wind had died away completely, and here we were becalmed again, with everything set, and no motion whatsoever through the water. Recently, our spirits had been as high as the wind. In fact, one day *Olivebank* had done twelve and a half knots, a record for her, despite the barnacles and seaweed on her hull below the waterline. No speed now. Just waiting again. Maddening.

"As we neared home, I enjoyed more than ever my duty as look-out man up on the fo'c'sle head. Here one was alone and could commune in privacy with oneself and the effects of the night sky and the early dawn; perhaps dream, too, of white sheets and a tasty meal. One could listen to the sounds around – the slipping of the wash at *Olivebank's* side, or the calling of lone sea birds. Sometimes, in a fog, one was posted as look-out even during the day. It was eerie not being able to see the other end of the ship or the tops of the masts.

"We were now some two hundred miles from the Irish coast and already talking of Queenstown* where we would pick up our orders for the discharge of our four and a half thousand tons of grain. But the Westerlies which we'd expected seemed mythical. They just didn't seem to exist, and the days dragged on while we wallowed.

---

* Queenstown was originally called Cove of Cork but its name was changed after a visit by Queen Victoria in 1849. It was re-named Cobh in 1922, but it would seem that *Olivebank's* crew had not adjusted to the change.

A South Pacific Blow (*Olivebank*): *oil*.

above: *Viking* on tow in the Thames, 1948; painted from the tug *Rumania*: *oil*.

below: A Low Dawn and Wet in the Waist: *oil*.
(By courtesy of Sir Robert McAlpine and Sons Ltd.)

"Then, another boost of wind at last came out of the West and up went our spirits again. At the same time, out came the shore-going clothes. 'Tomorrow – Queenstown,' we said. But not the older hands. 'No use you bring out your clodes so near to port. It bring bad luck – calms and headvinds!'

"One afternoon, as we now bowled along, I was aloft working when I suddenly sighted some trawlers ahead. When I reported this to the Mate he didn't believe me, but he went aloft just the same to see for himself. They were indeed trawlers, which meant that we were rather closer to land, in fact, than we'd reckoned. Our chronometers must have been slightly out. But we didn't worry about that. It meant that any time now we should sight the Fastnet Light. When night fell, I went aloft to do some spotting and met Hellberg coming down. 'No need to go furder,' he said. 'You can see her.' I knew he referred to the Light. I looked out ahead and there, sure enough, was the beam of the Fastnet, describing its white arc above the horizon. One flash every five seconds. A cold, yet exquisite, shiver crept down my spine; the sort of emotion that courses through one on hearing a sublime piece of music. It was the height of joy and the depth of sadness all in an instant. It was the elation that had caught me out on that distant day with my father, giving me a watercolour lesson on the lawn when I'd laughed to prevent myself from crying.

"This was the climax to nearly 15,000 tempestuous miles of toil and discomfort. How many times we had envisaged this Light, wondering when and under what conditions we would first see it. Now, here it was. The old girl had got us there.

"A zephyr of a breeze carried us forward through the night and when day broke, there was the land. How beautiful it looked as the sun rose and steeped the emerald green with its golden glow. And how delicious was the scent of heather and the peat fires burning. But alas, close as that land was, we could get no nearer. Our stately ship with her still sails lay like some graceful white bird, asleep on the ocean. The day passed, and only the tide drifted us back and forth within tantalising reach of the coast. The next day, too, the calm remained with us, so that we resorted to an age-old custom for raising the wind. We stole a pair of the Cook's trousers and threw them over the side. But it made not a single cat's paw of a difference. After a few hours, we took a pack of playing cards, tore them in half and threw them after the Cook's trousers. It was generally agreed that it was this that enticed the light airs to waft out of the West at last, and gently nudge us towards Queenstown. I wonder if any man has ever been so welcomed as that Pilot was when he stepped aboard with some mail and our orders. Our excitement knew no bounds. As we'd realised that his little boat was actually heading out to us, we'd cheered and cheered.

"We now learned that our port for discharge was to be Cardiff. This was wonderful news. With a fair wind, we could sail across to Wales in twenty-four hours. So, as a sickle moon sank behind the Irish hills, we squared away for Cardiff. It was then that the wind came. A fair wind for Queenstown right enough; but a dead muzzler for Cardiff.

"For some ten days we beat about the Irish Sea, or went down south again into the Atlantic. The familiar sight of decks filled with surging waters was again our lot. The Cook's galley was washed out once again; he lost yet more pots and pans; and the Mate's dreaded two whistles came piercing at us through the howling shriek of the night wind in the rigging.

"But it couldn't last for ever. Even this black easterly which had brought us such despair shifted at last, and the wind went round into the south-west. We brought every knot of it to bear, and it took us up the Bristol Channel and on to Cardiff. We dropped anchor in the Barry Roads to await our docking orders and after a night there were finally taken into a berth at Spiller's Wharf. The next morning I was at last paid off and received my wages, just under £9; most of which I paid over to the Carpenter for a model he'd made of *Olivebank*.

"It left me enough for the train fare home, though. Frank came to see me off at the station, and when I shook hands with him through the window as the train moved off, I felt I was shaking the hand of one of the best friends I'd ever known.

"The train passed close to Spiller's Wharf and I had a last glimpse of *Olivebank*. As I looked up into her rigging and yards and thought of the times I'd fought up there, saw again the graceful lines of her rusted hull I realised what she'd meant to me. It was just a little bit difficult to say 'goodbye.'

* * * *

"I now took stock of my surroundings in the dining car. How clean and fresh it all looked. How white the table cloth. How the cutlery sparkled. I folded my hands on the table, then realised with horror how begrimed and scarred they were, and that what remained of my finger nails was a disgusting sight. I hid my hands between my knees. They were hardly the hands of an artist. But what need to feel ashamed? My hands, after all, were only the outward symbol of honest labour. Hands don't matter all that much when it comes to painting. One can paint with the toes, or by mouth if necessary. What does matter is what goes on inside one's head. If there is nothing on top and no feeling in the heart, nothing meaningful or sensitive will find its way on to paper or canvas. There will be no message.

"Nevertheless, as I sat back waiting to be served lunch, certain questions arose in my mind. Had it all been worthwhile? Had it been anything more than an interesting episode? Was I a better man? Was I richer in perception of physical effects only, or had it taught me something deeper? Endowed me with a greater wisdom and understanding of myself and others? And, perhaps as important as anything else so far as my work was concerned, had it given me incentive to paint better than I had ever painted before? If that were so, and I believed the other considerations could be answered in the positive, then nothing had been wasted.

"But I had a suspicion that the task which now lay ahead of me might prove an even greater challenge than serving in a sailing ship, round the Horn before the Mast."

Chapter 7

Storm Clouds

In contrast to windjammer living, even in primitive Sutton, he felt cloaked in luxury. The cool, clean water drawn up eighty feet from the well was an elixir after the brackish rain water from the ship's tanks and his mother's cooking now seemed ambrosial.

At night, when the wind roared through the great elms that edged the garden and the rain hammered against the windows, it was pure luxury to have a warm, dry bed and to sleep without the fear of "two whistles" calling out the watch to take in sail. In future, he decided, he would go to sea only when he chose, and the easy way.

Then the old trouble with his stomach suddenly flared up again, was this time diagnosed as appendicitis, and he found himself in hospital. By extraordinary good fortune the real emergency had waited till he was ashore. He was wheeled into the operating theatre singing sea shanties, which were held by some to be none too tuneful.

He went to see his girl friend, more out of duty now than desire. But her circle no longer seemed to attract him so he wasted little time in getting down to painting. First, he worked a big canvas of *Olivebank* rounding the Horn in mountainous seas. It was painted on a piece of sail cloth which had served as his eiderdown, when it had got bitterly cold down in the southerly latitudes near the Antarctic. Another canvas he entitled "Rolling Her Easting Down"; a third, "A Low Dawn and Wet in the Waist". These were amongst the finest oil paintings Muncaster ever did. They capture dramatically, yet with deep poetic feeling, the spectacle of a lone sailing ship forging her way through that savage wildness of ocean. He recorded that "climbing out along the yard, it was cruelly impressive to note the boiling sea far below, wherein it appeared scarcely credible that any ship whatsoever could survive. The wind continued mercilessly and, whilst we were climbing up blew us flat against the ratlines."

Two of these oils were exhibited in the Royal Academy and there is no doubt that the artist hoped they might accelerate his election as an A.R.A. He certainly considered them important works. But the pictures received little attention. Marine paintings were seldom popular at the R.A., and no votes were cast for his election.

Also during this period he carried out a series of lecture tours, and wrote a book on his experiences on *Olivebank, Rolling Round the Horn*. This was published by Rich and Cowan in 1933. Moreover John Masefield asked him to illustrate his book *Bird of Dawning*, which was published in an edition limited to 300 copies. All were signed by author and artist.

At about this time he went to a tennis party in Petworth one afternoon, and met Primrose Balfour, then seventeen, a vivacious girl with blue eyes and flowing blonde hair. He said afterwards that she had all the attributes that attracted him, but with something more; her face expressed a spirituality and an inner beauty of soul which spoke to him immediately. They fell for each other completely, and a fortnight later were secretly engaged. But while she excelled at tennis and he at golf, her father, Sir Arthur Balfour (later Lord Riverdale of Sheffield) had to be tackled. He did not actually oppose the marriage, and Muncaster found this wealthy man much more amenable than he might have hoped. But Sir Arthur insisted on one thing; that his future son-in-law should at least prove himself solvent. Whether this was intended to scotch the marriage or not one cannot tell. But Muncaster did achieve some kind of solvency; anyway enough to satisfy his father-in-law, and he was married at the end of September 1933, at Fernhurst in Sussex. It was quite an occasion, and to celebrate it, the villagers tied large bunches of flowers to all the telegraph poles.

Their first house at Tillington was one of among a dozen identical bungalows, and not a little different from Ropes at Fernhurst where Primrose had been brought up. While she practised gastronomy on a temperamental paraffin stove, he had a wooden studio built in the tiny garden. There he held a small exhibition of watercolours which paid for the construction at least. They lived happily there for just over two years. I arrived in the world during the sweltering July of 1934 leaving my mother very weak.

In the autumn of that year my father held his fourth one-man exhibition at the Fine Art Society in New Bond Street. This was by no means a failure. He sold thirty-two works. But when all the expenses were deducted, the usual thirty-three and a third gallery commission, and framing costs, the profit amounted to only a few shillings more than one hundred and ninety-eight pounds. He began to wonder whether it was worth the effort.

Apart from the Fine Art show, he continued to exhibit at public exhibitions and also the R.W.S. for which Society he had already served on the Council and had on a number of occasions acted as hanger. This was a job he very much enjoyed, and was good at. Arranging pictures sympathetically on a wall is an expert business. But he did like to be left alone when doing it and hated being fussed by hangers-on. The public exhibitions to which he sent works included ones at the Royal Academy, the Royal Scottish Academy, the Royal Glasgow Institute of Fine Arts, Bradford, Southport, Worthing and Brighton. He usually sold at the Royal Academy, but his success at other exhibitions was mixed. He almost always did best when he could be on the spot to talk personally with prospective buyers.

It was at about this time that he began to be increasingly concerned by the advance of the modern idiom in painting. He was suspicious of much of this kind of art and couldn't understand why dealers and Press should champion what seemed to him such ugliness and distortion of the truth. Oliver Hall called a good deal of modern art "a cancerous growth from the underworld," and his forthright opinions about it obviously went against him. When he held an exhibition of his works at the Fine Art Society in 1936, he disposed of only one small canvas. Muncaster wrote: "This was purchased rather from pity than for any other reason, by his life-long friend and patron, Charles Oakey (of sandpaper fame). I was grieved at my father's ill fortune. It seemed sad that such a distinguished painter should suffer such an indignity."

The following year, after the arrival of my brother Clive, whose birth all but killed my mother, the Muncasters moved to a new house, built for them, near Petworth.

Four-Winds, half tiled and whitewashed, lay in the centre of a small farmstead, which when they arrived, was owned by a bent old lady who kept a white horse, a few cows and chickens and employed just one labourer. The corn was sown by hand. The farm buildings, situated in a worked-out sandstone quarry, consisted of a fine timber barn and some ancient outhouses. On one side grew a tall and graceful ash tree, on the other a very aged wych elm. It was all marvellous painting material which Muncaster was to use many times. From where the house stood, there were panoramic views in almost all directions but the site was also open to the elements from equally as many points of the compass.

It was to be the family home for many happy years.

*　　*　　*　　*

Those with any vision could see by 1937 what the next few years would hold. "If there was going to be a war I had no desire for foot-slogging or trench warfare!" He thus recorded his feelings at the time and decided to join the Royal Naval Volunteer Supplementary Reserve.

The R.N.V.S.R. was a force of some two thousand men with a practical knowledge of the sea. The Headquarters were at H.M.S. *King Alfred* at Hove, in Sussex. When Muncaster joined, he told the Lieutenant who interviewed him that he hoped he might be permitted to use his professional abilities as a painter to record the Navy at sea under war conditions. The Joining Officer was sceptical. He thought it a good enough idea, but doubted whether "Their Lordships" at the Admiralty would evince similar enthusiasm. They would perhaps have greater need for seamen, gunners and navigators. But because he had so much seafaring experience, Muncaster was in the event accepted into the Service, and just to keep things nice and tidy, was signed on as Sub-Lieut. Grahame Hall.* He went to a few lectures at H.M.S. *King Alfred*, though he felt very unenthusiastic about attending.

Before long, however, Muncaster followed through his ideas for getting naval history recorded in pictorial form. He proposed that he should accompany the Fleet on its Spring Cruise to the Mediterranean as the official naval artist. Much to his surprise, the request was granted, and he was invited to be a guest aboard the battleship, *Rodney*. Perhaps an authentic sailing ship man was a curiosity, though more likely his acceptance had something to do with the fact that his mother-in-law had naval connections. He recalled: "I was most apprehensive about joining the ship. I knew naval etiquette was of supreme importance and that there were certain things one just didn't do. For instance, on stepping aboard the quarterdeck one saluted if in uniform or raised one's hat if in civvies. I never wear a hat, so I bought one specially for the occasion. Unhappily, it blew off when I was looking out of the carriage window, and as I arrived in Devonport well after dark with the shops closed, couldn't buy another. This really worried me dreadfully, as I was unable to raise my hat or salute. So when I arrived at the top of the gangway I affected a sort of deferential lowering of the head as one does when meeting Royalty. The Officer of the Watch did look a little sideways at me, but nobody shouted or anything so I presumed I was acceptable. In fact, the Navy turned out to be a marvellous host, and I was very soon made to feel thoroughly at home. Everything was done to help me adapt to a strange life and to help me find my way about this massive ship which, both below and on deck, was labyrinthine. I lost my way to the wardroom so many times that I began to get quite nervous about asking for directions."

This great ship generated enough electrical power to light a fair-sized city. She had her own bakery, which turned out one thousand five hundred pounds of delicious bread daily; five telephone exchanges; and for spiritual needs, her own oak-panelled chapel carpeted in mauve.

After he had gone aboard, on that memorable evening "negative headdress" Muncaster had been shown to a cabin aft and at the same time was introduced to the occupant of the cabin next door, Sub-Lieutenant Lawrence Hornby. Hornby recalled this meeting in *Rodney*: "I joined at Devonport, feeling pretty down because of injections. I was taken to a cabin and found I was next door to a charming, kindly, humorous dark-haired civilian Claude Muncaster. We shared a Marine WRA (Wardroom Attendant) so got into the habit of wandering into each other's cabins and yarning. On our first morning aboard, we decided to have breakfast in the ward-room together, myself having no idea that it was a sin to utter at this hallowed time.

* Although his name was not changed to Muncaster by deed poll until 1945, he had taken the nom-de-plume, Claude Muncaster, in 1922, and for continuity we will keep it as such in spite of the fact that he used the name Hall while in the Navy.

"I sat down, Claude alongside, with the Commander across the table contemplating a copy of *The Times* and testing a cup of very black coffee. I said brightly: 'Good Morning, Sir.' He glared at me and replied: 'Good Morning' seven times, ending by saying he hoped this would last me the rest of the week.

"Claude spluttered into his porridge, but gripped my left leg to prevent me swearing back. We finished our breakfast in silence."

Later the same morning when Muncaster was making a tour of the ship on the lookout for likely subjects, he came upon the Commander consulting the Navigator about the weather forecast:

"Gales on all coasts, Sir."

"Fine! That'll blow us down to the 'Bay' all right. But it won't do my paint much good."

"You don't have to worry about that, Sir, we've got a real live artist aboard now. He can repair any paintwork!"

"Ah yes," said the Commander, now addressing himself to Muncaster. "I've been talking to the Captain about you. He suggests you start painting the starboard side of the funnel at six bells (7 a.m.) in the morning watch. Will that suit you?"

Once again he found himself used as a sort of safety valve for sailor's banter. Even the Captain, now on his own ground, did his share of chipping, with remarks about the ship's painter receiving "bottles" (reprimands) from himself and the Commander if his work didn't fulfil regulations laid down in Admiralty Fleet Orders.

At first the seas had not affected *Rodney* all that much, but as she turned the corner off Ushant, the swell came on to her beam. Now she began to roll very heavily and moving around was most difficult. He wondered how the gunners could possibly have been accurate if they'd had to engage in such weather.

Exercises were carried out during the run down to Lisbon, and there were some enthralling sights of ships in various formations and weather conditions. Particularly memorable was the sight of a destroyer lit up by the sun and seen through a heavy rain shower. She looked for all the world like a phantom ship.

He was keen to draw something of every department in the ship. Many things did not justify even a note in the sketchbook, whilst others demanded a watercolour such as the engine room, the gear room, the Admiral's Bridge and the chart room. He found the engine room spotless, less hot and quieter than expected. But the gear room was noisy and when the ship was getting under way the din was unbearable. While he was taking notes in the engine room one day an Engineer Lieutenant made himself known to the artist, asking for lessons and criticism. This was by no means the first such request on board and Muncaster found that he was getting quite busy as an Instructor.

Meanwhile the conditions for carrying out his own work were proving very difficult. Many times, in order to see the subject properly, often through high scuttles (portholes) he had to work standing up. Watercolour painting can be well-nigh impossible when standing because the particular technique demands very considerable control. He preferred to sit on a stool, supporting the folio on his knees. The blacksmith constructed him a very ingenious extending steel stool with which he experimented. But when this was fully extended he found it difficult, with the rolling of the ship, to balance and draw or apply a controlled wash from such a perch.

In his fervour to note every subject he could, Muncaster began to have an irresistible inclination to climb the mast. He realised it would be difficult actually to draw or paint up there, but at least he could take a photograph as a record. It would just be a matter of getting permission from the Officer of the Watch on the bridge.

As he started steadily to climb, he very soon discovered that it was not quite the simple task he had expected. A sailing ship's mast was bad enough with all its rigging, but this mast was a mass of intricate, spiky electrical gear, and all of it very grimy. About two-thirds of the way up, he became conscious of a good deal of shouting going on below. Looking down, he saw the quarter-deck thick with officers all staring aloft. "What the hell do you think you're doing up there? Come down this instant." Muncaster took his photograph, then obeyed the command, though taking his own good time about it. One didn't rush things when aloft.

The Commander, a tall man at the best of times, looked taller than ever stiffening his lean height before the stove in his cabin. Putting his hands behind his back, he glowered at the culprit.

"Now then . . . what the bloody hell do you mean by climbing the mast without first reporting to me?"

"I er . . . I did inform the Officer of the Watch, Sir. I understood that was sufficient."

"Well, it wasn't reported to me. Nearly every department in the ship must be informed before the mast is climbed. Do you realise what would have happened if we'd started to transmit?"

"No, Sir."

"You'd have been knocked off and killed by the current. Now, don't imagine that small fact would have worried me. What would have concerned me would have been my quarter-deck. Ever since we left Devonport, I've had my chaps holystoning the quarter-deck getting it snowy-white in readiness for the King of Portugal. I would not have wanted the first thing he saw on stepping aboard to be your bloody imprint all over the deck! It so happens that while you are in this ship, you're not under my command. If you were, you'd be in the cells by now. Before you start any more of your monkey tricks, you first report to me. Is that clear?"

"Yes, Sir."

"Good. Then we'll have a pink gin; and from now on you can consider the matter forgotten."

And, indeed, it was never mentioned again.

The visit to Lisbon was a goodwill one and attended by every bit of pomp and ceremony which could possibly be crammed into such an occasion.

A ball was arranged for one evening to which he was invited. It was held in a house in Black Horse Square which contained the most elegant architecture. He was much impressed by the scene that night, as officers disembarked from the picket boats in their full dress uniforms with black cloaks lined with red and white silk. Both *Nelson* and *Rodney* were floodlit and the reflection of the twinkling lights on the water was all most romantic. But he didn't much enjoy the ball, finding it very formal. Not only had he managed to come without money, but later, while breakfasting off indifferent bacon and eggs in a cafe, he realised he had missed the last picket boat that night back to *Rodney*. He had to stay with some English people whom he met at the ball.

The following morning he arrived aboard with the milk, feeling rather crumpled and while still wearing white tie and tails had to account for his movements.

The next part of the cruise took them to Gibraltar and Madeira and by now hints were being passed that could not escape him. They were to the effect that he was living on board, and generally looking on and enjoying the hospitality offered without paying his way. He could do little about the hospitality except return drink for drink and order rounds. The paintings however were a different matter.

Although reticent about showing his work, especially when it was unmounted and unframed, he felt in the circumstances that he'd better hold an exhibition. The Commander seemed to think it an excellent idea, so he went ashore in search of boards. At long last finding something approaching what he wanted, he cut about twenty mounts of various sizes, in which he put selected watercolours and placed them about the ward-room. The number and variety of subjects was a general surprise, and on the whole it was considered a creditable performance. At least they realised that he had been doing some work. There were critics, of course. One night he returned to the ward-room to find the Gunnery Officer discussing with a Lieutenant a picture illustrating a star shell put up at night over a destroyer. The bright glare lit up the destroyer in sharp relief. He heard the Lieutenant remark "if that's what he thinks a star shell looks like he must be ruddy well tight." But the Gunnery Officer thought differently, saying he considered it "a bloody good shot and a bloody good picture."

Each department made sure of some criticism before allowing any commendation. The Navigator, for instance, pointed out that he had not drawn his dividers and parallel rule in their usual places on the chart. But having voiced their criticism, most were happy, feeling that they knew better than the artist.

While at Gibraltar, Muncaster received news of difficulties with family business at home. He decided he could get no more work out of the cruise in *Rodney*, so booked his passage back to England in the *Circassia*, a small ship of the Donaldson Line. The voyage turned out to be uneventful and rather a relief from keeping up with naval tradition and working under very trying conditions. Nevertheless, the time in *Rodney* had been valuable. Though he was not to learn just how valuable until the outbreak of war.

Chapter 8

War

"The thought of war had always given me the absolute shudders. I abhorred any idea of killing, whether man or beast, but particularly man. Seeing the evil potential of Nazism and believing so completely in freedom, I was prepared to fight; but the thought of it was none the less repellent."

*   *   *

In the late summer of 1939, on a visit to Cardiff, Muncaster was thrilled to see *Olivebank* in dock again. She brought back such memories that he couldn't resist booking a passage in her. She was bound for Finland, and this time he would be a passenger. But Mrs Muncaster was horrified to hear what he had done and insisted that he dropped the idea. Her husband was extremely reluctant to throw away such an opportunity for more concentrated and leisurely painting under sail. Further, Captain Mateson who had taken over a few years before had made a much faster ship of the old windbag. The voyage would not take long. But in the end wifely persuasion won the day and he cancelled the passage.

It was well that he did. Just a few days after the outbreak of war, *Olivebank* struck a mine off the coast of Denmark. She went down, and there were only five survivors. Muncaster noted: "She had maintained her reputation as an unlucky ship. I felt sad that such beauty should meet with so sudden and unhappy an end. My survival seemed like a Divine Providence. This did not make me feel in any way special but, rather, that I had been given an extension of life in which to do things better."

He decided he'd better prepare for sea. If he was going to be called up, he would need some knowledge of navigation and communications. He set to and tried to teach himself something of these necessary arts. He made a creditable job of learning Morse and semaphore and the various signal flags that covered the alphabet, but the mathematical complexities of navigation stopped his brain dead in its tracks; he comprehended the subject through a fog. The more he wrestled with the problems of speeds, distances, angles, vectors, G.H.A.'s (Greenwich Hour Angles), declinations and deviations, the more he cursed his lack of mental agility and his maths master of long ago who'd so stupidly laid him about the head with a book.

His call-up papers landed on the Four-Winds doormat in February 1940. Back at H.M.S. *King Alfred* in Hove, the Navy was teaching young men to be resourceful officers in a few hours. If you had a mind for figures, that was fine. But Muncaster made his mark by singing sea shanties and telling Sussex stories at the Ship's Concert on Saturday nights; just hoping that his lack of prowess on the chart table would not be noticed.

In desperation, he requested to see the Commander to find out if there was any possibility of being detailed as an Official Naval Artist. The Commander promised to "see somebody at the Admiralty" and try to arrange something. But when Muncaster's time came for passing out, he was told that this proposition had gone by the board. Volunteers were badly needed for motor torpedo boats (M.T.B.s) and he was to be one. He was to a join celestial navigation class the next week.

An order was an order, and the following Monday he joined the class. The 'Schoolie' Commander addressed his pupils, informing them without bothering to conceal his pride too carefully, that the last class he had taught had passed out to a man. He expected his new recruits to do the same. He then explained something about the course, assuming that they were all well up in their coastal navigation. Muncaster raised a single-striped arm and explained that his coastal navigation was rather shaky. The Commander was undisturbed. "Not to worry about that. Coastal navigation is quite straightforward. You'll pick it up in a jiffy." He went on: "Now this course requires a knowledge of logarithms. I take it you know your 'logs'?" Again, an arm towards the back of the class was stretched skywards. Its owner explained that he'd left school early and had never done "logs." As the Instructor absorbed this information, a look of consternation unsettled what till then had been quite a composed countenance. He paused for quite a while. "Well, I'm sure you'll find somebody to put you wise to that one, it's largely a matter of looking up tables."

He now went a little deeper into the subject and explained that celestial navigation was to a considerable extent based on trigonometry. He averted his gaze from the body of the class as he asked in a tone loaded with expectancy: "I suppose there is nobody here who does not have any knowledge of 'trig'?"

An amused murmur drifted through the class as, once again Muncaster raised a hand. This time he only shook his head. The Commander, with eyebrows just a suggestion lifted, shook his head in return. "I wonder why you've been sent here?" he said slowly. "Well, we shall just have to see how you get on."

Muncaster managed to survive the fortnight, thanks to one member of the class, Douglas Probert, who took pity on him and offered to try and help. They got together and swapped experience. Muncaster helped Probert to locate the stars, which was second nature to him, while Probert in his turn tried to teach him how to work out sights. But the omens were not promising. When he tried to put the information into practice in the classroom after hours with the patient Probert, he worked out his ship's position as being in the middle of Rutland, when it was supposed to be off the coast of Ceylon. However, after more hours with the excellent Probert, and a liberal share of providence, he managed to scrape through. Now, on paper at least, a fully-trained Navigator, he was appointed Assistant Navigator, not to an M.T.B. but to H.M.S. *Andania*, an ex-Cunarder serving as an A.M.C. (Armed Merchant Cruiser) on the Northern Patrol.

Just before leaving to join *Andania*, notice of his promotion to Lieutenant came through, and, much to his pride, he had a second wavy* gold stripe sewn to his sleeve.

Together with three other officers, Muncaster arrived in wartime Glasgow one early April morning and changed on to a train for Greenock. Everything had happened with an air of the greatest urgency. They had to leave at short notice and had hardly even had time to say "goodbye" to their wives. When they finally reached Greenock, they searched for their ship, only to discover that she was not in and would not be for another week. They were to be berthed meanwhile in *Chusan*, an ex-P.&O. ship being fitted out as an A.M.C.

* Royal Navy Officers have straight gold braid stripes on the sleeve. During the War, Volunteer Reserve Officers had wavy stripes and were known as the "Wavy Navy."

Chusan was berthed alongside a dry dock in which another A.M.C. was undergoing refit and offered an excellent subject for a painting. Muncaster had in fact retrieved some of his painting-gear from the studio cupboard before coming away. He was almost finishing a watercolour when a dockyard 'Matey' approached and looked over his shoulder. He studied the work for some time, then remarked; "Ye've done verra well. But why didn't ye take a photograph? It'd save a hell uv a lot of boogerin' aroond!"

The following day the Captain went off on a spell of leave, having commissioned a watercolour of *Andania*, and Muncaster started the picture from a vantage point on the quayside. Unknown to him, however, he had set himself up by the side of a dock where a ship was taking on personnel for a highly secret and important mission. He was noticed; reported, and very soon found himself being escorted by the dockyard police to a small shed and there locked in. To make matters worse, he had a camera with him. "I thought I'd better come clean about this, so told the officer I had a camera in my painting case as well as my artist's materials. The officer's response was "Oh my God. What did you have to tell me that for? Now I'll have to take all your gear in charge."

As soon as the arrest had been reported, the Commander of *Andania* came smartly along to the shed to find out what had happened. He then had to do some swift talking, and it was, in fact, only after lengthy discussions and pleadings that Muncaster was released and allowed back to his ship. Nevertheless he was locked in his cabin and a sentry was posted at the door. He was informed, without quite the usual courtesies, that he would be taken to Glasgow where he would go before the security people. The Commander accompanied the prisoner to Glasgow the following morning and explained the situation. Fortunately for his charge the story was believed and the artist was allowed to go on leave while the situation was reviewed, but he was ordered to report his movements.

On his arrival in London, he went straight to the Admiralty to report his first movement which he had hoped could be in the direction of home. By chance he was taken to see the very man to whom the Commander at H.M.S. *King Alfred* had spoken about his becoming a Naval Artist. Mr R. M. Y. Gleadowe was a most understanding and cultured person. He turned out to be the uncle, in fact, of an officer with whom Muncaster later worked a great deal – Robert Gooden. Gleadowe could do nothing further about the idea of becoming a Naval Artist, but he gave him a letter "To whom it may concern" which was an official request that Muncaster "should be given facilities to sketch and take photographs of subjects of a naval nature during the exercise of his duties."

After a couple of days' leave he repaired to Glasgow with this valuable document and took it to the Captain of *Andania*, most concerned that he had caused him embarrassment and keen to put matters right. To his amazement, however, the Captain on seeing the letter went puce with fury: "What the hell do you think I've been trying to do all this time? Keep it out of the Admiralty. Now you've gone and advertised the whole shooting match. And who the hell is this bloody little civil servant who's signed this letter, anyway? You'll attend 'defaulters' at 10 a.m. on the bridge tomorrow. In the meantime, I want your camera and all your paintings and painting gear. They'll all go into the strong room, and you won't do any painting while you're aboard my ship. Understood?"

Life on board *Andania* thenceforward was made most unpleasant. Whenever he was on the bridge with the Captain, he had to endure continual innuendos, about artists and R.N.V.S.R. officers, and arrests. It was a long fortnight before the patrol returned and he was much relieved to find news waiting for him at Greenock of an appointment to H.M.S. *Osprey*, the Anti-Submarine School at Portland. He was to report there in three days' time, but meanwhile could go on leave. His wife met him at Glasgow and they went back to Four-Winds together. She had 'flu and he had a cough and a nose-bleed which was something exceptional. After the first night home, he was found to be spitting blood and had an acute pain in the chest. The doctor came and diagnosed pneumonia and pleurisy. There was no going to Portland.

By a piece of good fortune, he was allowed to be nursed at home. Primrose proved an excellent and most competent nurse and before long he was better. Meanwhile *Andania* put to sea again, was torpedoed, and sunk. Fortunately, a lot of lives were saved. But, even so, as in the case of *Olivebank*, he was given to think.

When he did recover he was almost immediately struck down by an attack of phlebitis in the leg. I have a memory of him hopping round the house with the help of a home-made crutch, an upturned broom with a piece of old carpet underlay wrapped around the bristles. Even though at times he was in considerable pain, he made fun of the whole thing and even managed to play cricket with us.

Gradually he became fit again with the help of some physical exercise, gardening, digging, and rather more than the occasional round of golf. He also used the time to construct an air-raid shelter. He dug a deep hole at the bottom of the garden, covered it with corrugated iron supported on struts of wood, and turfed it as camouflage from spotting German aircraft. In fact, his building works were none too strong. The thing collapsed of its own accord one night after some heavy rain, smothering sundry knitted toys. Clive and I had put them carefully into the shelter because we thought they would be safer there than in bed with us. When they were finally retrieved, they were so damp and mildewed that we had to dispose of them. Father thought we should do so with proper ceremony, so we dug graves for them and buried them in the kitchen garden.

In October 1940, there was a phone call from the Admiralty ordering my father to report to a Captain Rivett-Carnac, Director of Training and Staff Duties. Accordingly, he presented himself for interview the next day at 11 a.m. and was told that there had been repeated requests from Captains at sea for some sort of camouflage which might prove effective against air and sea attack. Their Lordships had now decided to call in a camouflage expert to be attached to Captain Rivett-Carnac's Division (T.S.D.) and Muncaster's name had been put forward for the job. He had to admit at once that he knew nothing about sea camouflage and could hardly be called an expert. "Never mind," said the Captain. "We'll soon make you one."

Muncaster took up his appointment early in November and at the Mad House as the Admiralty was reverently known, found Commander P. W. Brock, who was dealing with camouflage, at his desk surrounded by sheaves of paper. He was busily compiling a report on oiling at sea. Muncaster recalled their meeting: "I knew he had probably been writing all night and was reluctant to disturb him. But he was the only person who knew anything about camouflage and there was no alternative but to encroach upon his concentration. The Commander was a man of few words, though I was later to find he had a most refreshing wit which was to serve us well in trying moments. On first acquaintance, however, he was not in any mood for congeniality. Here was somebody, I thought, who would not suffer fools gladly and any direction, once given, had to be understood as it would not be repeated. His instructions were brief. He told me I would be known as "C.1." (Camouflage 1). Office hours were from 9 a.m. to 6 p.m. Most officers worked longer. When there was an air-raid warning and whistles were blown within the building, anyone who wanted to could go below to the basement to take cover. He suggested that as a first step I should call up any papers in any way connected with camouflage and study them carefully. Then he took me along to introduce me to the Head Boy, and promptly left me to return to his report on oiling at sea. Later I heard that this report had been a valuable and constructive contribution to our maritime war effort."*

Having been put wise to one or two Civil Service administrative traditions and practices, Muncaster returned to Commander Brock's office as the Navy's Camouflage Expert for all Ships at Sea. Although he felt ill equipped for this grand-sounding appointment, it was a job he felt he could learn; but as to being a Navigator – never.

For a time the newly-appointed expert floundered. Never having worked in an office he was unacquainted with administrative terms, never mind the specialised Naval jargon. He had no idea of what constituted a paper; nor the ramifications of Policy, Strategy or Tactics, and to baffle him further, there were initials everywhere, on correspondence and memoranda, D.N.C., D.S.R., D.N.I., D.A.S.W.* Should he ask to be enlightened? Somehow it was an admission of failure in not being able to work them out for himself. Perhaps "T.S.D." would give him some clues! At least he had sorted out that one.

But the first priority was to get his bearings. The office in which he had joined Commander Brock was somewhat Dickensian; a dark place with one diminutive window, frosted with grime and wired against the effects of bombs and shrapnel. The single office table that served as a desk was expansive and black-topped. The floor was bare, the walls painted a dirty green. According to standard practice and irrespective of weather or temperature, on 1st November the heating had been turned on. In one corner of this welcoming apartment stood a grey cupboard for the safe-keeping of secret papers. At the table were two oldish wooden chairs, and furnishing the table's sleek black top, IN and OUT trays, a telephone and an Admiralty Directory. There were two wastepaper baskets for reception of the less intelligible memoranda and tomes of official prose that were part of the horrors of a nation at war; and his own wastepaper basket was usually full of crumpled-up balls of paper upon which he had made agonised efforts to compose understandable minutes expressed in the accepted jargon.

*D.N.C.   Director of Naval Construction
 D.S.R.   Director of Scientific Research and Development
 D.N.I.   Director of Naval Intelligence
 D.A.S.W.   Director of Anti-Submarine Warfare

* Another contribution to the war effort made by Brock at about this time was noted in his diary for 7 November 1940: "On leaving Admiralty at 2120, ran into a stick of small bombs being dropped by a very low raider. Nipped down behind sandbags. One bomb destroyed the blackout arrangements in Carlton House Terrace. Could not raise the occupants, so I collected a couple of Royal Marines, with rifles, from the Admiralty, who shot out the lights. Never imagined doing this to one of the stately homes of England."

Outsiders' Varnishing Day at the Royal Academy, 1939. The model ship in the painting which Muncaster is varnishing is the one he purchased with his wages from the *Olivebank* voyage. Below is Charles Cundall R.A.

The *Victoria and Albert Yacht* at the Coronation Review, 1937: *oil*.

He had been installed in his chair hardly an hour when a Commander Shattock entered and enquired of Commander Brock what was the latest camouflage policy in respect of aircraft carriers. Brock nodded his head towards Muncaster and said: "Ask him. He's the Camouflage Expert."

Muncaster explained rather feebly that since he had only arrived that morning there had been no opportunity to study the papers on camouflage.

Eventually he was moved from Commander Brock's office, but not before he had become much better acquainted with him. His first impressions had been coloured by his being scared stiff about the situation in which he had found himself, coupled with complete ignorance of how to go about things. Commander Brock proved to be a man of great integrity, dedication and humour. He retired from the Royal Navy with the rank of Rear-Admiral after a most distinguished career.

It was not long before Muncaster found he had committed another blunder. It had been decided that a certain ship should be painted a particular colour to help camouflage her. It was also his duty to see that these directions were carried out with the least possible delay. Investigations revealed that there was not enough paint for the job so he approached the manufacturers and ordered more, much to their delight. However, when Camouflage 1 reported progress to D.T.S.D., he stopped a most unpleasant bottle, "Money has to be voted for this sort of thing 'C1', and through the proper channels. You can't just go ordering tons and tons of paint on your own initiative. Cancel it at once."

He obeyed the order, but recorded that he did not think that was the way to get on with the War.

The first real camouflage job was to disguise a small Q-boat. Her role was to give the impression that she was a lame duck in the convoy and attract any attack from the air to herself. Q-boats had been used successfully against U-boats during World War I. Concealing their armament until the very last moment, they then let drop the disguise and suddenly became fighting ships. In this instance Muncaster decided to conceal the guns under what would appear to be the deck cargo of a large pantechnicon. When it had been constructed, the whole thing looked very realistic and was thoroughly approved of by the Captain of the ship and others who saw it. Unhappily the ship was sunk by a U-boat and there were no survivors. The air attack never came. He was most upset when he heard the news and felt responsible for what had happened.

The next assignment would have tested the expertise and imagination of the most brilliant of experts. The order was to make the one-funnel target ship, H.M.S. *Centurion*, look like H.M.S. *King George V* which was a battleship with two funnels, ten fourteen-inch guns and a third as big again. The job took him to Plymouth.

He left London after the night of the last of the great London blitzes. In the morning he crunched his way to the Admiralty along unrecognisable streets deep in glass and rubble. Smoke drifted blackly from the ruins. He found his Admiralty office a total shambles, only one object standing upright where the desk had been – his "midwifery case," as he called it (a doctor's case in which he carried all his painting gear, cameras, and those useful bits of equipment that an artist collects in the course of his trade). Other than a thick covering of dust and plaster, the case was unharmed. It had been a good friend over many years and he was delighted to find it intact. How fortunate that he had not been working through the night! He would almost certainly not have survived a blast that had caused so much devastation at the Admiralty.

Brock also noted his findings after that night, "office untenable – 4 bottles of sherry smashed all over me papers. Moved down to basement."

Later that day Muncaster made his way to Paddington to take the night train to Plymouth. Although that area had been laid waste as much as the rest of London, enough clearance had been achieved by late afternoon to enable a few trains to leave.

At dawn the next morning, after a slow and tedious journey, the train came to a halt a few miles outside Plymouth. "We were stationary for about an hour. We had stopped by a wooded slope and a little stream sparkled in the early sunlight. I felt the keenest desire to step down from the train and wander over the dew-drenched grass among the trees. Here was beauty and peace and it belonged to God, not to war. Yet, as we jerked into motion again and moved slowly nearer to Plymouth, it was war again all too starkly. A pall of smoke was rising from a bomb-racked city. It had been the first night of the Plymouth blitz." So it was out of one blitz and into another.

Having been shown his accommodation in the barracks he found the Commander of *Centurion* who explained the job. There were just three days to complete it, so the sooner he could present them with a camouflage scheme, the better. If possible it was to be finished before noon.

The main constructional differences such as the fourteen-inch gun turrets and bridge alterations had already been carried out. It was Muncaster's job to produce a painted design. Fortunately he had seen the *King George V* at sea. When studying her, he had noticed a white line which extended along her hull – rather like the ones on the British India Steam Navigation Company's ships. As far as they were concerned it was decoration, but on the battleship it was caused by the light reflecting from the line of the extra armour plating round the lower part of her hull. He incorporated this into his plan, together with other suggestions which occurred to him after studying pictures and photographs in *Jane's Fighting Ships*.

With his experience of working quickly in watercolour he completed the design in a couple of hours, and presented it to the Commander who seemed pleased with it. Painting began that afternoon. But that white line was not going to look in the least like armour plating the way the dockyard hands were doing it. Eventually he had a number of strips of wood cut to equal length, then attached at their extremities, suspended from the topside of the deck and stretched along the length of the hull. By this means the line could be followed exactly. Much vital time was wasted over this but it was only one of the jobs which had to be organised to make a successful job of disguising the *Centurion*. There was a good deal of other painting to be done to make it look as if she had secondary armament when in practice she had none at all.

During the next night incendiary bombs rained on *Centurion* and her Captain and Commander worked frantically to put them out. Their swift action saved the ship from being lit up as an obvious target and she was not bombed. This blitz turned out to be an extremely severe one and all naval personnel had to sleep in the air-raid shelters. The curious thing about that night was that only one or two bombs fell in the dockyard, while immediately over the wall there was terrible damage. Some of the men working on *Centurion* had lost relations and houses, but they all turned up on the job next morning and it was finished on time. Muncaster received the Commander-in-Chief's congratulations for his part in the operation.

A signal was sent from the photographic unit on shore requesting that the main armament should be trained on a certain bearing as the ship left port. Training immovable wooden dummies would have been a problem! Later, he was given to understand that *Centurion* was mistaken for the *King George V* and the whole weight of a blistering air attack was concentrated on her. Muncaster's name stank! But the convoy got through. After that it was thought the enemy would have tumbled to the fact that *Centurion* was a fake, and she was withdrawn from operations and sent to India to perform other roles.

When he had been familiarising himself with the workings of the Camouflage Section during his first days with Commander Brock, Muncaster had read a paper about a unit attached to the Civil Defence Camouflage Establishment at Leamington Spa. He thought it was time he made himself known there, and the Director agreed.

On arriving at Leamington he asked to see the Chief Camouflage Officer, Captain Sir Lancelot Glasson - in civil life a painter he knew well. They had often discussed each other's works at the Academy. Muncaster recorded:

"Here," I thought," was a 'friend at Court' who would put me in the way of things. Imagine my surprise when Glasson all but refused to recognise me. To make matters worse, I carried no letter of introduction from the Admiralty. The situation became quite tense and he took me to see the Director, Wing-Commander Cave-Brown-Cave. I seem to remember being asked to show my identity card and I suggested they rang my Director at the Admiralty. At this the ice melted a bit. Sir Lancelot promised to take me to see the Naval Section at the Art Gallery the following morning. I was left to kick my heels for the rest of the day, and decided to go to Warwick to have a look round for subjects to paint sometime. In a room at the Woolpack Inn I spent a very noisy night. It happened to be the night the Germans decided to flatten Coventry.

"At the Art Galley back in Leamington the following day I was introduced to the officer in charge of camouflage, Lieutenant-Commander Yunge-Bateman and his Deputy, Mr. Trice-Martin. Bateman, tall, lean, dark and taciturn, seemed suspicious of me. It became obvious that he considered me a trespasser on his preserves and he had no wish to divulge details of his special brain-child. I quite understood how he felt but I was there to further his interests as well as the Admiralty's. Nevertheless, the atmosphere was distinctly frosty and had it not been for the diplomatic efforts of little Trice-Martin the ex-soldier, wounded, gassed and shell-shocked in World War I, I might never have been able to break through. As it was it took many months to impress Bateman that I was there to help, but I never felt I was entirely successful in winning his confidence.

"Trice-Martin was a charmer. He stammered a little, had a bad limp and a very shaky hand as a result of his wounds. But if any of us wanted to know quickly the outline of a warship and the arrangements of its armaments, he would produce a perfect little outline in a matter of minutes.

"There were about a dozen of us at Leamington, male and female. The team also included Wilfred Shingleton, the film designer, who was a superb draughtsman and a great asset to our Designs Section. He later became well-known as a film producer. In the land camouflage section, we had the painters Cosmo Clarke, and Tom Monnington who was to become President of the Royal Academy.

"Yunge-Bateman was working on disruptive camouflage designed to confuse the outline of a ship when viewed from the air or at sea, but predominantly from the air. It was admitted that from an aircraft a ship at sea would almost certainly be spotted on account of her white wake. The object, therefore, was not to make her invisible, which was virtually impossible, but unrecognisable. It was appreciated that because of the changing angles and lighting, a ship was far more difficult to disguise than a static object on land, but parts of her could be made to vanish when they matched a background of sea at a given time. It was assumed that some seven to nine tones of grey, varying between black and white (colour shades were of no account) would by and large, be sufficient to cover the variety of tones which would be met with in nature. This was a plausible enough theory and when put to the test in the tank at the Art Gallery worked admirably. But the artist boffins were apt to paint a ship to a corresponding tonal background and then switch on the most effective lighting condition. Nature was not necessarily going to oblige so easily. Frank Mason, the marine artist, constructed the tank on much the same lines as the one he had made in World War I to test Dazzle Painting Camouflage for which Norman Wilkinson had been responsible. Mason also made models. "He was certainly wasting his great talents in making our crude camouflage models, but he never complained. I think Yunge-Bateman and Trice-Martin really did believe in the efficacy of disruptive camouflage. I was rather more reserved about my faith in it. Clearly, there was something in the idea, but there were limits to working in a tank, and we had to get the Admiralty to let us try out our designs on ships at sea. They agreed to trials on two ships, H.M.S. *Queen Elizabeth* and H.M.S. *Suffolk*, and I found myself responsible for carrying out these trials. But it would be some time before the ships would be ready. Meanwhile, my office resembled a paper mountain: I was becoming completely snowed under. Requesting an assistant, David Pye, an architect, was appointed. Pye, a little younger than I had an incisive mind which cut through the tangle of any problem. He was also blessed with a photographic memory, and he loved the telephone which I loathed. Later, as the work built up even more, another assistant joined us, Robert Gooden, also an architect, but with a scientific background. Gooden was quiet-spoken, humorous and cultured. He could write minutes which were a delight to read. An Admiralty Fleet Order which he compiled on Camouflage of Ships at Sea almost approached a literary work.

"Soon after Gooden, yet another architect came to join us, Dick Russell, brother of Sir Gordon Russell. Dick had an enquiring mind and a gift for asking disquieting questions. On the rare occasions when we thought we were doing rather well, he would bring us down to earth with a bump. He became responsible for camouflage of Coastal Forces and a very good job he made of it.

"Captain Rivett-Carnac left T.S.D. having been appointed to *Rodney*, so we had a new Director, Captain Symonds-Taylor. It was a great privilege to be a member of his staff. I was not, however, on such good terms with our Deputy Director, whom we could only think had been sent to shake us up. He was one of the youngest four-ringers in the Navy and a Torpedo man. He obviously had a brilliant brain; but was a thruster, hustler and shouter-at-er. I was so much the reverse of this that he got me down dreadfully. If it hadn't been for a timely fourteen days leave at Machrihanish on the West coast of Scotland, I believe I would have gone under.

"My wife came up to Glasgow by train with the two boys. I met her at the station and found her being helped with her luggage by two young naval officers who clearly had an eye for blondes. Somehow there was a muddle over the number of cases and when we got to the hotel after a tiring ferry and bus journey, she discovered that the case with most of her clothes and precious cosmetics in it had been left on the platform at Glasgow. There was no possibility in wartime of finding it and having it sent out to the wilds of Argyllshire, so poor Primrose had to make do for about two weeks with only the clothes she stood up in. She was not at all amused. I played some golf and even managed to do some painting. This was marvellous therapy and for a time I really felt in touch with nature again. The broad sweep of curling white waves chasing up the beach in the nearby bay, the blues and greens of the deeper water, the dark shapes of the rocks jutting out of the land and the heather hues of the hills that entranced the eye away to the distance, brought back all the poetry and feeling that I yearned for. I did a little water-colour of the subject and later gave it to Martin. He seemed to love it and tried to copy it several times. I wished he would finish at least one of them, but he always seemed to give up saying he could never get it good enough.

"I returned to duty much refreshed and feeling far more able to cope, even with the Deputy Director. When I presented a report I had written on our work, he considered it did not fall in line with the prescribed naval requirements and started shouting at me and crashing his fist on the table. But what really made me angry was his accusation that the artists were a lot of shirkers and thoroughly incompetent. I stood up to him. I told him that the artists got no joy whatever from sitting on their bottoms in the Art Gallery, or for that matter, in the Admiralty. They would far prefer to be out fighting, and all of us would very much sooner be at sea. If he did not like what I was doing, I was only too ready to find a ship, put to sea and get out of this Mad House. If he did not believe in the artists who had given their lives to observing, I did. And if their judgement alone could not be accepted, then I advised that a scientist should be attached to the Designs Section forthwith. I was very angry. The Deputy Director sat down and went quiet. 'Yes,' he said at last. 'I think that would be a very good idea. I'll arrange for a scientist as soon as possible.'

"He paused for a few moments and then smiled at me. 'Now we seem to have cleared the air, let's have another look at this report, Muncaster. You know, you have a lot of good stuff here, but it's all over the place. When compiling a report there are three letters to keep in mind, F, D, and R, in that order. They stand for Facts, Discussion and Requirements. Thus, anybody reading the report will know from the last paragraph just what is required. Now, what about having a go at re-arranging your paper on these lines?'

"This was valuable advice and I have never forgotten it. I re-wrote the report and with one or two small amendments he accepted it. From then on the Deputy Director completely changed his attitude towards us. We became his special baby and he couldn't do enough for us.

"A young and brilliant scientist, Bill Schuil (pronounced Scoyl), was appointed soon afterwards. Everybody liked him and he was of great service to us. He and I did much work together and we became very close friends. Incidentally, Schuil's accurate measurement of light by telephotometry proved that the artists' estimations of particular tonal values were correct; they coincided exactly with his scientific measurements.

"A great number of camouflage ideas were now arriving at the Admiralty; almost all were impracticable or completely ineffective. I was always sorry to have to write the usual letter of rejection to the authors of these schemes, but there were times when we received interesting and constructive suggestions. One such came from Peter Scott, the naturalist, who suggested that we paint ships (and in particular Coastal Forces) white, with patterns of pale green and blue.

"The idea of painting a ship white certainly put the cat among the pigeons. Ashore, objects were sometimes painted white with the express purpose of making them visible in the blackout. Surely the same principle would apply to ships at sea. It was here that our scientist proved his worth. Schuil, with his telephotometry and a tank which exactly simulated natural levels of illumination, was able to prove that a ship painted white merged with the sky background when observed from periscope level at night. It was the dark objects which showed up most, and ships painted in Home Fleet Grey were bad offenders. So, from that time, certain ships, and particularly those operating in the Western Approaches were painted on the Peter Scott recommendations. If sunlight or moonlight shone directly on them, however, they were still not invisible. In fact, in such conditions they could show up for miles. In grey or foggy weather though, these ships became a menace. They were extremely difficult to see, and some collisions occurred. In the end, we stuck to our disruptive designs but painted the shadowy parts white on the same principle by which certain herbivorous mammals have light undersides, which reduces the strength of shadow, and thus prevents them standing out in relief. That seemed to be the best compromise.

"By this time our designs had been applied to the *Queen Elizabeth* and the *Suffolk*, and it was decided to carry out some air trials. I managed to get an Anson aircraft put at my disposal and taking with me Yunge-Bateman, Trice-Martin, a Lieutenant Currie from D.S.R. and one designer, we flew to Scapa Flow.

"We were all brimming with excitement at the prospect of seeing the effects of our camouflage on real ships. During the first morning I chartered a trawler to take us out into the Flow where the *Queen Elizabeth* and *Suffolk* were anchored. We were disappointed to find them anchored close to the shore and our only view of them was against a land background and up-light, two conditions which rendered any camouflage quite ineffective. However, we hoped for better things the next morning when we were scheduled to view the *Queen Elizabeth* out in the Practice Area.

"Flying over the area and over the ship herself demanded the closest liaison with shore batteries. Failure to comply with the proper orders and signal codes could mean we would be shot out of the sky so I took every precaution to be at the rendezvous precisely on time. The general procedure was for us to approach and flash the code letter of the day. The ship would then flash back her recognition of us and allow the runs to commence. These were carried out at a series of different levels, from sea level up to about 8,000 feet and from different angles. We would approach, then fly on past the ship to the point at which she was out of sight below the horizon. As we flew I noted down against stopwatch timings any effects of the camouflage. Photographic shots were similarly noted, together with the lighting and weather conditions.

"For the first few flights I found all these requirements most difficult to meet. I desperately tried to keep my head, but I was continually missing something out, rendering the observation useless. I was not used to flying, but mercifully was never air sick. There was not room for us all in the cockpit, but that was the very place where we all had to be. Just to add to the comedy, the inter-com never seemed to work and we had to yell into each other's ears to make ourselves heard.

"I confess I was not enthusiastic about our first viewings. They did not bode well. The ship looked dark, perfectly easy to distinguish, and the wiggly designs did nothing for her at all. But these were early days. Perhaps with experience we would be able to improve things.

"We flew over H.M.S. *Suffolk* in the afternoon and were more encouraged. Her overall tone was lighter than the *Queen Elizabeth's* and she did not carry so much shadow about her. But there were still some mysteries. It was puzzling that her camouflage should be so much more effective than *Elizabeth's*. In the evening we were wined and dined aboard the *Suffolk* and given a warm reception. Her design had been well received but it was still their opinion that the only way to make a ship disappear was to sink her.

"After dinner, as we leisurely paced the quarterdeck discussing camouflage, the Commander enquired of Bateman why he had thought fit to incorporate in his design, and on the quarterdeck of all places, a vast penis and scrotum. Bateman's expression was a picture, but when the phenomenon was pointed out there was no mistaking what the Commander meant. Bateman offered hastily to modify the design.

" 'Oh, for God's sake don't do that,' the Commander replied. 'It's a marvellous talking point and I'm sure it's lucky!' "

"Lucky or not, during the hunt for the *Bismarck*, H.M.S. *Suffolk* was able to get close to the enemy without being observed, and she claimed it was on account of her camouflage. Nothing would make them change it after that.

"Following exhaustive trials at Scapa, Pye and I got together and compiled as detailed and objective a report as we could muster. It resulted in our disruptive camouflage being accepted as the general standard. From then on, designs began to pour in. The Designs Section worked flat out and so did we. There was a huge amount of clerical work connected with each job and careful records had to be kept. We also had to find out from OPS the destination of each ship and the tactical requirements. More and more trials became necessary and these it was my business to arrange, carry out and assess. There was not much sleeping time going spare in those hectic days.

"During one of these trials we had to make runs over a ship commanded by my friend, Captain Lawford, in one of whose trawlers I had once done a fortnight's painting trip off Rockall. At dusk we were still at it, and he flashed: "You'd better make tracks for home, old friend. This is the time the enemy likes to attack.' We took his advice and flew back in our Hudson to the Irish base we were operating from, getting fired at by our own people on the way. It was the first time I had seen tracer bullets streaking up to a plane. Fortunately, we managed to establish our identity and all was well.

"An important consideration now arose and one which was being very much stressed by Pye. He was anxious about our designs being suitable in foreign waters where lighting conditions could be so very different from those in our part of the world. I thought he was right and mentioned it to the Deputy. He saw the sense of it and decided as a matter of urgency that I be sent off on a sort of Naval Camouflage Cook's tour. I welcomed the idea. It would at least be a break from the 'Mad House.'

"My terms of reference for the tour were:
  (1) To observe meteorological conditions and levels of light illumination so far as they affected the camouflage of ships at sea.
  (2) To arrange trials from air and surface, and as a result of the findings advise Commanders-in-Chief on Foreign Stations as to the best camouflage for the prevailing conditions and tactical requirements.

"My first reaction to these stipulations was that the first should be the province of a scientist, and the second should be my responsibility. My request for Schuil to accompany me was granted, and for me this could not have been a happier arrangement. We were to sail in early March, 1943, in the cruiser H.M.S. *Kenya*, destination Freetown, on the West coast of Africa.

"I had been promoted to Lieutenant-Commander in August 1942 and, together with Primrose, Lieutenant and Mrs. Schuil, and Lieutenant and Mrs. Lodder with whom we had made friends in the *King Alfred* days, arrived in Plymouth on the 27th and booked rooms in an hotel up on the Hoe with a fine view seawards. After tea I thought it would be wise for Schuil and me to make our number with the *Kenya* and get our gear on board, and, promising the girls an evening out when we got back, we went off to the ship in the picket boat. We discovered that once aboard, that was it! We were not allowed any further contact with the shore, as the ship was now under sailing orders of the utmost secrecy. It was quite heart-breaking. Primrose and the others waited and waited. There could not have been a sadder parting. Fortunately, Mrs Schuil who had not been married very long, was not to know that she would never see her husband again.

"Meanwhile, feeling as we did, Schuil and I decided we would try to smother our anguish by getting down to some work. First, we had to plan our routine and decided on a basis of four hours on and four hours off so that one of us would always be on watch. Our observations, which had to be made hourly and carefully logged and tabulated, required some dozen entries including sextant angles of sun and moon; levels of light illumination of sea and sky; amount of cloud, type of cloud and the general weather condition; and a note of which card, from a range of differently toned cards, most nearly matched the background of sea and sky, looking 'down light.' Light measurements had also to be taken by telephotometer, together with photographs.

"H.M.S. *Kenya* was painted 'Mountbatten Pink,' or as the Americans preferred to call it, 'Nipple Pink.'* Lord Mountbatten had first taken notice of this colour painted on the hull of a Union Castle liner when in company with some destroyers at sea. He noted that just after sundown, the Castle boat disappeared sooner than the destroyers which were painted Home Fleet Grey. He immediately concluded that there were special properties about this pink colour which would solve our camouflage problems. Schuil and I now knew that the colour as such had nothing to do with it. What had happened was that the colour at dusk resolved itself into a tone of grey which was lighter than Home Fleet Grey. This was the only magic about it.

"We kept strictly to our watchkeeping and found it was all we could do to keep abreast of the work. But we found life in *Kenya* very pleasant, although it was obvious the officers considered our observations so much rubbish. We became the target for tedious inquisitions and ragging. Schuil bore with this much better than I did and was always prepared to give sensible answers to what seemed to us the most stupid questions. I liked Schuil immensely and had the greatest respect for him. We got on extremely well and had one particular thing in common; we both missed our wives dreadfully.

"At Freetown we left the *Kenya*, and joined the *Edinburgh Castle*, a very ancient Castle boat which served mostly as a transit vessel. The ship was anchored some two hundred yards offshore which meant freedom at least from mosquitoes. Otherwise she was more like a convict ship. Punishments were continually being ladled out and courts martial were the order of just about every day. The Commander had long exceeded his spell of Freetown duty and it was as well to keep out of his way.

"When we arrived it was still the dry season. Even so, it was desperately hot and humid and whenever one got out of a chair, one's bottom was soaked. Every colour in my watercolour box was soon covered in a coat of mildew. Buttons dulled and shoes went mouldy. You could change three or four times a day and still be soaked through.

"The day I arrived I went to the bathroom next to my cabin and found a bath filled with cold water. I have never been a cold bath fan, but this was just what the doctor ordered. I thoroughly enjoyed that bath and went back to my cabin afterwards and slept soundly. I was awakened by a coloured steward.

" 'You let de water out of de bath, Sir?'

" 'Of course.'

" 'You let out de whole supply of cold water for de officers for de day, Sir.'

---

* One of the letters received while compiling records for this book came from Lieutenant-Commander Roy Casement, R.N. (Ret.). He was in H.M.S. *Kenya* when Muncaster was on board and told me that he christened him the "Fleet Chameleon." He was Officer-of-the-Day when Muncaster and Schuil joined at Plymouth and had been instrumental in not allowing them ashore again because the ship was under sailing orders. He well remembered the Camouflage Expert being up most of the night "taking readings with some obscure instrument." Casement had been in the pink painted *Kenya* on one of the Malta convoys and they had been torpedoed in the bows; completely demolishing the white painted bow wave section. This gave rise to a superstition amongst the ship's company that pink was a lucky colour – "ships painted pink don't sink." Imagine their dismay when Muncaster decreed that all ships should be painted two shades of grey. Near mutiny!

"There were just two pleasures to be enjoyed when one was off duty in that outpost of Africa; a swim from a sandy beach about three miles along the coast, and golf on a small course there. I partnered Roy Casement. We'd often played together on the West Sussex course at Pulborough. But my sport was short-lived. The greens at Freetown were mostly hard sand and even quite a good approach shot would go skidding on into the surrounding jungle from which I dare not retrieve the ball because of my fear of snakes. I couldn't afford a new ball at almost every green.

"When we had completed our trials in Freetown, I applied for air passages to Lagos, and thence to Khartoum, Cairo and Alexandria for trials in the Eastern Mediterranean. We waited days for a flight, and even when one was fixed some V.I.P. would always be put on it ahead of us. Then I decided on a sea passage, though this also seemed hard to come by. Eventually we were offered two berths, one in a submarine, the other in a motor-minesweeper of a class which had been built in Canada. When I asked Schuil which vessel he would like to make the passage in, he expressed no preference.

" 'All right,' I said. 'If you really mean that, I think it would be as well for you to go in the submarine. You've already done useful work on optics and periscopes and I think you would find the trip beneficial. It's not an operational trip, so you won't be in the firing line.

"Schuil was absolutely delighted.

" ' I didn't like to say so,' he said 'but I was longing to go in the sub.'

"So off he went, as cheerful as a cricket, waving me farewell with his face wreathed in smiles.

"When I reported this arrangement to Commander-in-Chief's staff they were aghast. 'Really,' they said. 'You a two-and-a-half (Lieutenant-Commander) putting yourself in a wretched little minesweeper and your junior in the sub. You must be potty.'

"They were to eat their words.

"On the afternoon of sailing, I went to inspect the ship and meet the skipper, a bearded Scot and Lieutenant R.N.V.R. He had been appointed only that morning and was a very worried man. What he had to say about that little minesweeper and its previous Captain is best left unprinted. Apparently, his predecessor was an R.N.R. Commander who had acted as Commodore to a squadron of six of these boats and had used his ship as a cocktail-bar-cum-brothel. He had left that same morning, together with the Chief Engineer and the Coxswain, two key men. Before he went, he had thoughtfully spread abroad the rumour that a German Pocket Battleship was on the prowl in the area, which did everything for the morale of newly-joining crew. I found the ship filthy and in no way ready for sea or action. The gun was jammed and the wireless in need of repair, none of which instilled confidence in the good order of vital working parts such as the engines.

"When I came to my tiny cabin, I realised just why they had considered me crazy. Yet I felt almost as glad that Schuil had not had to endure such discomforts. The ship's lively movement, the tropical heat in that confined space, and hundreds of cockroaches for bedfellows were not likely to induce tranquil sleep, even for the most hardened sailors, let alone scientists.

"We put to sea after dark with a monsoon beginning to blow. The minesweeper was being tossed about like a toy boat and I was finding it difficult to keep my feet. I turned in for a while to try to sleep before my turn of duty at twelve o'clock, but there was little rest to be had. Soon I was struggling out on deck for the four hour stretch. By now it was blowing hard, and a heavy, inky black thunderstorm was in progress. In one of the flashes of lightning I saw the conning tower of the submarine. It looked light in colour which worried me, but there was always some condition in which a ship showed up. In this case it was probably the glistening water.

"At 4 a.m. I went below and turned in to try again to get some sleep. But it was hopeless, so I went back up on deck. It was still very dark, though the wind had eased and a few stars had appeared. As I climbed the ladder to the bridge, the First Lieutenant said: 'We've just had three torpedoes under us. Didn't you feel her jump?' As a matter of fact, I had felt a rather unusual motion, but had thought little of it. We were battling through a monsoon, after all.

" 'We've had to break radio silence,' the First Lieutenant went on. 'We managed to get a signal through to the sub. but her Captain replied that he doesn't think they were torpedoes, just porpoises.' 'Number One' was a trawlerman in Civvy Street and growled his contempt: 'If I don't know the difference between real live fish and tin fish, I'm never going trawling again.'

"Then the Captain appeared on the bridge to tell us he had repeated the signal to the sub. but had received the same reply. Though the skipper did take it seriously enough to promise to make an enemy report.

"All this was stomach-turning news. If that slight lifting of the ship I'd felt had been the result of torpedoes, we can only have been saved from being blown sky high by the fact that this was a new class of minesweeper with a very shallow draft and the torpedoes were set too deep.

"When day dawned, we were comforted to see our sub. about a quarter of a mile off on the starboard quarter. The sun rose in a clear sky over a perfectly calm, blue sea; a beautiful morning, no land in sight. Were we really at war?

"At about 9.30 a.m. a ship was sighted right ahead. This was unexpected as the Captain had been assured that there were no ships in the immediate vicinity. All eyes and binoculars became fixed on this strange vessel. She was making steady progress towards us and would not answer our signals. What the devil was she doing here?

"I glanced across to the sub. to see if she was taking any action; and in the moment of that very glance saw a sudden tall column of white spray shoot up from her. I saw the bows lift heavenwards, hang for a few seconds as if suspended in time, then slip backwards – and she was gone. No sign remained to show that less than a minute before a proud ship had sailed there.

"Schuil! God, poor Schuil! I poured compassion out to them all, but Schuil's name burned into my brain. It was I who had told him to go in that ship. While these accusing thoughts raced through my mind, I recalled also that shimmer of lightning in the night that had picked out the colour of the submarine's conning tower. How light it had seemed. Then the truth focused. It hadn't been our submarine at all. Number One had been right; they had been torpedoes.

"I turned to tell the others what I'd seen – but they wouldn't believe me. There'd been no sound of explosion and they were giving their whole attention to the vessel bearing down on us from ahead. Eventually, I got through to them and they scanned our starboard quarter for reassurance, only to search miles of empty sea.

"The Captain was now deeply worried and turned to me, as his senior officer, to ask my advice. But I was feeling more than a little devastated and, try as I might, couldn't clear my head for judgement. I thoroughly distrusted the ship ahead, now much nearer, and still not answering our signals. As she drew closer we saw her alter course and turn broadside on to us, and we thought we were in for it. Already Number One was frantically collecting the Confidential books ready for jettisoning. I remembered my own briefcase packed full of my logs and secret information about ships and their whereabouts. I rushed below, grabbed it from my cabin and heaved the thing overboard, but it just floated gently astern, looking dreadfully conspicuous. I consoled myself with the thought that the case would soon fill with water and all the entries, thousands of them, would quickly run and become illegible.

"At length we established by light that the ship which had given us so much drama was a British merchantman some fifty miles off course. We told her there was an enemy close to us and advised her to take zig-zag evasive action. Either she did not understand or she chose to ignore the message for she came steadily on without any attempt at zig-zagging. We watched her with concern; a sitting duck for a U-boat. Then, when she was about a mile astern, up went that deadly spout of white water, and she became another victim.

"The Captain now appealed to me again: 'What the hell do we do?' 'What are the instructions, in an emergency?' I asked. 'To make an enemy report to Freetown.' he replied. 'But how can I? Our wireless is jammed; though Sparks thinks he might get something through if we can get close enough inshore. But what about the survivors?'

"I told him I thought the survivors could wait. The crew seemed to be abandoning ship in a leisurely and disciplined manner, and the ship had only been damaged by the look of it. She probably wouldn't sink for quite some time. If we went to pick up survivors now we would only present another target. It was crucial at this stage to make an enemy report. He agreed, and we altered course for land.

"The next few hours were charged with anxiety; our nerves at busting point. As we pushed on to Freetown shoals of fish would suddenly flurry along the top of the water, breaking the calm surface. Each time we saw a shoal, we expected the bows of a U-boat to surge up into the sunlight. Then we sighted a thin, menacing-looking object on the horizon and close to it another one. Again we imagined it to be a U-boat and were relieved to find as we got nearer that the objects were palm trees on a spit of land. At this stage somebody spotted an aircraft. It turned out to be a Sunderland and we called it up on our Aldis lamp. The plane circled and we were able to ask her to report that the submarine had been sunk and that we required help for survivors from the torpedoed merchant ship. A second aircraft appeared a little later and we repeated the message to her. I learned afterwards that our first signal had been taken to mean that the submarine had submerged, and no action had been taken. On receipt of the second message everything available had been rushed out. But too late. The damage had been done and the enemy got clean away. Meanwhile, we returned to pick up the survivors. In fact, there had been no casualties, though the ship had now sunk.

"We returned to Freetown hot and dusty. I had hoped never to see the place again. As soon as I got ashore there was much reporting and interviewing to be done which kept me active and delayed some of the distress which inexorably bore down upon me. It hit me in the end, with full force and a dreadful reality. I just could not get out of my mind the idea that I had been responsible for Schuil's death, and began to wonder whether I should proceed with my mission; secretly hoping that I might be ordered home. I had lost my scientific adviser and even if I did manage to obtain another telephotometer would I be able to use it? So I sent off a long report to the Admiralty and received a reply that I was to go ahead as planned. I doubted the wisdom of this directive, but perhaps the intensive work that lay ahead of me would help me to forget.

"Death had touched my shoulder and I had been spared six times at least now. The more I pondered, the more I came to believe that I had been given these extensions of life as a responsibility. This gave me new hope, new strength and a conviction that I must not fear for the future. When my time came, it would be not a moment too early nor a moment too late."

Three days later, Muncaster was on his way to Lagos for a tour of intensive duty which was to take him to many parts of the Mediterranean, down to Capetown, up the East Coast, and on to Ceylon, India and Burma. At the start of this daunting itinerary, he was on board a Flower Class Corvette in which he had enjoyed an extra warm welcome. By coincidence his brother Philip had until recently been its Anti-Submarine Detection Officer.

During the following months, he was to travel in several different types of aircraft and many different classes of vessel; by ferry, by train, by lorry. His journey then took him from Lagos and Khartoum to Cairo, and on to Alexandria where he worked for the Commander-in-Chief Eastern Mediterranean for some six weeks; arranging a number of different passages, flights and missions to study camouflage in varying conditions. One of the ships he joined for trials in convoys was the *Muncaster Castle*; another, an armed merchant trawler. In the trawler the Number One was a Welshman. They got talking about ships one evening and he described how he had once been nearly run down in thick weather in the Bristol Channel by a sailing ship. They worked out the date and there was no doubt at all that it had been *Olivebank*, when Muncaster was aboard her wishing at that moment that he could be in the trawler so that he could photograph the ship that had brought him round the Horn.

In a Motor Torpedo Boat making for Beirut, they had kept close to the land most of the way. Much of this he found most attractive and did a few light-hearted sketches. He had managed a dozen or so since leaving Plymouth.

They also acted as one of the escorts for a convoy heading South. During the morning, a beautifully clear and sunny one, a U-boat surfaced right in the middle of the convoy. It was an amazing sight. Her Commander immediately tried to crash dive, but he was shot up before he could submerge.

Later on, Muncaster also saw action off the Italian Coast.

Recently Admiral Sir William Davis has recalled: "He visited Naples in late 1943 and early 1944 and came to sea with me in H.M.S. *Mauritius* whilst we were bombarding the Germans who were attacking our Anzio positions. He was enormous fun and painted a delightful picture for me of *Mauritius* supporting the Fifth Army off Gaeta and Anzio in February 1944. This now hangs in my dining room."

But to return to July 1943: By the end of that month he considered he had done all he could for the time being on the Eastern Mediterranean Station and decided to move on. He prepared an assessment of all his activities and findings so far and presented them to the Commander-in-Chief. The record continues:

"On 8 July, I left by plane for Karachi. An intensive programme lay ahead which was to take me to Bombay, Colombo, Trincomalee, Calcutta and Chittagong; then Mombasa, Durban (where I had the luck to meet my brother Philip and have several runs ashore and games of golf with him) and Capetown. Then up to Aden and the Med. again. Back to India and Ceylon for a spell and thence home again where I was due to arrive at the end of March. This itinerary may read quickly on paper but it meant months of exhausting and concentrated work and travelling in war conditions when there was always anxiety. Added to this I was none too well much of the time with a bad stomach and a good deal of pain and sickness. Yet the demands of the job still called for hourly observations. I got very little sleep for long periods at a time. Psychologically, physically and mentally the pressure was immense. Each new ship I had to travel in and each one I had to visit, and they seemed legion, I was asked to explain my mission many times and needed always to worm out facts and information. At the same time I had to be a sort of hail-fellow-well-met kind of chap who had to make his way anew in to every wardroom and mess. Ashore there was paperwork by the mound, arrangements for trials, staff work and conferences, though I did towards the end rely on Dick Russell who was sent out to help me. What a relief it was to have him.

"In all these comings and goings I believe I only missed two connections – once because my driver lost his way to the R.A.F. Station, the other time when my transport failed to turn up. The next morning I went to see the Transport Officer to find out why. He explained that he had taken over the day before and the chit had only just been passed to him. 'But you know,' he said, 'it was damned lucky for you that you didn't go. The aircraft pranged and they were all killed!'

"Of course, against all this tension there were the lighter moments. I was in Trincomalee for the Christmas season aboard the repair ship, H.M.S. *Resource*, where we enjoyed ourselves as best we could. Just after Christmas Day lunch, my friend Lieutenant-Commander Casement was seen to come up on deck, mount 'Y' turret of *Kenya* (berthed nearby) and dive over the side in full uniform. The cheers from those who witnessed this remarkable display of valour echoed round the harbour."

The Navy's Camouflage Expert now had to report his conclusions and make recommendations. There was no doubt that light painted ships were less visible than those painted in darker tones, especially during periods of low level illumination, at dawn and dusk. The parts of a ship most free of shadow were bows and stern. By painting those parts white or light grey, at certain times anyway they could be made to disappear. Clearly, a ship was going to be seen in some lights; but they must be painted to meet conditions when camouflage was effective – at dawn and dusk in particular which were specially dangerous periods for attack.

His recommendation was that ships should be painted all over a medium grey, except for portions of the bow and stern, which should be painted white in home waters and a very light grey on foreign stations. The fore end of the dark area, he suggested, should be painted to represent the lines of the ship's bows; the after end of the dark area to represent the ship's stern. If the light painted bow and stern could be made to disappear by this means, the enemy might be deceived into thinking that the ship, appearing to be foreshortened, was on a different inclination to the actual one, and any torpedoes fired at her would be wrongly angled and therefore miss.

This seemed a simple conclusion, but its very simplicity proved its practicability. Trials were carried out, the Navy was pleased with results. It worked.

Camouflage designs:	above:	Cruiser; sunny weather
		C class cruiser
	middle:	County class cruiser
		R class battleship
	below:	V-W class destroyer

above: Gale brewing in the Pentland Firth (Armed Trawlers) 1946: *oil* (Muncaster's Diploma picture for the Royal Society of Marine Artists)
(By courtesy of the R.S.M.A.)

below: Lochnagar from Bush Lawsie, Balmoral 1947: *watercolour*; presented to H.R.H. Princess Elizabeth on the occasion of her engagement.
(Reproduced by courtesy of H.M. The Queen)

Demolition of Hay's Wharf, 1925: *watercolour*
(By courtesy of the Trustees of the Tate Gallery)

Aboard the *Rodney* at night; Gibraltar: *pastel and watercolour*.

"When I arrived home, after over a year's absence Primrose and the boys rushed to meet me. Clive taking one look at me, cried out: 'that's not my Daddy' – and ran back screaming into the house!"

I can remember that moment as if it were only a week ago. I was only nine, but even now I can see my father's drawn and yellow face as he stood before the fire in the sitting room at Four-Winds warming his hands behind his back. He was a very sick man.

Next day he went to the Admiralty. When D.S.R. saw his thousands upon thousands of tabulated entries, he asked in amazement, "But when did you sleep?"*

He was granted a month's leave. Only a few days after returning to his desk in London he was back in bed with a high temperature and double pneumonia. He was suffering, too, from the unpleasant effects of some tropical bug which was never diagnosed. When he had recovered, he went before a Naval Medical Board at Chatham.

The Chairman of the Board took one look at him and said "You're a pretty unhealthy colour, aren't you?" There was a pause, then: "We have, I'm afraid, come to the decision that we have no further need of your services."

So he was invalided out; his days in the Navy and in the war were over. It was now his sole aim to get back to good health. In this, painting acted as a kind of art-therapy. Out came his painting gear from its almost total retreat and he could only hope that whatever talent he might still have would emerge with it. He rather feared that all this time away might have put his hand and mind so out of touch that he would find it hard to contend with the demands of an exacting technique.

For a start, he chose some old pencil sketches, some of them drawn long before the War, and tried out his hand on these. Rather to his surprise, he discovered that he had lost nothing through the enforced break and in fact, appeared to have benefited from it. He began to paint with a new vitality, both mentally and technically.

The several sketches he had done during the War he thought worthy of an exhibition, so with these and a collection of water colours that had been stored in his studio, he arranged a one-man show at Colnaghi's in Bond Street, in December 1944. He sold quite well, and a water colour of Freetown done from the deck of *Edinburgh Castle* was bought for the permanent collection in the Graves Art Gallery, Sheffield.

The object of the exhibition as much as anything else had been to put himself back on to the map in the art world. There was still a market for traditional and representational paintings, for some people at least were feeling the need for the peaceful beauty of nature after the devastations of war. But influential factions of the art world were now pushing such painters as Picasso, Moore, Piper, Sutherland, Braque, Rouault and Matisse who were becoming household names. He felt no jealousy; only sadness that an art form for which he felt so little sympathy was making all the running. Whatever the current fashion, he determined to stick to his own style. If he was to continue to be a landscape and marine painter, he had to paint nature and the sea as he knew and loved them. So he decided on a spell of painting Nature in his beloved North Country, the land of his blood.

"With petrol in such short supply I had to count every mile and coast down every hill. I managed to get over to the Duddon Valley and down to Bardsea a time or two, and up on to the moors. The joy of that re-entry into the atmosphere of this fellside district was intense. To be free to paint again, and to see something of the effects I loved appearing on the paper before me as my own creations which would not have to be subjected to the scrutiny of some Admiralty Department, made me conscious of the privilege of being a whole time, free-lance artist. I was responsible only to my Maker, and to the ideal of attempting to create some small interpretations of His infinite beauty, which might perhaps afford some pleasure to my fellow men. Here, war was forgotten. I had played my part in it and had given all I could: very nearly, my life. Now, at least for a spell, I could forget it. I could pause and watch and contemplate, and draw and paint. I could see, I could hear, I could smell. I could observe the changing effects of cloud and colour over sea, mountain and fell. I could scent the freshness of the earth, the grasses and the peat. I could hear the wind in the oak, the ash and the thorn and listen to the black-faced Herdwicks answering to the bleat of their lambs. There was the music of the water in the becks as they flowed fresh, clear and sparkling to the sea. This was Nature. This was reality, because it was closest of all to beauty, the fulfilment of which is God."

*A note in the Admiralty records based on a report prepared at Leamington Spa (on 21.4.44) was critical of Lieut.-Commander O. Grahame Hall, RNVSR and queried both his method of approach and the accuracy of his conclusions: "When O. G. Hall confines his attention to observation and collection of data and information, he is very interesting and helpful, although accurate scientific readings are sadly missed. At other times one is almost alarmed at the apparent looseness of his thinking and his unscientific attitude. It is a great pity that he is alone and that no one accustomed to scientific discipline is with him."

Chapter 9

All the King's Castles

Windsor and Sandringham

(This and the following chapter are taken from Muncaster's own records).

On an afternoon in May 1946, when Primrose and I returned to tea from a walk, our post awaited us and among sundry bills a long envelope caught my eye. There was a certain distinction about this envelope. It was made of the kind of paper only seen before the war. On the front was stamped a large G.R. in red, and on the back was a noble crest, also in red, and the words "Windsor Castle."

I had nearly finished reading the letter when Primrose, who reads much faster than I, snatched it out of my hand and taking me in her arms and kissing me fervently exclaimed excitedly: "Darling! Don't you realise? You're *made.*"

I had my own opinion about this, but the news contained in the letter was indeed thrilling. It read:

WINDSOR CASTLE
2nd May 1946

Dear Sir,

I hope you will forgive a letter from a stranger, but I have long known your work, which I have seen at various exhibitions for a number of years.

The trees on either side of the Long Walk from Windsor Castle through the Park to the equestrian statue of George III have recently been cut down. They consisted of elms, nearly all of which were afflicted by disease, but since they were planted by Charles II, I suppose it would be captious to complain of their decease. Other trees are being planted, but there is now disclosed a view of the Castle and St. George's Chapel which has not been apparent, I suppose, for over two hundred years. There is revealed an outline of great beauty, and it deserves on this ground, as well as for historical reasons, to be suitably commemorated.

It is the practice of Their Majesties' Household to give the King a Birthday present annually, and it has been suggested that nothing would be more appreciated than a water colour sketch of the view I have described. I am wondering whether you would care to contemplate this: it would, I think, provide a subject well suited to your skill. I approach the matter with some diffidence for the sum available is no more, I am afraid, than thirty or thirty-five pounds, and it may well be that you would not care to undertake a task of this kind, despite its interest, for so modest a sum. I am emboldened however, to suggest my confidence in what would be the result, if the proposition proved agreeable to you.

If this should be the case, I would suggest a personal reconnaissance on which it would be a great pleasure to accompany you. I do not know whether you are often in London, but if you are, we could easily motor down and back within a few hours and you could locate the most favourable site.

There are still lying in what is left of the avenue the trunks of these fallen monsters, and I think it is possible that you will favourably consider incorporating them into the foreground of your sketch. They would be appropriate to the purpose of the picture and I have no doubt that you would make them very decorative. If I remember aright, there is a picture in the National Gallery by Hubert Robert among those lent by Mr Gulbenkian representing the building of Versailles. In the foreground a number of workmen are engaged on the sawing of some enormous trees and they compose very agreeably to fill the foreground.

Their Majesties return to London on Monday. Perhaps you will write to me there.

Yours very truly

Signed. Arthur Penn.
Private Secretary to The Queen.

Had I even been expected to undertake the picture gratis, I would have considered myself foolish had I declined such an attractive and exciting commission.

I replied to the letter, suggesting a date for Primrose and me to visit Windsor with Major Penn. The date proved convenient and we set off from London with Major Penn, on the day fixed, in one of the Royal Daimlers.

Having chosen a suitable viewpoint, Major Penn took us into the Home Park and pointed out some of the more attractive views of the Castle. He remarked, that if I felt disposed to paint scenes other than the Long Walk, he would see whether they too might be sold.

Although it was my private opinion that Major Penn could have little idea as to just how difficult it is to sell pictures, I took notice of his remarks and determined, when the time came, to stay at Windsor for a prolonged period in order to carry out his suggestion.

Eventually I stayed at "The White Hart" for the best part of a fortnight. The weather was kind and I enjoyed the only spell of heat that unlucky summer of 1946 could boast. I was about early each day, painting in the Home Park while the dew still sparkled in the early morning sun, long before the green-keepers came to whip off the dew and wormcasts from the greens of the little nine-hole golf course in readiness for the golfers who never played.

I completed ten watercolours which may not sound many for the hours I worked, but they were exacting works as architectural subjects always are. Also, they were required to be as topographically correct as possible, and I was anxious that they should be the very best I could do since much might hang upon the success of my efforts.

My endeavours were made lighter and more pleasant through the kind assistance and encouragement of Sir Owen Morshead, the King's Librarian who, steeped more deeply than anyone in the history of Windsor, could add interest to all the things he showed me by the amusing anecdotes he would recount so humorously. I enjoyed the privilege.

I believe I had never before felt so nervous about starting a watercolour as I did when starting the one of the Long Walk. Suddenly I imagined my artistry forsaking me, but after several evenings of concentrated effort during which the sun continued to shine and the effect remained constant, I completed the picture. As I had by this time completed several other works, I thought it as well to show Sir Owen how the Long Walk progressed. I did so hesitantly. I was not at all sure how good or bad my efforts were, particularly the one of the Long Walk, and I feared the worst. But his reception of them all was so favourable that my fears were allayed and I felt encouraged to proceed with some further views.

By the end of a fortnight I could paint no more and so decided to give Sir Owen and Lady Morshead another private view before I left for home. It was then that he informed me that Major Penn wanted to show the collection to the Queen if I would agree to this suggestion.

I had the pictures framed and forwarded to Buckingham Palace on the instructions of Major Penn and a few days later received a letter from him which set us all in a turmoil of excitement. It read:

BUCKINGHAM PALACE
31 July 1946

Dear Muncaster,

I have, as I promised, now shown your sketches to the Queen and you will, I am sure, be gratified to know that Her Majesty was so pleased by them that she wishes to purchase them all.

I should like to say how glad I am that this combined operation has had so happy an issue.

They are all delightful and the principal example – that of the Long Walk – will fulfil its purpose admirably, which was, as you know, to provide a Birthday present which Members of His Household give to the King.

The Queen further said that she hoped you might find it possible to do some more sketches of Windsor in the autumn when the trees are changing colour. If this would conform to your inclinations perhaps you will make your own arrangements to suit your convenience.

If you do go, as I hope you will, and would let me know beforehand, I think I could suggest two or three views which Her Majesty thinks you might find appropriate.

Morshead, I am afraid, may be disappointed, since I think he coveted some of your work for the Library, but I think it is the Queen's intention that this shall ultimately prove the home for some of the examples which she is now happy to acquire.

Yours sincerely

Signed. Arthur Penn.
Private Secretary to The Queen.

I recall a remark of my niece who was staying with us at the time. She said, "I wonder what it feels like to be successful!" I gave her a pound note for her remark and distributed other pound notes round the table, not that I particularly considered myself successful, but just because I had done a job of work which had been so fully and practically appreciated. And of course I was thrilled to think that the purchaser was the Queen. There are those who say an artist should not care a fig whether he gets any appreciation or not. But most artists do care a fig.

I visited Windsor again in the autumn, but things did not go right. For a start, my car broke down and had to be towed home. I went on in a hired car and arrived at Windsor on a bleak wet evening. Having no car of my own meant that I had no shelter from which to work. Moreover, the wind began to blow from the North East, that worst of all winds for artists. When my car did arrive the rain came with it, and there followed a fortnight of the murkiest October weather that I ever remember. The dull and sodden greens of that wet summer died on the trees the same dull green, and only on a few horse-chestnuts did some precious gleams of gold appear. I completed one pen drawing and two large watercolours in ten days, the smallest amount of work I have ever completed in a similar length of time. The two watercolours were shown to Her Majesty. She professed to their giving her great pleasure, but one she considered insufficiently characteristic of Windsor to merit its being added to her collection, and the other had not been done from the position she had indicated to Major Penn. The outcome of it was that the first picture portrayed some trees which were great favourites of Sir Owen Morshead and I offered it to him and his wife as a small token of my appreciation of all their kindness to me. The second picture Sir Owen purchased for the King's Library.

The second Windsor expedition was something of a sad anti-climax. I felt after the success of the first visit I had failed dismally, and that would be the end of it.

But it was not so.

* * *

One day in January 1947 Primrose and I were lunching at Brown's Hotel when I was summoned to the phone. Knowing that it could only be from home, since nobody else knew of our whereabouts, I had visions of the kitchen stove having blown up or some such domestic tragedy. It appeared that nothing at home was wrong, but they were in a flutter as Buckingham Palace had rung up to say that the Queen would like me to visit Sandringham on the following day to discuss with her the possibility of doing some paintings of Sandringham. Would I ring up Major Penn who would give me further directions?

Naturally, I was greatly excited, but I was also in a panic. I had so little time to prepare. This was probably just as well for had there been more time to think about it I believe my nerve would have failed me and I would never have got to Sandringham at all.

As it was, armed with a few hints from Major Penn, now the Queen's Treasurer, as to the suit and dinner-jacket which I should require, I set off.

It started to snow heavily in London and the journey to dreary Liverpool Street Station became something of a feat of navigation. The snow piled densely on the taxi's windscreen, but we made it. That is, the taxi-driver and I. My wife, alas, was not invited – a cause of great sorrow to me.

As the train crept northwards that gloomy afternoon, the snow fell faster and lay thicker as we proceeded. At Wolferton station, the station-master took my bag, and preceded me through the booking-office on the floor of which was laid a crimson carpet, the first I had seen in any railway station.

I was met by the chauffeur of a large Daimler who handed me a fur to wrap up in.

We swept out of the station yard in a flurry of snow, and proceeded uphill for some distance between unbroken borders of rhododendron trees until we reached some high wrought-iron gates at which a uniformed policeman stood sentinel and saluted us as we passed. Immediately there came into view through the snowflakes the lights from the windows of Sandringham House which, with the snow-laden firs surrounding it, looked for all the world like a Caldecott illustration to Washington Irving's *Old Christmas*.

Hardly had the door opened when I was met by Major Penn; and I was right glad to see him. He quickly put me at my ease, introducing me to the male members of the house-party which included the Queen's nephew, "Fergy" Bowes-Lyon and Colonel Gordon Lennox. The Equerry-in-Waiting, Capt. Sir Harold Campbell, was also one of the party, and when I had been refreshed by drink, it was from him that I enquired the programme for the evening.

"It is a very simple ceremony," he told me. "We shall gather in the drawing-room about a quarter of an hour before dinner, and you and the Vicar and his wife, who have also to be presented, will be placed a little apart from the others. As the Princesses, and the Queen, Queen Mary and the King come down the stairs in that order, they will come up to you and you will extend your arm and, taking their hand, lower your head. There is no need to say anything, but you will answer appropriately if they speak to you. At dinner, should the King talk first with the person on his left, then the rest of the company will follow suit until the King changes direction. You will address the King as 'Sir,' and the Queen, Princesses and Queen Mary as 'Ma'am.' That's about all there is to it. Now, if you wish I will show you where the ceremony will take place, and after that I'll show you your room."

Sir Harold led me out of the library towards the drawing-room. In doing so our way led us through the large hall which at one end was curtained off by high curtains. I gained an impression of this hall being a partially panelled but otherwise ornately decorated room in some light coloured wood. I had little time to examine its architecture before I observed a figure in a purple frock seated at a table with her back to us whom I recognised as none other than the Queen. She turned as she heard our steps, and seeing us, arose and approached us. Sir Harold Campbell whispered to me, "Come and let me present you to the Queen." "Ma'am," he said, bowing his head as he spoke, "May I present Mr. Muncaster." In the unexpectedness of this presentation I feel sure I forgot my directions and neglected to extend the arm and lower the head in the prescribed fashion. I was so fascinated by the Queen's gracious smile and friendly approach that I felt I must look her in the eyes as I took her hand. "It is so nice of you to come, Mr Muncaster," she said, "Were you frozen on your journey?" I replied in a mumbling manner how exceedingly kind I thought it was of her to ask me to Sandringham. "I thought it would be so nice if you could do some paintings of Sandringham," she continued, "I did so like your Windsor drawings, but I'm afraid the weather is not very helpful to my showing you round. Perhaps tomorrow will be better."

At that moment the door opened and Princess Elizabeth and Princess Margaret came in out of the snow. They wore fur coats and scarves over their heads.

"Oh! Darlings," exclaimed the Queen. "Aren't you frozen?" And turning to me she said, "Let me introduce you to my two daughters."

Each of the Princesses gave me a friendly and charming smile. They had been to a local Women's Institute party. "Did you have a good time, darlings?" the Queen asked. "No, Mummy, not awfully," Princess Elizabeth answered. "Hardly anybody came."

I now caught Sir Harold's eye which hinted that we should leave. This we did and he took me into the drawing-room. Here I was reminded of some museum, but this room was lighter and brighter and warmer, for a glorious log fire blazed in the large grate. Numerous glass cases stood around in which were arrayed priceless and varied specimens of Queen Mary's collection of antiques. The ceiling, if my memory is correct, was of an ornate white plaster stucco. Of the pictures and other furniture I have little or no recollection. My mind was in far too much of a flurry to absorb details of this nature. All I could think of was my meeting with the Queen and the Princesses. Yet I needn't have been nervous. The ordeal thus far had been nothing but pleasurable, and the manner in which I had been received must have put the most gawkish oaf at his ease.

At last upstairs, I relaxed sufficiently to look about me. My bedroom was not large, but long and narrow in shape. There was no system of hot and cold taps but a wash-stand with a marble top and the usual utensils. The walls had every spare inch plastered with watercolours of a late Victorian period, many of them rather refreshing after the ugly, so-called advanced, modern art. Thick curtains were drawn across the windows, and my feet sank into a carpet of a thick pile. The fire, the greatest luxury of all in a bedroom, burned brightly and gave an air of great comfort and homeliness. I undressed leisurely. I was tempted to lie down on the rug before the fire and stretch my limbs like a basking cat. But I dared not be late. I thought I had better have a bath. Everybody else would, so perhaps I ought to. So I wrapped myself up in a vast bath towel and staggered in it to the bathroom which was off the passage outside my room. Here I found the bath water already run and at the correct temperature. After some searching I also found the rest of what I needed beneath the seat of a huge kind of wicker armchair.

I bathed and felt refreshed, and then anxious as I realised too late that I was expected to share the bathroom with Col. Gordon Lennox. I should certainly have let him use it first. But he was so kind about it I did not worry for long. I had brought a stiff shirt and collar. I thought I might as well wear a stiff collar while I still had one, and a shirt that required studs down the front, though all my studs were odd ones. Subsequently I found myself the only man so dressed. All the others had soft collars and soft shirts with buttons.

Having dressed, I made my way cautiously downstairs and into the drawing-room. I was well in time. The room was deserted; only one low voltage light burned and the room was lit further by dancing light from the blazing fire. I rather wished it could remain so, but it was not long before Sir Harold came in, switched on the lights and the curtain was up. The Countess Spencer, a Lady of the Bedchamber to the Queen, and Lady Cynthia Colville, one of the Women of the Bedchamber to Queen Mary, entered the room and I was introduced to them. The Vicar and his wife arrived and the other gentlemen of the party, including Major Ford, an assistant secretary to the King. The Vicar's wife, the Vicar, and myself were stood apart in line, for all the world like a fatigue party on the deck of a ship awaiting an inspection by the Commanding Officer. The company was now all present, the stage was set and waited only the arrival of the Royal Family.

Their Majesties soon appeared and approached us in the drawing-room; the ceremony of presentation was over in less time than it takes to tell.

As the King advanced to me I really did have the feeling of a parade inspection. He seemed to pass around me and behind me, and I felt sure my tie was riding high on the back of my collar. He spoke to me immediately about the Windsor pictures and put me at my ease, stating graciously his appreciation of *The Long Walk* picture. "But you know, Muncaster, those trees in the foreground were too perfect. You should have shown something of the rot in them." In my nervousness and amid the babble of conversation which immediately broke loose, I did not hear him clearly, and putting the best face I could on the situation, guffawed hopefully. It was not the most polite thing I could have done. The King, with great understanding, repeated his remark loudly and more clearly, adding that the whole purpose of cutting down the trees was because "they were afflicted with disease" and should therefore, when fallen, not be depicted as perfect specimens. I recovered from my obviously ill-timed guffaw to admit that His Majesty was perfectly right, and suggested that since such an error would be likely to worry him whenever he saw the picture, and as it would be but a small matter to make the necessary alteration, it would give me much pleasure if he would permit me to make it.

We then proceeded to the dining-room, Their Majesties leading the way. They were followed by the ladies, and the gentlemen in informal order formed the rear-guard.

As we entered the dining-room I had an impression of an immense number of footmen dressed in a livery of dark blue standing behind the chairs placed around a long polished table pleasantly lit by small table lamps and beset with a formidable array of glittering glasses; of white table-napkins made up in decorative patterns, of flashing cutlery and decorations. It was a momentary impression immediately expelled by a sense of extreme perturbation as I observed the Queen smiling at me and saying with a gracious gesture, "Will you come and sit by me, Mr. Muncaster." I did as I was bid, and the Vicar, having given a blessing, the company became seated. I found myself between the Queen and Princess Elizabeth with the King seated at the centre of the table on the other side, almost opposite me.

The conversation buzzed. The King spoke to the Vicar's wife on his right and it therefore became my duty to speak to Princess Elizabeth on my right. I soon found it was a delight to converse with her. I cannot remember much of what we talked about except that some of it was of dogs. She told me of her distress at losing her own Corgi which was run over by a lorry. Distressed as she was, she had to say that it was "quite all right" to the lorry driver, who must have been as much upset as she. We talked a little of painting; a little of the forthcoming trip to South Africa; a little of her love of England. She always remembered a visit to Ireland when sunlight had followed her everywhere, but when she returned to England one early morning, the weather was grey with a misty rain and it had seemed to her that that was England and she still loved it.

Then the conversation changed and I conversed with the Queen. I had always understood her charm to be electric and was not disappointed. It was the most delightful experience and I discovered myself talking about all sorts of subjects as naturally as I would have talked to anyone else. We discussed painting, and her remark that she thought so much good talent was being wasted by painting in the modern style, impressed me. More than anything else her love and understanding and belief in her own people was refreshing and inspiring.

I could pay little attention to the food and drink offered me. I know I had excellent sherry followed by fine champagne, and thereafter a choice of port, brandy or liqueurs. I was the only one to choose brandy, and found myself served with the biggest brandy glass I had ever seen. It seemed so terribly conspicuous, particularly as the Queen asked me if it really did taste much better out of such a glass. If I suffered embarrassment at this remark it was speedily eclipsed as there arose a sound of pipes in the next room. The doors were flung open and the Pipe Major marched into the room, twice encircled the table and disappeared again through the doors where the remainder of the programme was played to its finale.

The first round of port having been consumed, the Queen rose, and she and the Princesses moved towards the drawing-room; the other ladies turned at the door and made low curtsies to the King before passing on.

The King then told me to draw up my chair, and Major Penn engaged me in conversation until we all arose to go to a film to be held in the ballroom.

The film was of no special merit. When it was over we wended our way to the hall where drinks were awaiting us. We discussed the film in light conversation, and took part in solving a vast jigsaw puzzle laid out on a table. The Princesses were adept at this and fitted in more pieces than the rest of the company put together.

The ladies then retired to bed, and it was something of a touching family scene to see the Princesses kissing Queen Mary, and wishing her "good night."

Sir Harold then told me that the King would like to see me and I went into his study where he had arranged around the room a selection of the Windsor pictures. These he discussed with me, and particularly the one of *The Long Walk*. He again repeated his criticisms concerning the fallen trees and I repeated my suggestion of introducing some vestige of rot in them should he wish me to do so. I also ventured that this picture be submitted to the Selection Committee of the Royal Academy, a suggestion which seemed to meet his approval. The King then showed me some other pictures in his possession representing some views of the Sandringham Estate, among which was one by Mrs Fellowes, wife of Captain Fellowes the King's Agent at Sandringham. Mrs. Fellowes had presented it to the King as a Christmas card. It was an illustrated map of the Estate, beautifully coloured, and the lettering carried out in a neat hand, whilst the illustrations of the King's favourite shooting stands and other favoured spots were most artistically conceived and executed.

Just before midnight we went to bed. I slept lightly and was awakened while it was yet dark by domestic noises about the house – carpets being hoovered and stairs being swept.

I lay listening to these homely sounds and watching the grey light dawning. I drew the curtains apart and could dimly see a snow-covered lawn and pine wood beyond. It was still snowing. I considered that it would be most unlikely that Her Majesty would wish to venture out to show me the sights if this weather persisted. Perhaps it would break and the sun would shine; the country would sparkle in gleaming whiteness and all would be well.

But it didn't. After breakfast, which was attended by the Princesses but not the King and Queen, although the snow had ceased falling, the black north-east clouds refused to break. They hung like a funeral pall which was only relieved from time to time by desultory snowflakes drifting on the chill breeze.

As the clock chimed nine, the Pipe Major commenced his piping. He piped for some ten minutes, marching up and down in front of the house. The colouring of his kilt and highland uniform looked particularly rich against the snowy background.

The shooting party collected in the library about 9.30 a.m. The King arrived and said a few words; to me he remarked, "It isn't much of a day for sightseeing," then to all the others, "Well, we'd better be off." I was left for some time on my own. I scanned the papers but absorbed nothing of what they contained and then began to browse among the books on the library shelves. I found here, to my delight, some excellent books on the Norwich School of painting, and one on J. S. Cotman which I had seen before and had often tried unsuccessfully to acquire.

At length a footman arrived to inform me that Her Majesty considered the weather unpropitious for an expedition. He asked me if there was anything he could suggest for my amusement. Was I warm enough? Would I like some hot refreshment? I answered that I was really most happy and comfortable and did not feel the need of any refreshment, but I told him I thought I would go out to explore a bit on my own. "Very good, Sir," he said. "If I might suggest it, Sir, the little church here is well worth a visit."

I thanked him and said I would certainly pay it a visit. "Yes, Sir, I think you'll enjoy it," and adding that luncheon was at 1.15 p.m. he put some more logs on the fire and withdrew. Shortly afterwards I donned some suitable clothes and stepped out into the snow.

I was now able to gain some impression of the house from the outside. The evening before I had been shown a photograph of the original house which had been a modest structure of goodly proportions. I believe the present mansion, constructed of yellowish stone and red brick in an Elizabethan style was completed in 1871. I cannot say truthfully that its overall design afforded me any aesthetic enjoyment. The style appeared bastard and the general effect was fussy and too reminiscent of the later Victorian era to be really satisfying. I felt I should have my work cut out if I should be asked to make a picture of Sandringham Hall. Maybe, later in the year, it would look happier and more comely, but as I turned my back on it and passed along the path towards the church under the dark canopy of pines through which the bleak wind soughed bitterly, I determined that whatever else Her Majesty might demand of my prowess, I would certainly give this subject a wide berth if it were possible.

The church of St. Mary Magdalene is of a different calibre. It is in perfect preservation, and built of local Carrstone. Perhaps it is neither so interesting nor so well proportioned as the majority of Norfolk churches, but it is a friendly building. Even in those bleak conditions I saw in it possibilities for a picture. Otherwise, but I must confess I didn't venture far afield, I saw little that lent itself pictorially, and I returned to the library a little despondent. There I renewed my spirits with a glass of excellent sherry, and as it was nearly one o'clock I made my way to the hall.

It cost me a good deal of effort to impel myself thither under my own steam, but needs must when the devil drives. When I got there I found myself once more in the presence of Her Majesty, Queen Mary, the two Princesses and the Ladies-in-Waiting. The Queen approached me to express her regrets that the weather had been so unkind as to prevent her from taking me out. She would speak to Jane Fellowes, and when the weather was kinder, she hoped I might return to Sandringham and, under the direction of Mrs. Fellowes, discover some subjects on the Estate which I might feel inclined to paint.

At luncheon, which was a much less formal meal than dinner, I again sat next to the Queen with Queen Mary on my left. I conversed mostly with Queen Mary, finding much in common with her in her knowledge and love of painting and the arts. I found myself talking easily with this grand old lady and I appreciated the fact that it was she who was really responsible for my ease.

Luncheon being over, the shooting party again set out. The Queen and the two Princesses had promised to grace a Women's Institute meeting with their presence. My train was due to leave just after 3 p.m. I therefore bade farewell to Her Majesty expressing, as far as I could, the pleasure I had experienced from my visit and the hope that I might return in better weather to do some painting.

I passed through the wrought-iron gates and glanced back at the house. As the guard blew his whistle and the London train steamed out of the station, away from the snow-bound marshes I breathed a sigh of relief. The ordeal was over. I had been intensely nervous, yet the kindness of these great people had calmed and encouraged me.

January gave place to February, but February was as bitter a month as its predecessor. In March the snow still lingered and the sun remained as bashful as ever behind the black north-east clouds. I never remember painting in my studio under such consistently severe conditions. The medium I use for oil painting remained so stiff in the dipper that only by holding the palette over a Valor stove as I worked could I get the medium to thaw. My mind and fingers seemed numb.

However, I got my winter's work completed, among which were three large oils and one smaller commission. I intended to send two of the oils to the Academy and also the King's watercolour of *The Long Walk*. I knew the oils would be slow starters, but I thought the King's picture would get hung and others of my own profession seemed to think it a certainty.

I had arranged with Capt. Fellowes that I should visit Sandringham the last fortnight in March, but during the first part of March there was no let-up in the weather. We spent most of it cutting logs from fallen trees in the valley below the house and lugging them up with immense labour through the snow. I decided to delay the visit to Sandringham for a fortnight. It was as well I did so, for when the thaw came the floods which followed would have made it almost impossible to reach Sandringham by road except by the most devious route. So that it was the first day of April before I set out. It was mild and sunny when I started and white clouds sailed lazily across the April sky. Spring had come at last. Beyond Brandon, however, the wind veered into the east and there was no longer any hint of spring in the air. When I arrived at Hillington, a village some two miles from Sandringham, where I was to stay, a steely grey sky and still air betokened snow.

The Ffolkes Arms, where I was to lodge, dated back to 1500. Some parts had been partially modernised, but for the rest, it was damnably inconvenient. Nevertheless, the warmth of welcome from the landlord and his wife did much to dispel the chilly atmosphere. The food was excellent, and the cellar of good quality and in fair supply. Even so, by the second night I had such a fit of ague, or some traces of an obscure tropical complaint which attacks me on occasions of extreme cold, that I could scarcely speak comprehensibly with my hostess and was forced to retire to bed early with some aspirin, whisky, a hot bottle and as many clothes as I could muster. I stayed in bed the next day, but by the day following I seemed quite recovered, and I determined to brave the elements. I donned almost as many clothes as I possessed including sea stockings and a couple of pullovers. Then, in the confined but sheltered space of the Morris 8, I started to draw in a group of silver birches on the edge of the Princesses' Drive. It snowed heavily from time to time and I could scarcely see my subject. My fingers became stiff and numb with cold and I found difficulty in drawing the birch stems and the delicate tracery of branches and twigs.

In the afternoon I sought other subjects in the blackness, but what with the cold and the dreary effect over the face of all nature I was unable to find much. Mercifully, after a few days the wind suddenly switched round and it became warmer, but the arctic conditions evidently felt cheated and only permitted the advent of the south wind in the form of violent gales and drenching rain. It was impossible to work most of the time and by the end of the first week I had completed very little, but the elements gradually became less boisterous and even a few April skies drifted up from the west and I was able to set to with renewed will. The air never really cleared, and since only one day was typical of the hard Norfolk light of those areas, I tried to make the best of it.

By the end of a fortnight I had completed some seventeen works, seven of these being smallish watercolours and the remainder large ones. I showed some of these to Capt. Fellowes on one occasion and his reception of them was most encouraging. Both Capt. and Mrs Fellowes assisted me in various ways, not the least of which was driving me round the country to show me some of the Queen's favourite views.

I enjoyed the work at Sandringham. Although at first I thought I should never get away from the thick woods which ring Sandringham Hall and block out the distances, explorations further afield led me to more promising subjects. There is a character and charm about this countryside which is different from anywhere else I know.

On returning home I cut and wash-lined the mounts for each picture and showed them to Major Penn so that he could advise me which to send in for Their Majesties' inspection on their return from South Africa. Major Penn suggested my showing them the whole seventeen. So I got them framed and delivered at the Palace, after which we awaited Their Majesties' return with some impatience.

Meanwhile, April advanced and I still had no news of the fate of my pictures at the Academy. There is usually a good deal of "buzz" going round in professional circles at such times. In clubs or at exhibitions or at other places where artists congregate there is a good deal to be overheard of such remarks as: "Any luck at the R.A. old man? I hear poor old so-and-so has had all his chucked. Too bad after all these years. They've been pretty drastic with the watercolours I'm told. Have you heard? No? Oh, you'll be all right then. I've had my large oil chucked. Funny people, aren't they?" One sympathises, applauds, and still hopes. The Royal Academy is a wonderful place to men who have their works accepted. Such a target for raillery for the less fortunate. But those who rail and those who are fortunate still have great hopes for another year, and a sneaking feeling that however much the Academy is going to the dogs, if they could only be elected, they could do so much to pull it back again.

The day before Outsiders' Varnishing Day I heard news of my pictures. My two oils were on the line and, therefore, if I chose I could enjoy the privilege of having a glass over them. The King's picture was out. Funny people these R.A.s.

But it was not a funny situation at all for me. In fact, I was most concerned. I would rather have had one oil chucked and the King's picture in than both my oils on the line and the King's picture out. I thought perhaps there had been an oversight, since on the sending-in form I had plainly stated, "Lent by the gracious permission of His Majesty the King." Much as I was loath to ring them up at the R.A. lest the Academy should consider I was cajoling or complaining at having a picture chucked, I determined to do so. The answer was, "The Academy didn't like the picture. There was no official instruction from His Majesty that he wished the picture to be hung, and the King must take pot-luck with the rest." This answer I considered short-sighted policy on the part of the Academy, and an insult to the King.

Very much concerned, I informed Major Penn over the phone. "I wonder why they should have done it," he returned. "Unhappily, the situation is complicated by His Majesty's absence abroad and we can do nothing about it. But if it's any comfort to you, I can assure you that this news will in no way affect the pleasure that I know Their Majesties will derive from the charming set of watercolours you have just completed of Sandringham."

Major Penn's reassuring reply was most welcome, but it made us realise that so far as the Royal Academy was concerned I had queered my pitch and I would never be elected. The R.A. frowns upon outsiders with important commissions.

The King and Queen arrived back in England on the day and at the hour prescribed. The country welcomed them back, delighted to see them looking so well. For our part, we began to wonder how soon it would be before we heard news of the Sandringham pictures. We knew we would have to be patient. There would be a host of engagements and duties for them to fulfil and we reconciled ourselves to the fact that they might not have time or the interest to look at the pictures for months.

We were mistaken. Within three days of their return I received a letter from the Queen's Treasurer informing me that Their Majesties were so delighted with the pictures that the Queen had decided to purchase all but two, and those two she did not wish to keep because one was not typical of Sandringham, and the other was a subject which she realised was not pictorial. Major Penn added that though the idea was not official, Her Majesty had suggested that I might be interested to do some work at Balmoral later in the year. Here was great news indeed. Fifteen out of seventeen water-colours purchased and the possibility of some more work at Balmoral. The Royal Academy could jolly well go to blazes.

The garden parties came and went, and we were invited to one of the later ones. We were so near to the Royal party at one time that we could have touched them. But either they didn't look my way, or they didn't recognise me. We thought the whole thing was done with, Balmoral and all.

Again, we were mistaken.

above: H.M.S. *Hood* in the Pentland Firth: *watercolour*
below: H.M.S. *Mauritius* supporting the 5th Army at Gaeta and Anzio: *watercolour*.
(By courtesy of Admiral Sir William Davis)

Claude Muncaster

Chapter 10

All the King's Castles
Balmoral

A letter dated 31 July 1947, with the now almost familiar crest of Buckingham Palace arrived and read as follows:

BUCKINGHAM PALACE
31st July 1947

My dear Muncaster,
 The Queen was recalling this morning the possibility of your visiting Balmoral this summer. If you would like to essay this, could you let me know what would suit your plans best?
 Her Majesty will, I think, be away from September 8 to 12, or thereabouts, but apart from this, any time between, say August 14 and the end of September would be appropriate.
Yours sincerely,
Signed. Arthur Penn.

I rang up the Palace at once and got through to Major Penn. I told him that I was under the impression that I was to visit Balmoral just for the day.

"Not in the least," Major Penn informed me. "It is Her Majesty's wish that you should stay as long as you choose."

"But do I stay actually in the Castle with them?" I asked in astonishment.

"That also is Her Majesty's wish," replied Major Penn.

The last few days before leaving became something of a gamble with clothes ration coupons. Somehow I contrived to buy a dark blue suit, some grey flannel trousers and a bowler hat for church. Equipped thus, and with impedimenta now including a trunk, a typewriter, painting gear, a second suitcase, a large brown paper parcel and my ration books, I set out for Pulborough station in a hired car, my own having been sent on ahead by rail

At Aberdeen my car was waiting for me. The Station Master had everything ready. After a good breakfast in the station restaurant I fitted the luggage and myself into the green Morris 8 and started out on the last lap for Balmoral, which lay some fifty miles inland up the Dee.

That sense of unreality did not diminish as the miles sped by, despite the glorious sunlight and the fine-weather haze. I cursed this haze for hiding the countryside when I was so interested to see what it was made of. I passed through Ballater and shortly afterwards found Crathie church. Opposite the church I swung left over the Dee and was almost immediately confronted by a lodge-keeper who directed me through the gates to a uniformed policeman further up the drive. Trying to swallow my nerves, I swept (as much as a little Morris 8 can sweep) up the drive towards the policeman. To my surprise he knew my name. Somebody had evidently been organising things.

The policeman directed me to the Tower door. Following his directions I emerged from the trees, and there with its white granite gleaming in the sunlight, was Balmoral Castle.

A footman in the dark blue livery with which I had already become familiar at Sandringham appeared and I asked for the Equerry-in-Waiting, Lt. Commander Peter Ashmore, who had taken over from Sir Harold Campbell. It seemed the Equerry was engaged at a conference about the new fire stations. So I suggested that if I could be shown to my room I would wait there until the Equerry could see me.

The footman took my tip and told me to follow him. This I did along a sunlit passage carpeted in rich red. I noticed Landseer prints on the walls, and above them numerous stag heads mostly shot by the Prince Consort. The general colour of the wallpaper was off white with a pattern imposed upon it in bold relief of some felt material in a beige shade. The pattern was a repeating design composed of a crown, a thistle and the letters V.R.I. Later on I was told that every bit of this pattern had to be applied by hand. The doors and window sashes were of a light-coloured wood – a local pine wood which at one time had been varnished; but Queen Mary had had much of the woodwork pickled and the effect was certainly a great improvement on the varnished wood, some of which still remained.

Half way along the passage we turned left. Here the carpet changed to a tartan pattern with a background of pale yellow and green. Turning left again we entered the room facing us. "This, Sir, is the Prime Minister's room," the footman informed me, and he added that it was only reserved for very special guests. I was amused at this remark thinking that I must surely be the least important guest who had ever slept in the room. I glanced around at the photographs of Prime Ministers hanging on the walls and seemed to see their indulgent smiles at the footman's remark.

It was not a large bedroom, but large enough. It was decorated with a plain light-coloured wallpaper. The furniture was of ample proportions of a late Victorian order of a yellowish timber, highly varnished.

above: Arun Valley in Flood, 1935: watercolour
(By courtesy of Worthing Museum and Art Gallery)
below: A view on the Balmoral Estate: watercolour
(By courtesy of H.M. The Queen)

The pattern of the carpet and of the curtains was the same tartan pattern as the carpet in the passage. There was a table with several bottles of different coloured inks upon it, pens to match, and a supply of crested paper on a blue leather-backed blotter. I discovered this paper to be of such good quality as to inspire me to write a letter home each morning before breakfast.

The outlook from the two tall windows was charming. One faced south-east and looked over the drive on to a wide expanse of lawn which was bordered on each side by a variety of types of trees.

An earlier house once stood on this vast lawn but the building was demolished in 1853 when the present Castle was constructed. Part of the old site had been transformed into a sunken garden which cannot be seen at ground level from the present Castle. But rising sharply beyond it I could see a hill. This was once completely covered by Scotch firs which the present King had cut down, and although there were still scars and not all the timber had been tidied up, the general improvement was obvious. Some trees on the summit have survived the axe and deer still thrive in this remnant of the ancient forest. Some three-quarters of the way up stood a flagstaff and Princess Helena's Cairn. On the summits of some of the surrounding hills there were other cairns, each a memorial to one of Queen Victoria's children.

The second window faced north-east over a garden arranged with flower borders, gravel paths and a fountain playing in the centre. On the left rose the Tower and beyond, over the curving balustraded wall, was a thick wood which obscured any further view.

Through the bedroom was a bathroom, a luxury I much appreciated. The furnishings of this bathroom were somewhat old fashioned having two wash-basins of a tip-up type not dissimilar to those found in ships. The arrangement of the lavatory paper intrigued me, being set out in its mahogany receptacle in a series of fans, which was most decorative. The bath still retained the six-inch mark for the limit of hot water, a reminder of the good old days. In its operation it was the quietest bath I had encountered. After the first splash of water there was no more sound as the water issued from a disc at the bottom of one end. The water was always piping hot as was also the towel-rail on which was spread a bath towel of some eight feet by ten feet; an enormous thing and quite difficult to manage.

While I was investigating these apartments Peter Ashmore appeared. I liked him at once. A typical naval type, he made me feel at home immediately and seemed to know all the answers before I asked them. To my considerable relief he explained what I should wear and do and when and what I should say when I renewed my acquaintance with Her Majesty.

He then took me on a tour of inspection and gave me further clues as to what the programme was and who the guests were. The list of residents with their room numbers was on a table at the Tower door entrance. There were twenty-three residents of whom I was the twenty-third. It was a formidable list and consisted of:

H.M. The King,
H.M. The Queen,
H.R.H. The Princess Elizabeth,
H.R.H The Princess Margaret,
H.R.H. The Duke of Kent,
Lord and Lady Eldon, and their two sons,
Lord and Lady Halifax,
Lord and Lady Salisbury,
Lord Porchester,
Lady Jean Rankin (Lady-in-Waiting to The Queen),
Lady Margaret Egerton (Lady-in-Waiting to Princess Elizabeth),
The Hon. Margaret Elphinstone,
The Hon. Giles St. Aubyn (Tutor to H.R.H. The Duke of Kent),
The Hon. David Bowes-Lyon,
Major Arthur Penn,
Major Adeane (Assistant Private Secretary to The King),
Lt. Commander Peter Ashmore (Equerry-in-Waiting),
Mr. Claude Muncaster.

I was the only guest without title or rank. I suppose I could have used the rank of Lt. Commander R.N.V.R. But I decided to call myself simply "Mister."

On the way to the Equerry's room we met the young Duke of Kent. Ashmore introduced me, saying "Eddy, this is Mr. Muncaster, he has come up to do some painting." I gave this young lad my hand and remembered to call him "Sir" just in time. He gave me the once-over in no uncertain fashion and I think he was a little at a loss to understand why he should be expected to speak on equal terms with a painter and decorator – for which he evidently mistook me. I passed on with Peter, a little uncomfortable and a little amused. In point of fact, I was later able to show the Duke some short cuts to drawing ships.

But the ice had been broken somewhat before then because a few moments after my first introduction to the Duke, I was inveigled by him into participating in a game of trying to place a ping-pong ball on the top of the water-jet of the fountain. It was a hazardous undertaking. The supply of water to the jet was controlled by turning on a tap on the lawn by means of a spanner. The Eldon boys and the Duke alternately manipulated the spanner while Ashmore and I were expected to climb the fountain in turns to place the ball on the tip of the jet of bubbling water. Only half a turn of the spanner was sufficient to transform the quietly bubbling jet to a spurt of water some twenty feet high.

On returning to my room to change my sodden clothes, I was relieved to find my belongings unpacked and no sign of my trunk, suitcases and brown paper parcels. Later, Ashmore, with ingenious foresight insisted on my paying the head chauffeur a visit to discover where my car was to be garaged. So we went to see Hurl, the Queen's chauffeur.

The chauffeurs' quarters and garages formed a block of buildings some two hundred yards from the Castle. Here we found a hive of industry with chauffeurs industriously servicing and washing a fleet of already spotless Daimlers, shooting-brakes, private cars and lorries. My own car was nowhere to be seen. Eventually we found it in a garage at the back. We also found beneath it on the floor a widening pool of petrol. Examination revealed a leak at both ends of the tank, evidently the result of rough treatment on the part of the railway. This was a tragedy as I would be lost without a car, and a repair of this kind might take weeks. But not so at Balmoral! One was not a guest of His Majesty for nothing, and the car was sent into Ballater and was returned, repaired, within thirty hours.

At noon the party assembled in the front hall to await the Queen and the Princesses. Peter Ashmore introduced me to everyone and encouraged me by saying that I would soon get them all sorted out. I very much doubted it. Waiting there for the Queen I felt like a new boy at school. The fact that I had met her and the Princesses before didn't help! I was as nervous as ever. The Queen asked me if I had got very wet at the fountain, and I replied that I had been sprinkled but no harm had been done. I was soon more at ease.

We then set off in two brakes for a shoot which was in progress that morning. The Queen invited me to sit next to her and as we drove along she pointed out various viewpoints in the landscape which she thought I might find suitable for painting.

The shoot was in the Gairnshiel district, a country of magnificent grouse moors on the north side of the Dee. The King rents this countryside for shooting; his own land lies on the south side of the river.

The heat haze persisted to such an extent that it was difficult to see much of the country, but even under these conditions I could see great possibilities for painting.

The Queen's interest and love of the country was most evident. She knew the history of all the places we passed. Gairnshiel itself is a cluster of scattered cottages bordering the river Gairn. It is the remnants of what had once been a much larger village prior to its community being attracted to the towns or the wars from which it never recovered. It is a special love of the Queen and of the Princesses. A year or two previously the Queen had discovered in Gairnshiel the ruins of a cottage which she purchased for a very small sum and had done up into an attractive little house to which she refers affectionately as "the cottage with the long ears" – the ears being the two tall chimneys. This tiny cottage on the banks of the Gairn river is said to be the Queen's only bit of personal property. She uses it as a sort of picnic summer-house. There is no furniture except one chair, so the rest of the picnic parties – Princesses, Ladies-in-Waiting and guests – either remain standing or sit on the floor.

There is some interesting history connected with this area. It was here that General Wade came in the 1720's to start work on the military roads, paying his five hundred highwaymen, as his working soldiers were called, sixpence extra a day for the work. One of his forty stone bridges, of which the Old Bridge of Dee is a magnificent example, spans the river at this point. It is a semi-circular one-arched structure of granite, most pleasing in its bold simplicity. The river flowing beneath is fast running and as clear as crystal. The grey granite boulders are a delight. There are rough heather banks, ancient larches bordering moors with patches of chasing sunlight and shadow when the south-west winds laden with the scent of heather scatter the clouds before them.

On this first morning, however, I could give little heed to such plays of fancy. My mind was far too occupied in my immediate responsibilities and awareness of my present company. How was it possible to let my mind wander off into heathery imaginings when I was riding beside the Queen? It was all so dreamlike; so strange and impossible, yet real. So I couldn't go wool-gathering.

When we arrived at the shoot I almost began to wish that I had accepted my father-in-law's many invitations to shoot. Then I should have known better what was expected of me. A drive was in progress. By straining our eyes we could just make out several of the guns far away up on the moorside. An army of beaters advanced towards them in perfect open order waving white flags. Judging from the scarcity of shots there could not have been many birds.

Meanwhile, chauffeurs and gillies carried the picnic baskets, drinks and rugs down through the heather to a spot about a quarter of a mile from the road. Here the party gathered. They conversed about the weather, the heather and what you will. Cameras of every description came out and their owners got busy with stills and movies. Mostly they were snapshots of the Queen or the Princesses, who were usually aware they were being taken and thoroughly entered into the spirit of it. The Queen was particularly proud of her summer hat which she said everyone laughed at. As a matter of fact, it was rather comical. It was a straw hat, in shape rather like an inverted soup-bowl with a surround of buttercups and cherries. It looked too small and really didn't suit her, but she seemed to enjoy being photographed in it. She brought out a camera herself, but considering the scene insufficiently animated she commanded them to do a Highland fling. The Princesses and Lady Eldon in their tartan skirts and the two Eldon boys in their kilts looked perfect for the part. Fortunately I was not in range, so I did not have to attempt the dance.

The food was set out by the Princesses and the Ladies-in-Waiting. Peter Ashmore circulated with the sherry. Lady Salisbury and myself found common ground in discussing Cartmel, Holker and the Ulverston district, discovering we had several mutual friends thereabouts.

The first drive being over, the guns could be seen wending their way through the deep heather. First with Lord Halifax, came the King bare-headed, kilted, wearing a tartan over his shoulder and carrying a long Highland staff. As they approached. I was introduced to each of them.

Then lunch began in earnest and I longed for an appetite, as I had quite forgotten how good food could be. But I was still far too nervous to appreciate the quality or quantity of this superb picnic lunch. All I wanted to do was to go and hide myself in a juniper tree and watch from a distance, but not be one of the party. Charming as they all were I could not get over the incongruity of my presence there. Yet they included me in their conversation and once Princess Elizabeth remarked how they had thought of me the day before when the landscape and the effects had been so much more interesting. The Queen observed that it was a pity that when they brought Mr. Muncaster to see the sights there was a heat haze and it was the dullest shoot of the lot.

Immediately lunch was over a search began for all the cameras, camera-cases, filters and whatnots which seemed to have been scattered willy-nilly in the heather.

By now it was hot. The next drive was near where we had been lunching, and since all the gentlemen seemed to have divested themselves of their hats and jackets, I left mine in one of the shooting-brakes. I followed the party and eventually found myself at a butt at the summit of a hill with the two Princesses and Lord Porchester. The Princesses seated themselves at either corner of the butt with sufficient view forward to enable them to mark down the birds as they fell. I was soon carrying on a whispered conversation with Princess Margaret, and being at such close quarters I was able to study her eyes which are both attractive and remarkable. Apart from their extreme clarity betokened by her youth, they consisted of three distinct circles of blue; violet blue at the centre, circled by grey-blue, and ringed by an outer circle of dark blue.

I have little recollection of our conversation, but I know we talked a little of the surrounding country, and she supplied the names of the hills sometimes giving the English translation of the Gaelic names. Notable among these was Lochnagar, The Lake of the Goats, which dominated the surrounding hills and could be seen faintly now that the haze was clearing. I came to know this hill a great deal better as time went on, and the more I became familiar with it, the more I came to revere it. Each time I returned I regarded it with new respect.

There was one more drive a little nearer home. This time I found myself in the lowest butt with the Queen's brother, the Hon. David Bowes-Lyon. With us were Peter Ashmore, the Duke of Kent and his tutor. As we lay on our bellies, Peter Ashmore who had seen my book, *Rolling Round the Horn*, wanted to know all about life in a windjammer. In whispers I answered his questions as best I could.

For the return journey I was asked to join the King and Queen in their brake. Other passengers, if I remember rightly, were Lord and Lady Salisbury, Lord Porchester, Lord Halifax and Lady Eldon. At first there was a general post-mortem of the shoot. Then it changed to an appreciation of the countryside and the changing light. "How can you paint this country, Muncaster, when the light is changing every minute?" the King asked. "Look. You see the light is completely different from what it was a few minutes ago." Then the King pointed out a particularly lovely view of Lochnagar. "There you are, Muncaster. What about that?" "Yes, Sir," I answered, "it certainly is a fine view. I'd like to have a go at it sometime." In fact, I did so on a subsequent visit and the picture I painted was the one which Princess Elizabeth chose for her wedding present.

Again the conversation changed – to a discussion on art. The King wanted to know what "all this modern stuff" was about. "When I see a picture of a place I like to recognise it," he said. His Majesty was no sympathiser with the modern movement.

On arriving at the Castle the procedure was for the men to change into suits for tea which was served in a smallish room between the drawing-room and the dining-room. Card tables were placed together in one long line. The Queen sat at one end to serve tea and Princess Elizabeth served tea at her end as well. It was an informal meal, and we looked after ourselves.

Tea, which had started about five o'clock was over by a quarter to six. I was still not really at ease. "What do we do now?" I asked Lady Eldon.

"Just whatever you like," she answered. "If you like demon patience, the Princesses will rope you in for a game. If not, you are free to do exactly as you choose. I expect dinner will be at eight thirty." I decided to take myself for a walk.

Rather forlornly, and feeling like an insect beside the Castle walls, I followed my nose and wandered off into the woods and climbed far enough up the hill to be able to look back and see the castle and a view westwards up the valley towards Braemar. The weather had turned gloomy with dark thunder clouds. Yet somehow it seemed to suit the grim grandeur of the mountains, even though the haze still clung about them. But it had cleared sufficiently to enable me to see their many possibilities for painting, a consideration which was naturally always uppermost in my mind.

How was I going to work in this atmosphere? It was obvious that I could not go shooting every day, even if I had wanted to. That would be quite hopeless for I would never get anything done. Somehow I would have to arrange to be on my own and be as independent as possible. I would have to ask Ashmore about it and see if this could be arranged without my seeming too impolite and unsociable.

I returned to the Castle. By the tower door I found Major Penn who kindly offered me an expedition by car, but we found the chauffeurs at tea and no car available, so we took off on our feet.

We crossed the vast lawn and passed through the sunken garden, fragrant with the scent of sweet peas, then over the road and up the twisting path to the flagstaff and cairn which I had observed from my bedroom, and on again into the deer forest above.

Major Penn's idea in taking me this way was to show me a particular view of Lochnagar. "We came up here last Sunday afternoon with Their Majesties," he informed me. "I would like you to see this view because if you can find the time or the inclination to record it, I know it will give Their Majesties the greatest pleasure."

Eventually we emerged from the deer forest on to the wild upland country which had been partially cleared of trees.

"There it is," said Penn, but added that "it looks nothing at all today."

The view had a wild foreground of primitive granite boulders; the felled trees and some stark survivors showed darkly against the distance and the nearer greens and browns and light greys of heather, juniper and moorland grass. Beyond, in the middle distance and to the right, the ground fell away steeply to a forest of dark green firs. On the left, a steep hill rose, barren of trees and mottled with boulders. In the centre were the moors, green and yellow ochre and brown, stretching away in gentle slopes until they rose to the steeper contours of the great central mass of hills by Lochnagar, simple in form now because of the haze which hid its slopes and jagged corries on this north-east side. In its grey-blue tones it was beautiful enough. Later, I was to see it in other moods, far finer and far more exciting. Even so, even in this light, the subject was there and I longed to be at it.

On the way back we discussed many things, not least of which to my way of thinking was the question of my nervousness amidst my present surroundings. I felt I could confide in Major Penn. He comforted me considerably by telling me how well he remembered his own extreme consternation when he first undertook his duties as one of the Household. He assured me I would soon get over my discomfiture and enjoy myself.

We returned to the Equerry's room for a drink and then to our rooms to change for dinner. There I found the water run in my bath and evening things put out with cuffs and links in the shirt. I lay in the bath just five minutes too long. It resulted in a struggle with my black tie and because of my haste lest I should be late, I finally had to discard it for a ready-tied one. It would at least look tidier and the other would probably have come undone anyway. But there was plenty of time after all, for I was the first to arrive in the drawing-room.

One by one the house party arrived, the ladies looking elegant in their long evening frocks; such a joy for eyes starved by Sir Stafford Cripps's austerity.

Seating at the dinner table was arranged beforehand by the Queen and the Princesses. Usually, if the latest arrival to the house party was a man, he sat next to the Queen; if a lady, she sat next to the King. This was the rule for "the greatest outside stranger." The positions for dinner were indicated on an oval table plan corresponding to the shape of the dinner table. It was of red leather with spaces for visiting cards which could be slipped in with the visitor's name typed on it. It could be elongated or shortened according to the size of the house party. This plan was placed on a table in the drawing-room before the guests assembled, so that as each one arrived in the drawing-room, he could ascertain his position at table. However, on arriving in the dining-room there was a further check in the form of a card with the guest's name on it in the place at table which he was to occupy.

A hush fell upon the guests as the corgies entered in single file in front of the Princesses who in turn were followed by the King and Queen. The Royal Family usually circulated among the company for some ten minutes and then proceeded to dinner.

On this first night I found myself sitting next to the Queen in accordance with custom as I was "the greatest outside stranger." I enjoyed this privilege. When remarking to the Queen on the excellence of the fare, she said, "Do eat plenty – as much as you can. It will do you good."

I noticed the King had two small decanters before him, one of water and one of whisky. He drank very moderately from these and did not take wine. Under the table above his knees was a bell which he could use to indicate for instance, a change of course.

The Queen ate very little. Never soup, and seldom game; sometimes she took some fish and usually a sweet, but no coffee. Princess Elizabeth also refused coffee, but helped herself liberally to the sugar – those lovely brown coffee crystals of which she made a little pile in front of her on the table and ate with her fingers.

So long as the ladies remained at the table one had to be careful to talk to the right person. The procedure at Sandringham was good for Balmoral too, that is to say, the King set the direction and the remainder followed suit. Sometimes when the King was particularly interested in the conversation of the lady at his side he forgot to change. Then the Queen tried to catch his eye, but if after some time she was unable to do so, she changed the direction herself.

So far as possible the arrangement of guests was evened out so that each one in turn had interesting companions. This could not always work out, as, for instance, when new and important guests arrived in numbers and had to be seated in the most important positions which ousted the less important guests to the corners and ends of the table. Thus, often enough, the Equerry, the Secretaries and I found ourselves together in Cad's Corner. I was quite happy to be so placed since formalities were rather less strict and we could exchange conversation between three at a time if necessary. The pipers in their full dress, who paraded twice round the dining table after the sweet had been cleared, gave an additional note of colour and resplendence. While they piped there was no talking. Indeed, it would have been impossible to have done so against the skirling at such close quarters. The King's critical eye surveyed each of the pipers in turn. He would have noticed the slightest maladjustment of any of their uniforms immediately.

Over drinks in the drawing-room afterwards, the King discussed the Grimethorpe strike. Having his country so much at heart, it was natural that he should feel the greatest concern over it. He was all for making up a party there and then and going down to Grimethorpe. Although, as Lord Halifax remarked to me, he believed the King might do a lot by his personal presence among the miners, the Monarch must keep himself above politics. Moreover, should the King's motives by some mischance miscarry much more harm than good would result. The King knew this well enough, but it must have been most aggravating to have to desist from his purpose.

The following morning I had asked for a call at seven. Accordingly, as the clock in the tower chimed seven my servant arrived with tea and biscuits and my clothes brushed and pressed. He ran my bath for me and inquiring what clothes I proposed to wear, put them out for me and, taking up my evening clothes, departed.

I had not slept very well. Excitement, nervous anxiety and perhaps the champagne and brandy found me a bit heady. I had fully intended to get up and write. Instead, I lay and thought and drowsed, and then got up and prepared my painting kit. It was a nuisance about the car, but I could at least do some more exploring on foot.

I shall always associate breakfast at Balmoral with the smell of methylated spirits, hot-plates and smoked haddock. Not that haddock was the staple dish, but it was there on the first morning, and first impressions last. I don't like haddock particularly, and in the ordinary way, where there is a choice, I avoid it. But Balmoral haddock was different from other haddocks.

Neither the King nor the Queen attended breakfast. I believe the Princesses did, but I never saw them as I always breakfasted early, often before most of the other guests. I had a double motive in this early breakfast because I needed to get away painting as early as possible so as to give me a long morning's work, and because I hate being sociable too early in the morning.

At nine o'clock the piper started piping. He marched bareheaded up and down before the Castle for some ten minutes. This practice was carried out every day irrespective of weather conditions.

I felt restive about the car, so immediately after breakfast I went in search of news of it and was told it would be back about eleven. This was encouraging. It also gave me an excuse for not getting mixed up in another shooting party.

The morning was fresh and clear. The haze had been driven away before a north-westerly breeze. I set off on foot westwards up the valley. As I passed the front door Princess Elizabeth was talking with Peter Ashmore. I said, "Good morning, Ma'am," as I passed. She returned my salutation and smiled deliciously. I can think of no other word to describe her smile. It was only after I had passed that I remembered I had neither bowed nor lowered my head, nor done any of the things I ought to have done. Perhaps that was why she smiled!

I passed on through the woods and came out on the side of the Dee. There was very little water in the river. Even so, a fast, clear running river which sparkles and twists between and around great boulders always holds me fascinated. The Dee does all these things and is marvellously clear, having come all the way over granite with no peat or mud to discolour it.

Nevertheless, it was not the Dee I wanted to paint, at least, not at close quarters. It was the moors I needed and the hills. I followed the road we had travelled to the shoot; up the steep rise past the farm and the mill-wheel (Bush Lawsie Farm), on through the forest of firs and out on to the moors above. The clouds were driving up now but the late morning sun broke through them and silhouetted the great range of the hills in simple tones of dark grey-blue. It was a magnificent piece of country and a magnificent view of it. As a subject for painting it was far too big to tackle in so short a time and before I had got my hand in and my mind attuned to the landscape. So I climbed on until I spotted a fascinating rough road twisting away to the left. I followed this for a mile or two and then stopped and looked back. Lochnagar still reared its dark shape above the moors. The valley of the Dee and Balmoral were hidden but there was a subject there. If I took a small sheet of paper I thought I might be able to complete something of it before lunch.

It was stupid how nervous I felt starting that first sketch. I had only once before had a similar feeling and that was when I started the picture of The Long Walk. I felt a kind of despair lest my artistry should suddenly forsake me and I should make a mess of everything. After all, it might happen all too easily. Fortunately something came and I returned to lunch encouraged.

In the afternoon I set off in the opposite direction, the direction of Gelder Burn. I had been longing to explore that district which Major Penn had pointed out from the summit of our walk on the previous evening. He had indicated a road which led from the Castle and I followed this. After climbing through a deer forest it emerged on to the open moors scattered with white granite boulders, which increased in number and magnitude as the road twisted towards Lochnagar. It ended at Gelder Shiel, a couple of deserted cottages in an isolated spinney by the side of the Gelder. Here a footbridge crossed the burn. Beneath it the water tumbled between the boulders and crags and the broken banks of deep heather.

I managed to do a quick rough sketch quite close to the Gelder Shiel looking back towards Balmoral. It was not a large watercolour, nor was it a particularly successful one. But both this and the one I did in the morning interested the King because he was unable to place where either was taken from. So much so, in fact, that he took the Gelder Shiel picture out with him in a car to find exactly where it was done from. I met the Royal car with the King at the wheel on the Gairnshiel road one morning. I did not realise it was the King's car, nor that the King was driving, nor, indeed, that he had my picture with him. Two cars could not pass abreast on the narrow road. Seeing the larger car ahead I was preparing to give way when I saw it pull into the side. I proceeded to pass and just as I had done so heard shouts from the other car. I thought I saw Princess Elizabeth in the back but could not be sure. What was I to do now? The question was solved by the King's car driving on. It was only afterwards when the King and the Princess arrived home very late for lunch, that they told me the purpose of their drive. Had I known

I could have told them at once that they were travelling in quite the wrong direction. It was Princess Elizabeth who discovered their mistake and who finally directed them to within a few yards of where the picture had been painted. Here they took it out of the car and compared it with the view. The sketch, as I have already indicated, was a rough one and the lighting quite different from the effect over the landscape when the King and Princess viewed it. Notwithstanding these differences, it was the small spinney reserved from the axe on the summit of the hill behind the Castle which caught the King's eye. Or rather, so far as the sketch was concerned, its absence was noticed: I had excluded such an insignificant object in my hurry to complete the picture. To the King, the spinney with its history was a salient object, and it was its omission that had foxed him. Afterwards I put the spinney in for him, but the picture was too hasty and insufficiently literal and not one which he eventually purchased. However, it taught me a lesson– to be more topographically correct. Inaccuracies of this nature might cost me the sale of a picture and worse, be responsible for the whole house party being very late for lunch.

After dinner, over the port and liqueurs, the King became engrossed in conversation with Lord Halifax. The ladies had retired into the drawing-room some time ago. Presently, Margaret Elphinstone arrived with a message from the Queen reminding him that there was to be a film.

"There you are," the King exclaimed, "the Queen is always late you see, but when I'm late she doesn't like it."

It frequently happens in strange surroundings when the first few days are crammed with new experiences that any period of time seems trebled in length. So it was at Balmoral. On the third morning as I awoke to the sound of swallows and the scent of stocks from the borders outside my bedroom, I could scarcely believe that I had been at Balmoral only three days. Certainly I had not spent many hours in sleep, possibly not more than ten at the most. And as the days passed I discovered that one lived on excitement, good food and champagne, rather than on sleep.

The day again dawned bright and clear with a north-westerly wind which gave a keenness to the air, which made painting in the open none too comfortable. I managed to complete a watercolour of Gairnshiel in the morning, and during the afternoon drew in a large view of Balmoral and the Cairngorms; a complicated subject with a host of pitfalls. It was vast and colourful and its light and shade continually on the move. I knew I had set myself a difficult problem, since I could not complete the picture in one sitting and it was doubtful if I would ever see the landscape in like circumstances again. One chooses a subject because of a particular effect of lighting. It is this lighting that gives the feeling and spirit of the subject and which is most difficult to recapture on a second visit if the scene is lit to an entirely different effect. In the case of this view, it was several days before I got anything like the same lighting, and how far I was able to achieve anything of what I originally set out to do is difficult to judge. But I got something, and when the King saw it he said to me aside, "I think that's marvellous." It may be imagined how gratified I felt at his remark, the more so when I happened to speak of this later to Peter Townsend. He said, "If the King really said that it should last you a lifetime. The King is a man of deep feeling but without a gift of ready expression. He often longs to commend a person but words just don't come. Sometimes it makes him a difficult man to work for because one never seems to get a word of praise. But he is a wonderful person to work for and it's the greatest privilege. In fact, the Royal Family are the most wonderful people and I have the greatest admiration and affection for them all."

That same evening when we joined the ladies after dinner, we found Princess Margaret playing the piano and singing in a powerful voice. She was doing a most entertaining turn which closely resembled a Gracie Fields act. Princess Elizabeth, who adores her sister and thinks all she does marvellous, was rolling on the rug by the piano in paroxysms of laughter. When this turn was completed, the Queen asked me to sing something. I could scarcely refuse a Royal Command so, greatly to my embarrassment, I gave my rendering of Deep River. I sang extremely badly and my bottom notes seemed to have disappeared. I suppose embarrassment and champagne had drowned them.

Following this unfortunate anti-climax to an otherwise most enjoyable evening, I was surprised to see a tartan shawl put over the firescreen; to hear that two detectives had been chosen; to find the lights suddenly turned out and the whole house party involved in a game of "Murders." When the last person had been murdered and the murderer discovered in the shape of Sir Alan Lascelles, it was well nigh one o'clock and everybody retired to bed.

Next day I set off over the narrow road to Gairnshiel, I had become most attached to this white road twisting over those wild moors. I loved the desolation, the vastness, the colour of the heather intermingled with the strips of warm coloured moorland grass, which swept around and up the sides of these minor hills, delineating their contours in varied colours. The clouds springing up from behind the distant hills or from behind the dark brows of the nearer moors cast their shadows on the deep-toned heatherland below.

But this morning that usually deserted route was thronged with traffic. Every few yards I met a car, a bus, or motor cyclist or a bicyclist – all bound one way – to Braemar for the Games. This influx of holiday makers seemed to alter the atmosphere of the country completely. Gone was the wild desolation and the primitive remoteness. I was kept busy skinning my eyes for bad drivers. I could no longer gaze rapturously over the country on either side of the road in search of subjects. If I did find a likely viewpoint there was sure to be somebody parked just where I wished to paint. I had the greatest difficulty in finding a subject at all. At last, by getting myself off the road into a most uncomfortable position in the heather where I was in continual danger of falling headlong into a burn below, I started on a subject looking down Glen Gairn. It was a big subject and I could do no more on the first morning than the sky and some of the drawing-in. I did the sky first because it was magnificent and I knew I might not see it again, or anything like it, during my stay; and I would certainly not be able to remember it. The decision to paint the sky before anything else was rewarded, for even before I had completed it, much of its brilliant pageantry had disappeared below the heavier clouds which had banked up. As I returned homewards there was every indication of rain. It always rained at the Braemar Games. But after thirty-six rainless days, an unheard of thing in Scotland, it would be too bad if the fine spell chose to break on just this day.

That evening, the Queen's brother, Michael, arrived. I liked Michael at once; nobody could possibly dislike him. The Queen was sweet to him. He suffers from asthma and as I entered the drawing-room I heard the Queen saying, "Darling Michael, what a horrid nuisance this old asthma is. Perhaps the change here will do it good. You must stay as long as you possibly can." Then, observing me, she introduced me to him. "This is Mr. Muncaster, Michael. He has been doing some delicious paintings. Come and look."

Michael Bowes-Lyon went over to the chair in the corner under the unfinished Landseer where my pictures were always placed for all to see when I had completed them. "Ah!" he exclaimed, "Lochnagar! Lochnagar in a stern mood. Now I've seen it when it's ablaze with colour, rich reds and purples. You must paint it like that. I wish you would." We then launched into a discussion on purples. Michael's love was for purples. For my part, I abhor them. We did not fall out on this score, and we often teased each other about purples on subsequent occasions.

Quite a large proportion of the original house party departed that evening. Only eight sat down to dinner; the King and Queen, the Queen's two brothers, Major Penn, Giles St. Aubyn, Lady Jean Rankin and myself. It was an informal meal and I sat next to the Queen.

When the Queen and Lady Jean Rankin had left the dining-room, the King lapsed into an amusing and reminiscent mood to which Major Penn responded with that dry wit and charming conversational power which he possesses. They recalled a certain diminutive gentleman whom the King had knighted. Penn remarked, "Yes, Sir! Indeed I remember him. He was so small he scarcely reached the ground." The King laughed and said that he had had difficulty in finding him as he knelt, and an extra long sword had to be provided. He added that he wished people would keep still during the ceremony as he was sure that one day he would chop off somebody's ear. He went on to describe the difficulty he had experienced in investing a gentleman who was wearing a particularly long and bushy beard. He was contemplating the unsavoury business of lifting aside the beard with his fingers in order to discover the hook on which to hang the medal, when a timely gust of wind brushed the beard aside and, pop, the medal found its mark.

On Saturday the Queen, Princess Margaret and Major Penn left for Edinburgh. It seemed strange without the Queen, and I was more than sorry that Major Penn had left and would not return. He told me before he left that there would be one newcomer. "A nice young fellow, Altrop, I think he likes himself pronounced. He's turning up by air today. And I think he's about all until the influx later in the week."

I found Althorp standing alone in the Equerry's room, idly turning over the pages of *The Tatler*. He was a pleasant looking, well-built youth, in his early twenties. He wore plus-fours in a heather mixture shade. It struck me that he looked a trifle pensive and lonely; even a little awed. Knowing so well how I had felt myself on first arriving and, to some extent, still felt, I considered I ought to do something about it. It seemed silly for us to stand there together and not speak just because we hadn't been introduced. I determined to take the initiative and break the ice.

"My name's Muncaster," I said, and added a little bashfully, "I'm up here doing some pictures for the Queen."

"My name's Althorp," he answered rather shyly but with a charming smile. I immediately took a very good view of Althorp, and, moreover, I thought to myself, here is a commoner like me, somebody in whom I can confide.

A few minutes later I passed the visitors' book in the Tower Hall and read the name of the latest arrival . . . Viscount Althorp! I might have known it. However, my first impressions of him did not change, and the more I saw of him the more I liked him. He was fresh, amusing, shy and naughty; but his naughtinesses were so charming that one forgave them and enjoyed them. He left on the same day as I did some ten days later.

There was a small shoot arranged for the Saturday morning but none for the afternoon when the King and Princess Elizabeth went off for some rough shooting near by. For my own part, I went off painting as usual.

That evening, the Master of Elphinstone, the Queen's nephew arrived. Another arrival was the visiting Minister who is always entertained at the Castle over the weekend. Major Ford, Assistant Secretary to the King, also arrived. He was to act for Major Adeane during his period of leave.

There are just a few people whom I have met from time to time who always cause me the same trouble, that of not knowing where I have met them before and therefore possibly mistaking them for somebody else. Major Ford is one of these people. I had met him at Sandringham, but for the life of me I could not imagine where I had met him before when I saw him again at Balmoral. He made it none the easier for me by shaking my hand and saying, "Hullo, Muncaster. We know each other, don't we?" Naturally I said I did, but he must have seen at once that I did not know who he was from Adam.

There was an occasion when Major Ford, Townsend and myself were having the usual life-saver in the Equerry's room one evening before dinner. The telephone rang and Peter said, "Your honour, Major." Major Ford took up the receiver. Now some people can say "hullo" in a manner which

Balmoral from Lochnagar: *oil*
(By courtesy of H.M. The Queen)

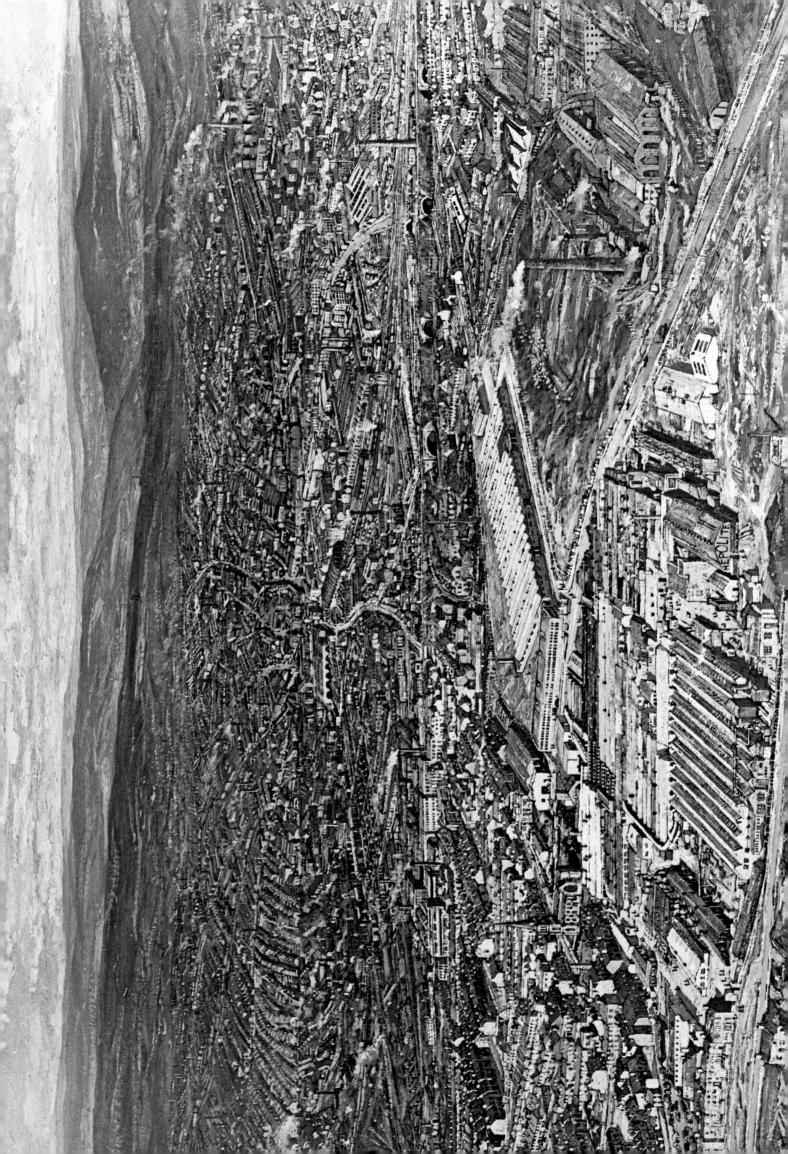

immediately puts the fellow at the other end at his ease. Some say "hullo" with exactly the opposite effect. Major Ford was a case between the two and his "hullo" was a mixture of levity and faint annoyance. But this tone immediately turned to one of concentrated deference and it was perfectly plain to us that the King was at the other end. The conversation became a lengthy one and Peter, in impish mood, found a London telephone directory and, opening it, tip-toed towards Major Ford and placed it gingerly on his head. The Secretary seemed quite unmoved (as indeed he had to be) at this absurd head-dress. Peter was not content, and seizing a blotter he added this to the directory. Still not satisfied, he poured out a glass of water and placed this on the blotter. Major Ford continued his conversation of respectful "Yes, Sir" and "No, Sir" and contemplative ". . . ers . . ." apparently quite unruffled by Peter's practical joke, although he must have been fully aware of the ridiculous figure he cut and of our obvious amusement. When the conversation ended I fully expected the glass of water to be directed at Peter's head and the blotter and the directory to be thrown after it. We were disappointed. Without a flicker of emotion he extricated himself from his embarrassment and in a perfectly everyday tone, asked me to have another drink.

At lunch on Sunday the King suggested taking me for a drive during the afternoon to show me some possible views for painting. As soon as lunch was over a shooting brake arrived and the King, Princess Elizabeth, Margaret Elphinstone and I set off to see the sights. The King drove. Princess Elizabeth insisted on my sitting in front with her father while she and Margaret Elphinstone sat in the less comfortable seat behind. She said I would see better in front.

We went first up Glen Gelder and then turned right along a wild rough road over which a smaller car with less clearance could never have travelled. But the rougher the road, the more the King seemed to enjoy it.

We continued to follow what road there was, down through an ancient deer forest to the Dee. We stopped occasionally to admire some magnificent specimens of Scotch firs. They must have been many centuries old, and twisted and wind-blown from the gales sweeping down the glen. At other times Princess Elizabeth spotted deer and we stopped to observe them through spy-glasses which had been brought for the purpose. Princess Elizabeth has a tremendous enthusiasm for deer-stalking and is often out for whole days in the forest pursuing this most exhausting and exhilarating of all sports. She certainly had an eye for spotting deer; they had to be much more obvious before I could see them.

When we reached the bottom of the forest slopes by the river we turned along a reasonable enough road and then up on to other ground. A little way up we passed Mrs. Adeane and her little boy and girl. They all curtsied as we passed. The boy should not have curtsied of course but lowered his head. The King may or may not have noticed this, but had he done so, I think he would have been amused. I certainly did not notice it and it was Mrs. Adeane who mentioned it to me afterwards. Major Adeane said it was easy enough to do; he had, himself, curtsied on more than one occasion. I wish I had seen him doing it.

After we had left the Adeane family, the road ceased to be a road and became nothing more than a track through the heather for ponies which were used for carrying down the shot deer. The King drove on up to the higher slopes where the road became more precipitous. We hoped we would not hit one of the large granite boulders lying hidden in the heather. We reached the summit safely and then turned almost back on our tracks to dip down into a forest of venerable birch trees and firs. On the right the slopes dipped steeply in a tangle of deep heather, outcrops of granite and fallen trees. On the left, the slopes of Creag nan Leachda rose sharply, at first in a tangle similar to that on our right until further up the forest cleared to give way to the barren wind-swept slopes of the hill tops. From time to time gaps in the trees on the right revealed something of Deeside with the bends of the river and the twisting valley. The conditions of fleeting sunshine and shadow and drifting rainstorms were ideal for viewing this landscape, and several times I had to exclaim at the beauty of it.

"Ah, but wait a minute," the King said, "we shall find a path soon up to the left and we'll walk up there and then I'll show you a real view. By the way, Lillibet, where is the path? We haven't passed it yet have we?"

"No, Poppa," the Princess answered. "Carry on a bit, but keep to the left of the track. I always think it will slide down here." And sure enough there was a large semi-circular crack in the road which seemed to indicate that at any moment an avalanche might start from this point.

"Here we are," the King said. "I don't think there'll be any traffic. I'll let her stop here."

So saying he brought the car to a standstill and we climbed out. The King, bare-headed, carrying his plaid over his shoulder and grasping his five-foot staff, began to lead the way. He had not left the shelter of the trees before a rainstorm swept down on us. The King unfurled his plaid and putting it right over his head wrapped himself in it. "There you are! Now you can see the use of these things," he said. The storm passed as quickly as it had come and we started to climb again. Princess Elizabeth, more active than any of us, raced ahead and called back as well known landmarks came into view. It was a breath-taking climb. From time to time we paused for breathing space and to admire the view. We talked of this and that but mostly of the country about us.

"It's a marvellous country," the King observed, "and one of the pleasant things about it is to be able to look upon it and know it is one's own. You see, we know it all so well." The King pointed with his staff to a gully on the side of a distant peak which had an unpronounceable Gaelic name, but which the King pronounced without the slightest hesitation.

"It's good to see that burn winding its way from source and to know every inch of it. Look at those hills. Those great features never change. You do, and I do; but they don't. The elements battle against them in fury through the ages but they remain steadfast."

Aerial view of Bradford, with St John's Works: *oil*
(By courtesy of Hepworth & Grandage Ltd., Bradford)

"The Castle's visible," Princess Elizabeth shouted from above. "Come on, Mr. Muncaster, you must see this."

We reached her at last where she was seated on the ground near a rough stone butt or shelter which I imagine is used in connection with deer-stalking. Then we turned round, and stretching out before us was a landscape of very great beauty. I understand this view to be a favourite of both the King and the Queen. The Queen told me that she always visits it at the end of the Balmoral holiday before returning to the arduous life of London.

"Now, Muncaster," the King said. "What do you think of that? Could you paint it?"

I replied that I should have great pleasure in trying to do something of it, but that it was really too vast for a watercolour and called for a large oil. If he would be interested to see what I could do in that way, I should love to try.

(The picture, completed by the end of 1947 is forty inches deep and one hundred and ten inches long. On the right is Lochnagar. The centre embraces the vast deer forest of Ballochbuie. The Dee is on the left with the main road from Braemar to Ballater. Balmoral can just be seen in the distance on the left. Behind the Castle rise the high grouse moors in the Gairnshiel district, and Brikhall is some eight miles down the river from the Castle but cannot be seen because of the high land intervening.)

On the day I first saw this view, and on the subsequent days when I visited it for the object of making studies, the colour effects were very fine and the sky formations a revelation in brilliance, form, and aerial perspective. I preferred the colouring of mid-September to that of October. In September it was quieter and more dignified without the lemon yellows which were so prevalent among the birches in the autumn.

On the afternoon I was there with the King, the mists capped Carn Beag, the highest peak of the Lochnagar group. This distressed the King somewhat as he wanted to show me everything.

On the way down, Princess Elizabeth and Margaret Elphinstone ran on ahead, ostensibly to seek shelter of the forest before another storm which threatened. But the Princess's real intention was to gather blueberries which grew in great quantities. By the time we had reached her she had picked a large handful for the King and myself. They were beautifully sweet and it was amusing to see the King chatting away quite unconscious that his lips and teeth were bright blue. It seemed rather like a fairy story, this receiving of blueberries from the hand of a Princess. In fact, the whole of that afternoon's drive was somehow unreal, and I can believe it less as time goes by – that there was I being driven round the country by the King himself and feasting on blueberries from the hand of the Princess Elizabeth.

I regard that expedition as the culmination of the memorable events which happened during my visit. Much else happened, of course, but it was that first week of experiences which remains indelibly stamped on my mind. After this, life developed into a more regular routine in which the outstanding incidents fade into a rather more general haze of recollections.

One such memory, and inevitably a more vivid one is my extreme bashfulness at bringing a new picture into the drawing-room. Usually I brought the day's work in at dinner time. If I could manage to slip in between cocktails at seven and dinner, when everybody was changing, I did so; or when everyone was out shooting and the drawing-room was deserted. I seldom joined the party for cocktails in the evening because I came back from painting late and it hardly seemed worthwhile changing into a suit for so short a time. Once I found the Queen walking about the room examining things in what appeared a rather distant and disconsolate manner. As soon as she saw me she was herself at once, and welcomed me with that wonderful smile of hers and enquired what I had been doing. I told her and suggested showing her some pictures I had done while she was away on her visit to Edinburgh.

"Oh, I'd adore to see them," she said. "Will you really show them to me? That would be kind."

I went and fetched them.

When I put them up, the Princesses and the Ladies-in-Waiting who were playing a game of demon patience, leapt up from the table and fell down on their knees before the pictures with loud exclamations of delight. Princess Elizabeth was particularly adept at recognising exactly where the scenes were painted. She often surprised me in this since many were painted in most remote places. Had I taken their appreciation at its face value, I must soon have become insufferably conceited.

Whether or not the artist and his pictures were something of an innovation at Court and served as a new source of conversation, was of no consequence to me. I felt that I was doing a little in my turn to repay them for the great privilege granted me.

After a fortnight, I felt that I had done all that was possible for me to do at that time. With what grace, or in what disgrace I took my leave, I am unable to say. I remember vividly the vast concourse of people there seemed to be in the drawing-room after lunch. One by one I had to say farewell to them all . . .the King, the Queen, the Princesses, the Dukes and Duchesses. Somehow I got through with it and, with a sigh of relief, passed through the door and fled to my room. There Dodd was waiting for me and he soon had my gear into the car, together with a present of a brace of grouse from His Majesty, some excellent sandwiches and a small bottle of whisky. In a few moments I was off.

How different this day of my departure to the day of my arrival. The sun had shone gloriously then. Now, a black and gusty north-easter had swept down over Gallaig hill obscuring all but the foothills. The rain drove past the grey walls of the Castle in sheets. The fountain still played bravely, but it looked dismal and out of key. A covey of autumn leaves blew from the trees and chased each other over the wide lawns. The swallows had flown and summer was over.

Chapter 11

On a Razor's Edge

After so much wartime gloom, dirt, destruction and depression, the ball which celebrated the engagement of Princess Elizabeth to Lieutenant Philip Mountbatten came as a treat; a luxurious abundance, in contrast to the meagreness and frugality of the past few years. Mrs. Muncaster, invited with her husband to this magnificent occasion, of course had "nothing to wear." Claude Muncaster himself was worrying about decorations. He had enquired of the Admiralty what medals he might be due for since he had served in so many theatres of war, but there had been no reply from them before the date of the ball. He therefore took himself off to ask the advice of that doyen of the medal market, Mr. David Spink.

Mr. Spink was most helpful, and after a few questions produced what he thought would be just the thing. It was a row of medals already made up. He explained what each was for and Muncaster discarded several as inappropriate. Even so, quite a glinting array survived and he bore them away, easy in mind. Of the evening itself he recalled:

"What a boost that ball was to our jaded morale; such spectacle. I wished it might have been possible for far more people to enjoy it and be inspired by so great a display of nobility. At one point during the evening the Princess's fiancé recognised me and came across to talk to us. I was able to present Primrose to him. He asked her whether she had met Princess Elizabeth, and on learning she had not, organised a meeting then and there. The Princess spoke to Primrose and then thanked me for the picture I had offered her as a wedding present and apologised for not having written sooner. She added, with that delicious smile, 'You see, Mr. Muncaster, I have really been rather busy lately!' We were amazed that she had remembered, and, what is more, that she quoted its title and went on to discuss the picture in detail.

"Next to me at one moment stood Sir Winston Churchill in conversation with the King. I noticed the King eyeing my medals and for a heart-stopping second thought he was going to ask me what they were. I hadn't been all that attentive when Mr. Spink had given me the particulars, and now could not remember which was for what. Only afterwards did I realise that, of course, the King with his astonishing memory for detail would have known perfectly well what they all stood for and would not have needed to ask for information.

"When it was time to leave and carriages were called, we stood on the steps outside until it was our turn for that little moment of personal publicity. I whispered the name into the ear of the page. Out into the night air, to reverberate about the pillars and hard stone surfaces of the palace courtyard, boomed his stentorian announcement: 'Lord Muncaster's car.' The inner glow lived hardly a couple of minutes. Just the time it took for our polished car to cross the forecourt of the Palace, and turn out through the gates and back into the world of commoners again."

The very next morning Muncaster opened an envelope from the Admiralty. The letter inside bore the news that he was, in fact, due only for the Defence Medal and the 1939-45 Medal. He never dared to wear medals again.

At the end of January 1948, Muncaster heard in a letter from Major Penn that the King had asked to view the oil painting of Deeside and would also like to know the fee. He had seen the photograph of the picture and now wished to acquire it. There was celebration over the breakfast table at Four-Winds; but later, it caused him a very great deal of professional pondering. "How much should I charge? This was a much more difficult problem than painting the picture. It is never easy to put a price on one's own work. One can only be guided by the general figures charged by contemporaries, though even this is an unreliable guide. Whereas one painter will charge two thousand guineas for a work and get his price, another will charge for a picture of equal size maybe two hundred guineas, or even less, and not get his price. Personally, I have never been able to bring myself to put a high price on my works. Perhaps I would have done better if I had. Some people like telling their friends about the high prices they've paid. There seems to be a sort of snob monetary value attached to this business of prices for pictures. My own view is that no picture, however good, has an intrinsic value of two and a quarter million pounds, as was paid for a Velasquez recently.

"However this may be, my problem was to estimate a fair figure which I might charge the King. I reckoned on the basis that I got three hundred and fifty guineas for a 30in. x 40in. canvas. If I reduced comparative sizes to square inches, the total of a 30in. x 40in. came to twelve hundred square inches; the King's, to four thousand, four hundred square inches. On these grounds I should charge the King well over a thousand guineas. This I did not like to do and decided on seven hundred guineas. I wrote to Major Penn to inform him of my decision, explaining that I considered that in the circumstances I would charge twice as much as I got for a 30in. x 40in. canvas.

"Major Penn's reply brought me out hot all over. He made it abundantly clear that I had committed gross breach of etiquette, for I had obviously tried to exploit the occasion for a most unpleasant piece of sharp practice. Of all people, he expected this least of me, particularly in view of the privilege I had received from Their Majesties and it was galling for him to think that he had been responsible for my introduction to them.

"This was absolutely shattering! What on earth had happened? What had I written which could possibly have caused such a misunderstanding? I carefully studied the copy of my letter to Major Penn. It all seemed perfectly clear to me. I wrote back immediately to try and clear myself; then telephoned him by way of follow-up. But I received a most cold and uncooperative response. It was impasse however I looked at it. I saw my career crumbling. Surely the price had been a fair one?

"About a week later a letter arrived from the Palace. I dreaded opening it and finished my breakfast first. Was it the Tower for me?

"To my immeasurable relief, and to Primrose's, too – for she had been as worried as I had – Major Penn revealed that revelation had come one evening as he lay in his bath. He had suddenly realised how he'd come to misconstrue the terms. The words 'twice as much as I would ordinarily charge for a 30in. x 40in. canvas' had been the offending ones and created the ambiguity. What he had not realised was that the King's picture was nearly four times as big as 30in. x 40in. He had now put my suggested price before His Majesty and the King had expressed a wish to pay me a fee of seven hundred and fifty guineas, being fifty guineas more than I had asked. At Four-Winds, the very house itself almost sighed with relief.

"The picture was exhibited at the Royal Academy that same year, but was removed before the close of the exhibition to be transported to Balmoral. In the blank space where the ten-foot picture had hung was pinned a notice the size of a visiting card. On it were the words: 'Picture removed by the express wish of His Majesty the King.' This succinct three-line announcement led to the sole Press mention that the painting received."

At about this time people in the United Kingdom were becoming increasingly concerned about the state of Britain generally. The war was over, yet life went on in a sort of grim, grey pessimism. There were shortages, there was rationing, there was the black market. As a nation we seemed utterly exhausted. We'd given our all and were paying the price. Indeed, prices were the constant topic of conversation. The *Daily Express* was soon to run a campaign against "Mr. Rising Price," a cartoon figure, inspired by the Labour Government's wiry Chancellor, Sir Stafford Cripps. "Mr. Rising Price's" picture appeared daily on the front page, his skinny form and long, pointed nose lengthening visibly into the columns of each day's news.

So hard was this atmosphere gripping the country that many people were seriously considering leaving the ship before it sank in despondency. The emigration figures climbed. Mr. and Mrs. Claude Muncaster and family were numbered among them. It had been decided that the family would try South Africa. During the war he had made friends there, and his brother Philip was now back at Michael House School near Pietermaritzburg. Major exhibitions were arranged at Capetown and Johannesburg and passages fixed for four in the grey-hulled liner, *City of Exeter*, an old coal burner which had survived the torpedoes. On Easter Saturday 1948 we left Four-Winds behind having rented it to friends. As we travelled in the train from Pulborough to Victoria in the early spring sunshine, I can remember wondering just how long it would be before we saw home again. My parents were prepared for seven years away at least. It was all rather sad.

My own most fixed memory is of our arrival at Madeira. My father shook me in the warm comfort of my bunk just before five o'clock in the morning and said "Come and look at this." I staggered out to the chill deck, holding a pad of cotton wool to my ear (which had been extremely troublesome and painful since the night we left), and peered into the darkness of the morning, my eyes watering.

"What am I supposed to be seeing?" I shouted against the rush of the wind in the rigging.

"Look ahead," he replied.

I blinked and focused again. As far as I could see, there was merely some dark cloud lowering on the horizon. Then, gradually, as the ship pushed forward into the swell, I became aware of an outline and a shape of deep indigo blue against the lighter tone of the sea.

"An island!" I said.

"Madeira."

It was a long time before I returned to my bunk. I suppose that emerging scene spoke to me in a way that so many hundreds of times, such moments had spoken to him in his years of observing the effects of nature. I was so fascinated by the marvellous contour and colour of that island in the sea that I forgot my earache, and watched till the emergence of dawn; and as we neared, saw the tiny dots of the lights of Funchal and its harbour, winking like a cluster of stars. He later painted an oil of the subject and, before he died, gave it to me as a present. It hangs in the dining-room of our cottage as a reminder of that unforgettable experience.

South Africa was not a success; though the exhibitions were. The emigrants were clearly homesick for a sight of a bit of England and sales were very good. But Claude Muncaster saw taking root the new idiom in art with which he could have no traffic. He doubted if his style of painting would be making him much of a living before long. Within six months the Muncaster family were back in green England.

On returning to England from South Africa he kept up a heavy painting programme; carried out many major commissions, and in between these did a considerable amount of writing. His records show that in these years he painted some 1,400 watercolours; a large number of very complicated black and white sketches for the *Sphere Magazine*; and completed nearly 150 oils, some of them large and detailed.

He also managed a great deal of teaching – particularly weekend courses and correspondence criticism; and even did a spell of art instruction at a Butlin's Holiday Camp.

He wrote articles; there were two further one-man exhibitions at the Fine Art Society, and he overhauled the records he kept of his works. He acted as Art Adviser to the Worthing Corporation; was elected President of the Society of Marine Artists (which was to become a Royal Society under his Presidency); became President of the Old Watercolour Society Art Club and the St. Ives Society of Artists, both of which presidencies demanded a very great deal of his time and energies, for he would never agree to being anything other than an active president. He was Vice-President of several art societies, and member of the Royal Watercolour Society, the Royal Society of British Artists and the Royal Institute of Oil Painters. He worked on a number of committees and was in constant demand as a hanger of exhibitions. He was a member of the Chelsea Arts Club and the Athenaeum for a while, but found that the pressures on his time were such that he hardly used them. Eventually he restricted himself to membership of the Arts Club in Dover Street, where he sometimes invited Clive or myself to play billiards with him, and always won.

His painting travels during these years took him to Antwerp, in a tug towing the sailing ship *Viking* from the Thames to Belgium; Portugal, North Africa, Italy, Sicily, Madeira and the north coast of Spain. In the U.K. there was a series of watercolours of the River Severn; some painting on the Thames; visits to the Orkneys and to County Kerry, in Ireland, three times. There were spells of painting in Wales, Westmorland and Cumberland, in Buckinghamshire and Dorset. When there was time, he kept himself fit with heavy gardening, tennis and golf.

There was no doubt that all these various activities and work demands built up the pressure, and many times my father suffered bad migraines. I remember, particularly, after some of the *Sphere* series he would be completely knocked out. It was during this period, too, that he contracted a very serious attack of measles. Then we all had to creep about the house without making a sound. Any noise literally made him physically sick. With my mother's nursing, he gradually got back to health; but I believe it was measles that affected his eyes and was to lead to so many problems.

In the mid 1950's Claude Muncaster began to work on a new oil painting technique. On a visit in the small Ellerman Wilson cargo ship, *Domino*, to North Africa and the west coast of Italy, he had found some outstanding architectural and shipping subjects in Algiers, Pisa and Naples. He had always been intrigued by Canaletto's technique and wondered how he had managed to achieve such precision of architectural features in the rather clumsy medium of oil paint. Muncaster determined to discover some means of overcoming the considerable difficulties he had encountered in portraying sharp edges and long, straight lines. After experimenting with taut string, fine wire and even metal strips of the type used for securing packing cases, he hit upon the idea of utilising razor blades bolted between strips of Meccano, which he borrowed from his sons' box of old toys. I well remember his excitement when he came up with this ingenious invention and found that it worked. Heath Robinson it may have been, but it achieved the precise effect he had so long been seeking. It enabled him to get even a hair's breadth line if needed, and sharp vertical or horizonal edges to buildings and architectural delineations. He discusses this development of technique in his book *Landscape and Marine Painting*,* and describes the painting of a large and complicated canvas showing a panoramic view of the rooftops of Algiers.

He made the following note about his new way of applying paint when working on pictures like the one of Algiers. "Although this technique could give me a knife edge effect when required, as I developed it I found I could get considerable freedom if necessary and a richer quality of colour mixings. But for more atmospheric effects, the brush was still the best. Whether or not works painted largely in this new technique are better or worse than previous ones, it is hard for me to judge. The answer largely depends on the nature of the subject. Most artists from early times have used a palette-knife for painting, but I feel that my own invention gives a wider range of ways of applying paint and it also provides a greater delicacy than can be obtained by the palette-knife technique."

* Published by Pitman in 1958.

Chapter 12

Other Men's Visions

The three years up to 1958 continued to be full ones. He visited Venice, which he found thrilling and later Taormina and Bellagio on Lake Como. At Bellagio he was instructor to a class of over fifty student painters. He found this unwieldy and worrying as he was unable to give to each pupil the individual attention he wished. He worked like a slave and ended up the fortnight absolutely exhausted.

Also, there was a commission to paint large watercolours of some outlying Post Offices. This involved a good deal of travel to find Post Offices which were not only remote, but which also served as attractive subjects for painting. At the same time he was working on an annual commission of six paintings for Hadfields, the manufacturers of marine paints. "These pictures demanded an exacting technique, but I enjoyed the travelling because I was nearly always able to find subjects and paint a few pictures for my own account."

Perhaps the most interesting innovation that Muncaster brought to the art world was his work from helicopters. He first had the idea when he was commissioned by Hepworth & Grandage Ltd., of Bradford. The company wished to commemorate their centenary and had decided on a picture of their works.

"When they approached me they made it quite plain that they were looking for something very special indeed. This concerned me, as I knew all too well that it would add to the anxiety of the commission. I would be expected to produce something of uniquely high quality. When had I ever done that? After a good deal of deliberation, inspiration came; how about a view from a helicopter? The company went into the cost of flights, and eventually agreed.

"It was quite some time before weather conditions were favourable and several flights had to be cancelled at the last moment. This didn't help in the least to set my mind at ease. I really had no idea what it was going to be like sketching in the sky while hovering over the subject, and had taken quite a gamble in making the suggestion. However, we got off at last in a Bell helicopter; a miniature type with seats for the pilot and just one passenger. It was a curious looking machine, rather like a glass bubble with a long tail.

"Special arrangements have to be made and conditions adhered to before a helicopter is permitted to hover over a thickly populated area. One of these meant we were not allowed to hover at less than two thousand feet. I really needed to get much closer to my subject than this."

Once up, Muncaster found that the height restriction was the least of his worries. The vibrations were such that it was impossible to draw a straight line. He also took some black and white photographs for the record, but of course they had to be taken through the perspex of the bubble cockpit, and that, together with the vibration, made for very poor results.

The subject which he had set himself was extremely detailed and expansive and the pilot had to keep the helicopter hovering for well over an hour while the artist did his studies. At one point the pilot tapped him on the shoulder and pointed to a small object in the sky, shouting "bat!" This seemed unlikely at two thousand feet. A few minutes later, he shouted again – "No. It's a hawk." Muncaster took his word for it and went on drawing. Then he felt another tap on his shoulder and looking up saw him pointing again. The creature proved to be a Red Admiral butterfly now resting quietly on the perspex. It stayed there for several minutes then gently fluttered away.

Muncaster admitted that the picture of Bradford was far and away the most difficult painting he had tackled so far. He spent hours piecing together the blurred photographs and getting them into their correct geographical relationships. This was vital if he was to get the scale, perspective and distances right, and quite apart from the factory itself, the correct representation of chimneys, churches, roads, streets, railways, bridges and predominant buildings. There was also the background of Ilkley Moor and undulating hills which took on quite a different aspect from this high angle. All had to be just right if this picture was to be a success.

In the actual painting of much of the architectural detail, Muncaster resorted to his new razor-blade technique and found it invaluable. It was essential to express with clarity the scope of the subject and the detail which the Works presented.

There was an amusing postscript to this particular commission. A special handing over ceremony was held in the board-room at the Works, attended by the top brass of the Hepworth & Grandage Group, a number of local dignitaries, and several art experts, directors of galleries and museums and the like. The picture certainly created quite a stir, and was written up under the heading "Masterpiece of Detail" in the September 1958 edition of the company's monthly paper, *The Messenger*.

It also made the *Daily Express*. The report ran: "Five thousand workers at a Bradford engineering firm were given time off to go art-viewing yesterday. They went in crocodile-line through the carpeted board-room of Hepworth & Grandage Ltd., to see what their factory looks like from a helicopter. The oil painting of the factory, with the city of Bradford as background, was painted, etc., etc."

The Messenger reacted with amused reserve. "Although it is the intention of the Directors that all our employees will eventually see the painting, we cannot for the life of us understand how the columnist associated 5,000 employees with a handful of art experts who, in themselves, were sufficient to fill the board-room.

"We pride ourselves on our ingenuity, but to accomplish such a feat in such limited space would have been comparable to the Biblical miracle when a multitude of 5,000 were fed on five loaves and two fishes."

The time scale of the painting of the helicopter picture is of interest. Muncaster often found himself being asked how long it took him to paint a picture, and he recorded that in the case of the Bradford canvas, which measured 40in. x 32in., there were a hundred and sixty hours of concentrated work. "This may seem rather a long time, but the amount of detail has to be taken into consideration. Other canvases of a similar size but of a sketchy nature might be completed in only a morning, or a day."

Another helicopter work, a 36in. x 24in. canvas, he painted for Westland Aircraft. This picture took him a hundred and twenty hours to complete. He wrote: "I found this subject most trying and difficult. At one stage of the drawing in, which I did with an HB pencil, afterwards accentuated by indelible pen work, I all but gave up. After twenty-one hours, I was thoroughly sick and tired of the whole business of what amounted to mechanical drawing on an unsympathetic surface."

He had to start work in early November 1959 in very bad light, and this persisted almost through the whole period of the job. Even with the canvas flat on the table right under the window and with the studio lights on, he still found it an effort to see. There were also many interruptions, including Christmas and he became exceedingly frustrated at the slow rate of progress.

In his diary, he wrote on 6 January 1960:

"Took advantage of better light at last to get a largish area of the canvas covered, both during the morning and the afternoon. But for some reason I just could not get the paint to work right and I was not at all satisfied with the results. Once or twice I had to remove certain passages and paint them in again. I very seldom have to do this. It may be that these particular passages are the very ones in which the most detail and precision are needed, as they embody the landing stage for the helicopters and the control tower and offices of Westland Aircraft. Being insignificant, these features are very difficult to express and make stand out. I cannot tell how far I have succeeded until everything is in, including several helicopters. When the paint is dry, maybe it will be possible to define the detail more exactly. There is still a week's painting before I can consider the picture finished. I have never been quite so long over a picture of this size, but I am determined to throw dust in the eyes of the Post-Impressionists and escapists, and try to paint London from the air as Canaletto painted it from the ground."

When Muncaster finally delivered his picture on 5 February, he found reactions to it most disappointing. He had to take the picture to the company's head offices at Yeovil, in Somerset, and set off in his car with a light heart; the picture on which he had lavished such infinite care, patience and time propped up on the back seat. He believed in this picture, and carried high hopes in his mind by imagining the warm reception it would receive. He arrived on the dot of 12.30 p.m. to see Mr. Penrose, the director who had been his contact. Instead he was passed on to the public relations man who had no clue at all as to why he was there. He took Muncaster off to lunch, saying in the meantime the picture could stay in the car. This was not a promising start. On their return, he said: "Well, what are we going to do with this old picture of yours? I suppose we'd better yank it out and take it up to the board-room."

There was nobody in the board-room when they arrived, except a gentleman of advanced years who sat at the end of the table munching sandwiches out of a paper bag. Presumably he was a director.

They propped the picture up on the floor against the wall and the "Sandwich" man was told that the painting was of the London Heliport. He glanced cursorily at it and asked briefly: "How wide's the river there?" Muncaster admitted ignorance. They then took the picture down to the PR office to await the return of Mr. Penrose. He arrived at last, looked at the picture for a moment; then saying he hadn't got the right glasses, disappeared out of the room.

The PR man brought up the matter of publicity. "I think I could fiddle it into some publicity stunt or other," he said. "The colour ought to be all right for that. All you want, after all, it to have the picture reproduced with your name alongside it." And that was that. He drove off with a leaden heart and never saw any reproduction or reference to it.

When he got home, Muncaster wrote up his diary for the day: "I tried to comfort myself with the lovely light and landscape as I drove homewards, and with the thought that it was a very good thing that I had not had to deliver the picture immediately it was completed, when I was all keyed up over it, and my own appreciation of it quite out of proportion. The trouble is with these commissions, one is so often having to satisfy somebody else's vision of the subject."

He need not have been so despondent. Soon afterwards a letter came from Sir Eric Mensforth, who had commissioned the picture. He was very pleased with it.

*   *   *

At the end of the 50's, Muncaster was commissioned by Sir Robert McAlpine & Sons to paint a series of big industrial subjects. The first of these was the new Atomic Power Station to be built at Bradwell on the Blackwater River, near Colchester, in Essex. The picture was intended for presentation to Sir Walter Citrine, and was wanted in a hurry. In fact, Muncaster had just a fortnight to get the job done.

This didn't particularly worry him, as he had the *Sphere* experience behind him, and in this case there was only one picture to worry about. Imagine his dismay, therefore, when he arrived on the site of the proposed Power Station to find nothing there but four poles sticking up in a grass field indicating the corners of the structure. Apart from that, all he had to work on was a blue print. For the rest, he had to use his imagination. This kind of painting was something quite new and proved a veritable nightmare. Somehow he produced something which was acceptable, but vowed never to work in this way again.

The initial visit to Bradwell was, however, to prove profitable. While he had been on the site, he had taken a photograph of the open field with its four poles sticking up thinly into the skyline. There was, on reflection, quite a reasonable subject there for a watercolour. He did one on spec and McAlpines bought it. From this and the Bradwell picture followed a number of commissions of a variety of subjects: dry dock construction, hospital buildings, iron works and several big reconstruction schemes. He also painted a large canvas of the three masted barque *Balclutha* rounding Cape Horn, which Sir Francis Chichester was later to use as the cover for his book *Along the Clipper Way*.

This latter was a joy to paint. He could let himself go a little. But he confessed that many of the other works in this series of commissions caused him much more worry than pleasure. There were roughs to be submitted as well as the finished pictures, and he found there was little artistic satisfaction to be had slogging away at scaffold poles, stagings and cranes, all of which have to be in proper relationship and perspective, while somehow preserving the overall atmosphere and colour effect pervading at the time. His endeavour was always to portray the scenes realistically but artistically. What he did find refreshing while carrying out these works was the happy relationships he enjoyed with Billy McAlpine and his brother, Alistair.

Muncaster wrote much about these commissions while they were under way. A note from his diary at the time he was doing a picture of the Cameron Iron Works is of interest: "... 6 a.m. in the Studio. More tricky painting and a new technique. A large passage of spidery girdering against the sky. To manage this kind of thing with any accuracy and delicacy in oil painting does present a nasty problem of technique. I decided on reducing the oil medium with turpentine to make the paint more fluid. Lines could then be almost ruled. It worked. Of course, some subtlety must be introduced; but the important structure is there. Always, there is something to learn."

* * *

In 1960 my parents had moved to the village of Sutton. For my father, it was a return to the actual house of his boyhood. Clive and I were both now married and raising families. The house had been converted by the previous owners and was much improved and modernised. There was also a small bungalow in the garden. After much deliberation he converted this into a studio. One room was to act as an office, another as the painting room. For the time being, the third room served as a store for pictures. Of his return to the old home he wrote:

"I was very strongly conscious of my father's presence when we moved in. Perhaps this was because his studio had stood only some ten yards from my new one. I was most conscious of my mother, too, and on many nights was awakened by her calling me. At first I must say this scared me, but I got used to it and after a time, in fact, welcomed it ... Our coming into this homestead with its beautiful garden and surrounding views has had the effect of bringing us a tremendous sense of being closer to the Divine. Things seem to be working for the enrichment of our lives. Of this we must take the fullest advantage, both for ourselves and other people. It is a great but welcome responsibility, and it is our aim that anyone coming into our home will go away feeling better for having been in it."

Soon after the move, a commission came from McAlpines to paint a large oil of London from the new Shell Building on the south side of the Thames. The company thought it would be an appropriate record for Shell when the building was completed.

In July 1961, he visited the site and met the Engineer who suggested that they ascend to the roof by means of the outside lift. This was not a welcome suggestion. In the event he persuaded the Engineer to take him up by the lift inside the building. When they arrived on the roof he was overcome by a bad attack of giddiness and was quite unable to approach and take hold of the one horizontal scaffold pole which surrounded the edge of the roofing. This rail was the only protection against a fall of some two hundred feet to the ground below. While the artist was trying to take in something of the view, the Engineer climbed up a ladder to an even higher level. From there he called down that the view from his new vantage point was superb and urged his guest to join him. Muncaster inclined just to take his word for it but pulled together some courage and gingerly climbed up. Indeed, the view from there was quite staggering for they were open to the sky. There was a kind of pill-box structure in the centre of the platform with an area of flat roof all around it. Precautions against disaster were the same as they were below – just a single, horizontal scaffold pole. They stood for some minutes with their backs against the wall of the pill-box discussing the view. As they moved to go, my father suddenly saw the Engineer slip and topple backwards. He grabbed at the scaffold pole and his face went ashen. Then he managed a laugh and said: "I trod in the runnel and it tipped me back. For a moment I thought I was over. It just goes to show how even a person like myself who is used to heights will react when something like that happens."

It was sunny and clear when a few days later he went up again to make some notes and take photographs. From these he worked out a rough sketch in oils. With some small alterations, McAlpines accepted this, and he was asked to proceed with the picture. It was to measure 8ft. by 2ft. 6in. He wrote

The Demolition of London Bridge: *watercolour*
(By courtesy of John Mowlem and Co. Ltd.)

Barlavington Down from Chanctonbury : *oil*

Panorama of London from the Shell Building, 1962: *oil*
(By courtesy of Sir Robert McAlpine and Sons Ltd.)

Drawings for the *Sphere*: above: Sea Hawks taking off from H.M.S. *Eagle*, 1953: *pen and wash*.
below: Liverpool Cathedral, 1952: *pen and wash*.
(By courtesy of Illustrated London News)

a detailed account of the picture, which is now considered historic, so dramatically has the skyline changed.

"The first stage of any picture is the moment of inspiration. This occurs when you first view the subject and decide what the final effect will be. Unless you can see clearly in your mind's eye the finished picture on the blank canvas, you will always be stumbling, for you will never know what you are after. Once having seen this vision and decided that it is the right one, by and large there must not be any diversion from it. Of course, one cannot envisage every small detail, and minor alterations and refinements will be made as the work progresses and unfolds. But on the whole the first vision must stand. There must be no changing of horses in mid-stream.

"Having decided on the size, I cut a panel of hard board and had this glued to battens by my framer so that it would not bend. I painted on the smooth side of the board and coated this with two coats of size. This was followed by two coats of plaster of Paris mixed with size and applied warm. This mixture dried quickly, rather like starch, and formed a hard gesso ground. I next applied a coat of foundation white mixed with turpentine and copal medium, and after a week or so, when this was dry, I applied a second coat. The panel was then put aside for some six weeks to allow the paint to dry thoroughly. If painted on too soon, serious cracking would result. I know Turner said of his works when they cracked that 'all the best pictures crack'; but I had no wish to emulate Turner in this respect. In fact, I did not start the work until 3 January 1962.

"The first job was to study very carefully my photographic records, piece them together and then paste them down on to cardboard. With this as a guide, I then determined the boundaries of the subject and made sure that the whole was of a size which would make for easy calculation when it came to enlarging every measurement to its correct magnification.

"I now divided this photographic reference into 84 squares, and numbered them. Next, I estimated my height from ground level, determined where the corresponding level would occur on the scale of the picture, and represented this by a horizontal line drawn right across the photo. All perspective lines of buildings would join at their respective points on this eye-level line.

"Now, I turned to the canvas and divided this into 84 squares, each square being twelve times larger than the squares on the photograph. I worked out a chart in centimetres from nought to a hundred with the relevant magnifications, so that when I came to prick off any measurement with dividers on the photo, I could see at a glance the correct calculation. As it turned out, this table, which included quarters, halves and three-quarters, saved me a great deal of time. The first attempt at ruling off the squares on the canvas had proved incorrect, and I had to rub them all out and start again. That cost me a lot of india-rubber.

"All this done, I had to make a special support on my long studio table to take the panel which had to be at a shallow angle; also, arrange a board above the panel to take a big magnifying glass, instruments, pencils, etc. Then, behind this, there had to be a little easel to support the photograph. There had to be battens, too, to extend the eye-level line for shallow perspectives, with a nail hammered into a board to take a length of string which, when pulled taut, would give the correct perspective lines. At times, the nail could be at least five feet to the right or left of the panel. Such preparations, and there were many others, were made for the drawing-in stage. There were to be even more gadgets and contrivances for the painting process.

"I started to draw in with a hard pencil but found the oily surface would not take it; so I sliced a raw potato and rubbed this over the surface. It did the trick. I worked square by square, and fixed the pencil work in each with an aerosol fixative spray as I went. Then I inked over the pencil lines with indelible ink. This accentuated the pencil lines so that they would be discernible through the first thin, transparent coat of paint when I came to the painting-in stage. I had to draw with the greatest accuracy, which required much patience, concentration and interpretation.

"I would have liked to work regular hours but this was never possible – it never has been in my life – with social, household and administrative demands, even ill-health, causing constant interruptions. I had estimated 21 days for the drawing-in. It took me 52; at a rough estimate, 108 hours' constant work.

"The painting-in was started on 27 February and completed the following day.

"For painting-in I use no white. The effect is transparent; the shades are rather brighter and the tones darker than they will appear in the final painting. At this point I could gain some idea of how the finished job would look. I was by no means happy about it, but hoped I would be able to pull it round as the picture progressed. I was happy, however, to have these two initial stages behind me. There had been times when my patience was all but exhausted and I was tempted to abandon any exactitude, resort to an impression and leave it at that. But this would never have appealed to me as my intention was to produce a faithful – yet I hoped artistic – record of the City of London in the year 1962.

"On 2 March, after having got everything ready to hand, I drew a deep breath and began to paint the sky. Between this date and 9 May I was to work at the picture on thirty-one days.

"I always tackle the sky first, as this gives the key to the level of light for the required effect. The McA. picture was certainly an anxiety. I'd decided, rightly or wrongly, on an uneventful sky, but one of smooth texture, to serve as an antidote to the complicated matter below. Such a sky has to be worked at one sitting. There can be no delay, or the paint dries and the smooth texture cannot be worked. In this case, any brush mark after the final painting was done would have left inconsistencies and blemishes in the gradation of blue on the left of the picture to the warm, yellowish light on the right.

"There are three definite processes in painting a sky of this nature. First, there must be a fairly heavy coating of white mixed with yellow ochre, graduated with some Indian red down to the horizon. Care must be taken not to get this coat too dry or too thinned with medium. The speed which is so essential is not easy to maintain when working round the architectural forms silhouetted on the horizon and which must not be eradicated.

"The next coat is a white and blue mixture composed of cobalt and Winsor blue. This is gradated off to very little blue towards the right, until at the extreme edge there is scarcely any blue in the mixture at all.

"The top sky is now gradated down to the horizon to a more warm and smoky haze; yellow ochre, Indian red, Winsor red, rose madder, cobalt, blue, French blue and Winsor blue may all come into the mixture in varying degrees.

"Now comes the final stage; smoothing off the brush marks with a large sable brush. The action here is a very light touch and can almost be described as a flick-and-a-sweep all in one. The trick is not to lick up the paint at the beginning or end of the action by one instant of uneven pressure. This light flickering which is applied over the whole surface of the wet paint helps to amalgamate the colours with, one hopes, a resultant quality and warmth through the blue, while at the same time minimising the effect of crudeness and too obvious brushmarks. I managed to complete the sky before lunch after two and a quarter hours of anxious and speedy painting which called for considerable physical exertion and mental strain, even though the final effect looks so controlled."

When I found and read these references, I realised that I had never really appreciated what personal professional battles he was often fighting in the secrecy of his studio; though the family usually got the feeling when he came in to lunch that he was less communicative than usual and on edge. This happened particularly when he was deep into a commission. I have a clear memory of his obvious frustration and impatience to return to the studio. "I must get back to work, darling," he would say to my mother, "while the light's good." And off he'd go. It must be said he was ever thoughtful of the constant chores that are a mother's lot and could for some reason always get a fire going when the rest of us failed; but he was not, on the whole, "good in the house." He kept a scrupulous record of his work on the painting meanwhile.

"The picture was worked square by square. Before each period of painting I had to estimate the amount of coverage I could achieve, and prepared mixtures of colours on the palette accordingly. Through experience I seemed to be able to estimate pretty exactly and little paint was wasted. I used razor blades and brushes, both sable and hog-hair, and these I laid out in strict order of sizes for quick handling. Usually I used about seventeen brushes a day. Any more than this was an indication that the work had not proceeded as well as it should have done.

"This process of painting square by adjoining square demanded much care in order to ensure that the square, or part of a square, painted each day would exactly match in colour and tone, but particularly in effect, the portion painted the day before. Otherwise the picture could have turned into a sort of patchwork quilt of squares that did not match each other, or carry on the general lighting effect. From left to right the gradual gradation of illumination of this view, which covered a hundred and eighty degrees, had to be maintained, and I had to remember that the sun was fully lighting Somerset House on the left of the picture, whereas Waterloo Station to the right was in silhouette against the light. There was also the difference in atmospheric effect between the distance and the foreground. The strongest lights and the strongest darks would occur in the foreground. I had to keep a reserve up my sleeve for these final plums which would serve to give recession.

"All such considerations are part of the artist's craft. The layman cannot be expected to be acquainted with them. He only judges the final result, but the artist has to judge the final effect too. Though he is perhaps the worst judge of all, for it is almost impossible for him to be objective. The artist lives his picture during all his waking hours and sometimes even in his dreams. Whatever he is doing, the work is always in the background of his thoughts and he often longs to see it with a fresh eye. I have found looking at it in a mirror sometimes helps. It gives one a new angle on the picture, and can reveal errors which are not obvious when viewed in the normal way.

"After many weeks at one picture, it would be unnatural for the artist not to gain some affection for it, and when the work is finally carted off to the purchaser the studio feels quite empty for a day or two. There is a sense of loneliness, as if somebody you have deeply loved for a time has gone out of your life for ever. But very quickly you are on to the next work. The old one is soon forgotten, and all energies are concentrated on some new endeavour; and always with the hope that this one will at last prove to be a masterpiece.

"I heard a little while later that 'View of the City' had evoked the comment 'fabulous' from Billy McAlpine, and that the company kept the picture after all and did not present it to Shell. So, I regarded this, at least, as a compliment."

Clearly this enormous technical proficiency demanded everything from him. But rather strangely, he was not good with his hands. If he ever had occasion to put a screw in, it would invariably end up crooked; if he hammered a nail, it unfailingly contrived to bend. My mother was ever rueful of the fact that Father could hardly mend a fuse. It amazed us that he had ever managed all those bends and hitches which are an integral part of a sailor's daily life. All the more surprising then to read of the meticulous care he took with the more mechanical and mathematical processes attached to the creation of a picture such as this big panoramic canvas of the City of London. Perhaps it was the very fact that these things didn't come easily to him which made it such an incredible strain.

Chapter 13

Some notes from sketching trips

Muncaster found his sketching trips invaluable. Two or three times a year, he went off for a fortnight or more, to get back to nature. These trips acted as a kind of artistic safety valve which enabled him to retreat from the predictable daily round and press of business, the boring necessities of correspondence and art administration, to be with himself and his painting.

The following is a selection from his copious notes in the diaries which he kept during these times of refreshment, and they reveal something of his character and the feeling he had for his art.

April 1959 A visit to the West Country
Wednesday, 8 April.

"Having decided to make Bridgwater, in Somerset, my base, I booked myself a room at the 'Bristol.' After tea, went for a tour of exploration to Glastonbury and back over the Polden Hills. There are very fine views from these hills, looking both over the Sedgemoor Marshes with the distant Quantocks and northwards to the Mendips. There is also much material, as I hoped there would be, among the dykes, pollard willows and villages scatterd over the marshes. The light, clouds and effects were magnificent. But I have come just a little bit too late. The willows are already three-quarters in leaf and the hedgerows are virgin green. The ploughland is sprouting young wheat so that the contrast which the winter colour gives has been supplanted by a monotony of acid greens of early spring. Maybe I shall have to treat it all with reserve and somehow introduce some greys into the greens, or at least some quality of warmth.

Thursday, 9 April.

"Studied the map over breakfast and noticed a little inlet from the River Parret at Combwich. I went out and explored this and found it attractive and paintable. I then proceeded to Stert Point, a couple of miles or so to the westward. Here I discovered a kind of country I had been looking for for years. It is marshland coastline of the Bristol Channel, with the distant Quantocks and Mendips beyond, and the Welsh mountains in the very far distance. There is a sufficient number of scattered farmhouses and buildings to give a human interest and bring the place alive.

"12.10 a.m.: To bed, with the pageantry of skies and the April colouring of fascinating and historical landscapes passing in quick procession before my eyes.

Friday 10 April.

"Another day of a hard north-wester, cold and stormy, but for the most part sunny in this locality. Not quite such a painter's day as yesterday, being rather too brilliant and the skies rather less interesting. Nevertheless, the effects were such that I felt it essential not to waste Stert Point. I was there just before ten o'clock with a subject in mind looking seaward to what I thought was Lundy Isle. Yesterday it was so clear in outline and solidity that it looked scarcely more than three miles distant. In fact, it is all of ten miles, and is not Lundy Isle but Steep Holme, with Cardiff another seven miles beyond. This morning, Steep Holme, despite the brilliant sunlight, was scarcely visible and the distant coastline unimpressive. But looking south-westwards to the Quantocks with a broken foreshore of timber breakwaters and the golden-coloured reeds reminding one of a field of stubble, the atmosphere seemed clear enough and was looking full of spring sparkle. I drove the car up on to the stony foreshore and started a big watercolour from it, but neither in the front seat nor the rear is there room for freedom, or for allowing the folio to lie at a flat angle, which is imperative when working skies. One can manage to draw in a subject, but after that it's necessary to get outside. This I did. But in the scanty shelter of the car I just could not hold the folio steady. The wind whistled over the bonnet and still caught me however close I sheltered against the car, making subtle draughtsmanship and precise brushwork well nigh impossible. Moreover, the wind made my eyes water so that only with the greatest difficulty could I actually see what I was doing; and the sun was full on my paper – almost always disastrous. So the final result was anything but a masterpiece.

"In the evening I returned to Stert Point and drew in with pen a subject of the gateway to the marshes. By the time I had finished the shadows were solid across the road, the distant storm clouds had drifted to obscurity, and the hills had flattened out to nothingness. It was already five forty-five, and to start applying paint now would have been a hopeless exercise. So I drove on to the little chapel at Stert, parked the car, donned my mack, for the wind was keen and boisterous, and stepped on to the hard road to the marshes. I had determined that somehow, road or no road, I must get to the end of the Point. Never shall I forget that walk. It is not that Stert Point is a spectacular landscape, it is a gorgeous estuary flanked by noble mountains. This is low-lying country, with far, undulating hills, soft in outlines and friendly. Yet there is something of the north about it, through the presence of twisting walls and the occasional collie which stands up on them deeply curious of any strangers.

"Beyond the last of the farms the road deteriorated to a muddy track deeply entrenched in places; but at length it became grassy and clean, ending in an enclosure of gates and fences associated, I suppose, with sheep penning and branding. Then only a few more yards . . . and the sea!

"From then onwards to the right, lush marshlands, grazing sheep, fragments of walls and thorns, yellow sedge, glimpses of the River Parret and the distant Sedgemoor neighbourhood and Polden Hills. Ahead, the estuary of the Parret, Stert Island, Burnham, and behind that the low, humping foothills of the Welsh mountains, too far distant to discern and shrouded now by low storm cloud. To the left, the golden sedge, even more golden in the low evening sunlight; the broken, pebbly foreshore, the sands and the sea. As I listened to the constant surge of it, I determined to make the furthest point, so that I could look down the twenty foot or so steep banks and observe the purple dun-coloured tumbling waters as they rounded the point and flowed inland to Bridgwater. On the way, slipping on the loose, shingly shore, I was amazed at the amount of timber strewn along the top of the tide mark. Some of these stumps were obviously of great antiquity.

"When I eventually turned from the extremity of the point and looked westwards, the sun was full in my eyes. It shone over the sea, the wet sands and sedgy foreshore. It was the kind of light which Turner, Bonington, Cox or Wilson would have delighted in and painted to perfection. As I watched, the air was full of the sounds of curlew, gull, plover, sky-lark and all the twitterings of a secluded sea-bird sanctuary.

"The sun sank in golden effulgency, the brilliance of light and shade gently softened and diffused. I offered up a prayer of thanksgiving for the gift of being able to see, hear and smell the glories of nature which surrounded me.

"For the gift of sight I was indeed grateful. But I had fears . . .

Sunday, 12 April

"My eyes are troubling me considerably and my glasses a problem to cope with. I have to change from tri-focal to bi-focal from time to time, as I find my left eye functioning very dismally . . .

Tuesday, 14 April

"Have found much to paint in the Bridgwater area, and now another area greatly to my liking – more or less an extension of the Stert country – Stolford. The place consists of little more than a large farmhouse and close-cropped marshlands bordering the sea. When I made this discovery the light was much the same as yesterday; the wind strong, warm and southerly. But the sun glowed with richer quality. There was a brilliant, jewel-like colouring, clean, and sparkling. Happily the trees round the farm were not sufficiently in leaf to obscure the delicate structures of branches and trunks. The skies over Bridgwater Bay reminded me of Boudin at his best. To the westward, the blue of the sky was continental in its intensity, though more limpid. I sat with my back to the sea and started on a watercolour of the farmstead.

"While I worked I began to enumerate the sounds of nature. First, there was the sound of the wind and sea breaking, more of a sigh than a surge, for the breeze was from the land. There was the occasional cry of a curlew. The cattle in the farm were making a fuss. There was the bleating of lambs and the baaing of sheep. A woodpecker yaffled insistently; a blackbird trilled in the blossoming thorn, and the larks sang as they soared high above me. There were the gruff commands of the farmer to his dog as he walked behind me. The dog came up to me and laid his muzzle on my shoulder, evidently intent on watching what I was up to! He was perhaps the first onlooker in my life to whom I had not felt a belligerent objection . . ."

In the summer of 1959, a long summer and exceedingly hot, Muncaster went on sketching trips to Wales and Newby Bridge at the foot of Lake Windermere. On the way to Wales, he stayed at the "Woolpack" in Warwick (glad to be safe from bombs this time), as he had to make studies of Warwick Castle and the Shakespeare Memorial Theatre at Stratford for the Hadfield's Calendar. He then went on to Criccieth, his chosen painting ground for this particular visit to Wales.

Wednesday, 9 September 1959

"Was much impressed with the country above Criccieth. From the contours of it, with its open, broken foregrounds and background of mountains, I knew this would be most paintable country. If *only* I could see it! But the set-fair heat haze reduced the far distances to milky blue silhouettes, and the middle distances to sickly hues of purple browns in which there was no sparkle or contrast in tonal values. In some respects the country reminded me of Mooi River, in Northern Natal, where we stayed in a house belonging to a friend of my brother during our trip to South Africa. This long summer of 1959 had burnt the landscape to a uniform brownness in which there was no vestige of green."

* * *

Sunday, 20 September

"While at Newby Bridge, I naturally wanted to visit Bardsea; in the first place to see my aunt, Mrs. Stephenson, but also to search for a subject or two in Bardsea Park. I knew almost all the trees had gone, but I thought I might find one group still standing. Indeed, I did; and it was the one of which I painted a watercolour when I was sixteen which was exhibited in the Royal Scottish Academy. This time I spent two evenings on the subject.

"As I made ready to climb over the fence when I had finished work on the second evening to gain the Birkrigg road, I was met by the village bobby.

" 'Ah, Sir,' he said. 'You're perhaps the gentleman who has been causing the local farmer so much worry.'

" 'Oh,' I said, surprised. 'Why?'

" 'Well, Sir, you see, this is private property, and . . .'

" 'Oh dear. I'm terribly sorry,' I replied. 'I never gave it a thought. I've worked up here pretty well since I was a child, you see, and my father before me. You might, perhaps, even have known him, Oliver Hall.'

" 'Oliver Hall!' he exclaimed. 'Say no more!'

"He put a friendly hand on my shoulder and then opened the gate for me.

" 'Oh . . . The stories I could tell you about Oliver . . . I mean Mr. Hall. You know it seems only a little while back that he came knocking at our door one evening and walked right in.' 'I don't suppose,' the policeman said, 'that you could ever teach him anything.'

" 'Not really,' I said; but added that I thought we had both learnt something from each other. My offering, though, had been in very small degree compared with what he had taught me while working in close proximity to him, and by reason of the constructive criticism he had so many times given me. The policeman was brimming with anecdotes. Now he was under way there was no stopping him. Another he recounted concerned Oliver Hall's Morris 8, which became quite famous in the village. 'He must have been one of the world's worst drivers,' said PC Hyde. 'Several times he turned the car upside down. Nobody ever came to any harm, thank goodness.' The constable went on to tell me that my father had become just a little absent-minded towards the end!"

Chapter 14

New Zealand

The winter of 1963 was as bad as any. The snow lay feet deep and icicles spiked down in long transparent fingers from the cottage gutterings. A persistent north wind scattered snow from a lowering sky. The Muncasters began pondering the possibility of a holiday in the sun, or even a cruise; but the idea faded as quickly as the winter afternoon light. Financially it was out of the question.

Then a remarkable thing happened. Alistair McAlpine presented himself on the doorstep at Sutton one day requesting to see what shipping pictures Claude Muncaster had on offer. He was shown round the studio and was delighted with what he saw – several canvases of *Olivebank*, and a number of sketches of other sea subjects. He was making a collection of marine paintings at the time and added these Claude Muncasters to his haul there and then, leaving no one more surprised and delighted than the artist himself. It by no means provided the whole of the money required to get them south of the Equator, but it was a promising start.

By the end of the year, and after further picture sales, the hope of travel was becoming rather more concrete. An important exhibition of paintings had been arranged in New Zealand, together with an extensive painting tour. It was to be a packed programme. 29 November found the Muncasters aboard the P.&O. liner *Oriana*, bound for Australia.

By the time they docked in Melbourne it was Christmas. In the heat and dust, the illuminations and decorations seemed oddly out of key to passengers from a frozen north.

Having spent Christmas in Melbourne, they left by air for Auckland on 28 December.

There at the airport, they were met by Allan Swinton, Director of the John Leech Gallery, who took them to his home in Auckland. Swinton warned Muncaster that he would be expected to talk to the Art Societies in Auckland, and that there were Press interviews arranged for the morrow on both radio and television. He told him, too, that it had so far been a cold unsettled summer, which was pleasing as it suggested that he might get some painter's weather.

The John Leech Gallery, Muncaster found was not, in fact, ideal for picture hanging. The white washed walls were very uneven. It was decided to obtain some large sheets of off-white material and suspend these from an improvised picture rail to act as backing for the paintings. The final effect was satisfying and, after the usual scramble to get things framed in time, both oils and watercolours looked well.

The show was opened by Sir Henry Kelliher who owned a chain of breweries in New Zealand and was a patron of the arts. The gallery was packed, and by the end of the evening the majority of the pictures had been sold. There were cases when people queued up for the same picture. Sir Henry, saying he wanted to give the exhibition a good start, purchased six large watercolours. He later invited the Muncasters to stay with him.

On 6 February 1964, the Muncasters left Auckland for home in the P&O liner *Arcadia*. The venture in the sunshine had surpassed all expectations. What was more, he carried an invitation from Sir Henry Kelliher to return a year later to judge the Kelliher Art Prize which had now become a major annual event in New Zealand.

* * *

On his return to Wellington in June the following year Muncaster was invited by Sir Henry to select and arrange the pictures for exhibition, judge them and award the prizes. He had also been commissioned to paint twelve oils of New Zealand subjects and had undertaken to complete these in the period between the two visits.

When he arrived at the hotel after the long and tedious flight from London, he asked if he might be left in peace for an hour or two for a bath and a little sleep. He managed the bath, but immediately afterwards was beset by the Press, radio and television which kept him busy until lunch-time when he had to join a luncheon party which had been arranged in his honour. It would have been discourteous not to have attended, but it was all he could do to make sensible conversation. Back at the hotel he was to be besieged by more Press representatives. By now he was so tired that, realising that he had made a complete nonsense of the last interview, he had to ask the reporter not to print the story.

"After a bite of supper, I went to my bedroom where the management had very kindly installed a television set so that I could see how I had fared with the journalists. After a few minutes I fell asleep and awoke to see myself on the screen saying: 'My father considered much of modern art to be a cancerous growth from the underworld, and I must confess that in large measure I agree with him.' I then went off into deep sleep again."

The National Gallery at Wellington where the exhibition was to be held was a fine main gallery and afforded ample space for a number of the pictures sent in. Muncaster adopted his usual procedure for selection and hanging; two classes – rejections and doubtfuls. Only from the group of doubtfuls would pictures be finally selected and hung. Then, only after the exhibition had been hung would the prizes and awards be decided upon.

"This method was contrary to general practice where the prize pictures were selected first and then all hung on one wall. That did not appeal to me. I pointed out that the best effect was achieved by placing the most suitable pictures alongside each other so that each was shown off to its best advantage, while at the same time a general overall and tidy arrangement was maintained. This idea had the further attraction of keeping the interest alive all the way round the exhibition. It was my opinion, too, that the best judgement of any picture from the award angle came from seeing it hung amidst a variety of works containing a variety of subject matter, colours and techniques. A picture of particular merit would stand out more readily in such surroundings."

Having made his awards he also had to make a speech, which once again caused him an acute attack of nerves. He urged that artists should make full use of their powers of observation. In New Zealand particularly, where the landscape was so fine, they had plenty worth observing. His worry was that they would turn away from "God's Own Country" as their natural source of inspiration, or that their painting might come too easily. He suggested in most cases a much more careful study of the objects observed to draw out their particular and individual characteristics. He continued:

"As for us artists, it is just as well to remind ourselves from time to time that we are privileged people to be allowed to live the life of creative artists. We have to remember that we have been given the gift of expression, each one of us saying what we have to say in an individual way. We are, in fact, communicators. But in order to communicate our message we must learn the grammar, so that what we do have to say is clearly expressed and will be of benefit to others. It is a sheer waste of time to put into the world incomprehensible language which nobody can understand – not even the artists themselves.

"This, then, is our responsibility – to improve our gift of expression to the fullest capacity. We must learn to draw, and develop our craft, always bearing in mind with humility that we are mediums of expression derived from a source of power much greater than ourselves.

"But perhaps the most privileged of artists are the landscape and marine painters, because their work and their studies take them out before nature; and you can't be long communing with nature before you become conscious of her wonderful balance of forces, her restorative qualities and her beauty. She is continuously working miracles around us if we will but take the trouble to notice."

After his spell in New Zealand, he sailed to Durban to meet Primrose, my wife Iona and me. We had sailed out separately, by way of a holiday, while he had a painting commission to do for the Union Castle line. Sir Nicholas Cayzer wanted a painting of the new *Southampton Castle* entering Durban, after her maiden voyage.

There was no doubt that he needed a complete rest after the New Zealand trip, but no sooner had we all met up in Durban than he was working on and worrying about the Union Castle picture. Indeed, he began the search for a suitable background for it almost at once. But he was thrilled and sustained by the prospect of the voyage home and several weeks' relaxation aboard ship, while he researched the Durban dockland area, sketching and taking notes.

With a lot of work done, on the night before departure he turned in late, very weary, but full of pleasurable anticipation.

By three in the morning, however, he was awake again, and lying in his bunk pondering and worrying. Had he done everything to explore all possible viewpoints for the picture? There was still just one angle he had not considered. Surely, from the upper floor of the Union Castle offices near the edge of the docks there would be a most interesting high view of the harbour scene. Why hadn't he thought of that before? He worked out that the light would be best for this particular aspect during the afternoon, and decided that there would be just time to slip ashore and take a couple of photographs after the official luncheon on board to which they had been invited.

The following morning, he was to have a curious encounter.

Another glorious day, sunny and windless, Durban's weather at its best. He went ashore early and strolled around the docks clicking colour shots with a Polaroid camera by way of taking a few reminders of harbour scenes. Perhaps there would be some subjects for future pictures. A ship had just come in from the Far East and was berthed a little astern of the *Pendennis Castle*. He was intrigued by the colourful saris and the display of colours against the more drab background of the ship. While he was taking some shots he noticed a tall man in crash helmet and leather boots observing him with obvious interest. After a while he approached and fell into conversation, asking about the Polaroid camera, and wanting to know what sort of results it gave. My father replied that the colour he got was only a guide and far too mechanical as far as he was concerned. He only used photographs for reference: when there was time, he far preferred to sketch on the spot.

"I'm a crane driver by profession," said the stranger, "but I'm very interested in painting. I have a bit of a problem, though. A little time back, I was painting a picture of a sailing ship in a rough sea. My little daughter was ill at the time and I hadn't finished the picture before she died. My wife liked the painting, and for sentimental reasons connected with our little girl she wouldn't let me part with it. Naturally, I was pretty upset about it all and didn't do any more painting for a bit.

"Then, being so keen, I started on another painting, and before I'd finished it, my father-in-law died suddenly. So again, I kept off painting for a while. Then, when I did start on another one, my brother was drowned at sea. I'm telling you, man, this is God's truth! Anyway, I didn't like to start painting again. I was getting a bit scared. But after a few weeks, I thought, well . . . you know, it's only coincidence. I was so keen on painting, you see. I sort of couldn't help myself. I couldn't resist starting on something else. Now, I know you won't believe this, but about half-way through that picture, my best friend was crushed to death by a shunting truck in the docks. What do you make of that?"

His listener could only reply that if he really valued his family and friends, he'd better stop painting.

"Ah, maybe," said the crane driver sadly. "But you know, I'm just too damned keen on this painting business to give it up. Do you think I should go to art school, perhaps. Have some lessons?"

The artist began to answer but a dock official came to move them on, saying they were just about to do some unloading there; and this remarkable exchange was terminated. By evening, Claude Muncaster was to find himself wondering if the crane driver had perhaps begun art lessons that very afternoon.

The official luncheon was finished by 3 o'clock, and Muncaster sought out the Union Castle company's secretary, Mr Tilley. Would he take him ashore to the company's offices so that he could take a last photo? Mrs Muncaster, however, was quite horrified to hear what he was going to do and implored him not to go. But Mr. Tilley was reassuring. "We'll have him safely back in good time; don't worry, Mrs Muncaster."

But half an hour later, walking alone round the promenade deck of the *Pendennis Castle*, Mrs. Muncaster was worrying. And as the minutes ticked off into the last hour before sailing, that womanly instinct of which we men should take much more account, began to form into a terrible reality. Where were they?

The Union Castle's freight offices in which Mr. Tilley worked did offer a marvellous view out over the harbour. Some of the big ships turned there, almost within a stone's throw, and if the *Southampton Castle* was placed in this position in the painting she would be shown off in a stupendous setting.

But not from ground level. A high angle was needed to get a view over the top of the ship and away to the docks and landscape behind. Perhaps there was a window upstairs which faced the right way? Mr. Tilley showed Muncaster to the top floor to a window which might fit the bill. So it would have done if the flags hadn't been there, blowing out from tall flagstaffs at each corner of the balcony below and showing off the Union Castle colours. They completely obscured the view. A photograph was impossible. There was only one way of getting the picture and this was from the balcony beneath the flags. It would be a bit of a drop and a climb back, but he hadn't been round the Horn in a windjammer for nothing.

Mr. Tilley was persuaded, and opened the window. Muncaster heaved himself up and made ready to jump down but suddenly slipped on the sill, lost his balance and fell all the way down to the balcony. He landed with a sickening crack on his left heel. In great pain he managed to get on to his hands and knees and do some deep breathing, which prevented him from passing out.

A chair was eventually brought to support him. While Mr. Tilley was arranging for an ambulance, he insisted on being manoeuvred into position to take the photograph he wanted.

When the ambulance arrived there were no stretchers, and he had to be lifted, bodily, back up through the window, put into another hard chair and carried downstairs to the street. Not only was he in agony, but his anxiety mounted as he realised that catching the ship was going to be impossible. It transpired that he had smashed his left femur and badly damaged his heel. (The resulting emergency operation also revealed a weak heart which was to become an increasing cause for concern.)

Mrs. Muncaster was recalled from the ship with minutes to go before sailing. White-faced and distraught she watched the ship sail, carrying almost all their belongings. There had hardly been time to snatch even a night case.

Iona and I had made our homeward journey by air; only to be met by a phone call within twenty minutes of arriving. Within hours I was on my way back to South Africa to assist with his return.

But for Claude Muncaster there was another side to this unhappy saga. Sometimes, when one is on the verge of consciousness (for example at the moment of waking from sleep) there comes a flash of spiritual insight, which in itself is closer to reality than either sleeping or waking. While being taken into the operating theatre in Durban, he wrote: "I lay waiting in full consciousness. Then they finally took me up and I was for quite a time in the room adjoining the theatre. I could not see into it, but I could hear the preparations going on. It was during this wait that I think I must have been in a kind of semi-consciousness. I remember thinking it rather astonishing that at the moment disaster struck and I knew that I'd seriously injured myself and what must be in store for me, I was aware of no feeling of fear. Rather the opposite. I felt there were spiritual beings cushioning me on all sides. I remember too, that these feelings were accompanied by a strange vision which remains clearly in my mind as I write even a long time later. I saw myself in a rather darkened room in the centre of which there were a number of acolytes in red skull caps, surrounding what I believed to be a long table; though this was hidden from sight by the acolytes standing round it. At the head of the table was a tall figure dressed in white who seemed to radiate light. From the table also there seemed to radiate another, though lesser, light. I felt quite certain there was a being on the table and that being was myself. This vision gave me a feeling of wonderful security. I now just longed for the injection which would release me from pain and allow me to pass into peaceful oblivion."

above: Clear Morning, Rhum and Eigg, 1937: *watercolour*.

below: Petworth from the Gog: *oil*.

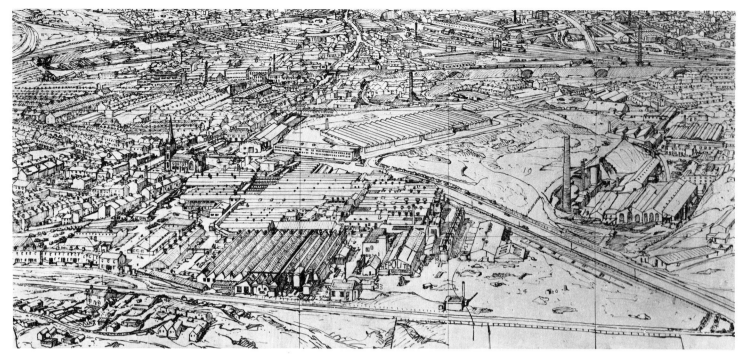

above: Detail of drawing of the Hepworth & Grandage Works: *pen and ink*.

below: Luton Hoo; from H.R.H. Prince Philip's helicopter: *watercolour*.

Chapter 15

Through a Glass Darkly

Although I saw all too little of him during his last years, I was keenly aware of the problems and tremendous professional challenge which now faced him. His grit on that tense journey home had been an inspiration. Most of those who came into contact with him were pretty soon smiling or laughing. Crippled as he was, he still managed to see the ridiculous in a situation.

He laid great store on the freedom he would have when he was rid of the plaster. He thought he really would be able to get around. I remember he set off for Haslemere Hospital on the appointed day in great spirits to have the plaster removed. But without the support of the plaster, he found walking even more difficult and painful than before and he became dependent on his crutches for movement. He insisted on struggling over to the studio to start work long before he should sensibly have done so. This put great strain on the equilibrium of the household. There were other commissions on his mind, in fact, apart from the *Southampton Castle* picture. He was quite determined to deliver on time.

"The works I had been called upon to do each had about them a great deal of detail, requiring much precision which in itself demands absolute control of hand and brush. Although not such large works as the 'View of the City,' they each needed similar arrangements of devices and materials before the canvas was firmly on the table and ready to work on. Even in full physical command of one's limbs, this preparation takes time, some strength and considerable activity. To have to do this under conditions of extreme physical disability and pain called upon all my resources, and there were many times when I sweated in agony in my efforts to reach some piece of equipment which was essential to my needs. Often I had to think out some way of obtaining it without having to get to my feet. I discovered that a crutch could act as an effective puller or pusher, and that two used together made a very practical grappler. Beyond all this, I had to find some way of sitting which was sufficiently relaxed to allow me to work. Many artists stand at their work, even when painting in water-colour. I was thankful that at least this was never my own practice. I could not have stood for short spells, let alone the long periods needed for the work I was doing now."

But it was not until 6 July, just a year after the accident, that he was able to walk without a stick; though this was still a painful proceeding. There had been many times in the past year when he had almost given up hope. He had started out with such optimism, imagining himself soon back on the lawn, striding up and down with the mower, or walking the golf course again. But he dreamed.

One of the priorities in the studio was a painting of *Southampton Castle*, not at Durban, but in the Solent off Cowes. This picture was to be presented to Princess Alexandra who had launched the ship. The launching had been a particularly happy occasion, and Sir Nicholas Cayzer (who commissioned the painting) had decided that some picture of commemoration would be the best way of showing the company's appreciation. The ship steaming past Cowes with the Royal Yacht in the background seemed appropriate.

The greatest problem about this commission was getting workable pictorial references of the Cowes background. Muncaster spoke about it at the time, saying that he never did get what he really needed and that his imagination was stretched to the full. He certainly found this picture quite a headache to paint. But judging from the appreciative letter he received from the Princess, the result was evidently successful.

The oil of the *Southampton Castle* entering Durban presented many problems. He had photographs, but had never actually seen the ship in that situation. Again his imaginative powers and sense of scale and perspective were very fully stretched. He did not, in the end, choose the view from the Union Castle offices; though this decision had nothing to do with crane drivers or falling out of windows. The view from the Bluff (land stretching out to sea by the harbour mouth) turned out to serve his purpose much better. The complications were manifold. He did not know how big the ship would appear in relation to her surroundings, or how much background would be blanked out by her form. But he could not be content unless he had overcome all the problems and presented a picture of correct proportions while displaying a reality of form and effect.

He started the work on 4 February 1967 and completed it on 10 April. BBC television gave it a showing which he found encouraging, and Sir Nicholas seemed very pleased with the finished article. So that story at least, had a happy ending.

Meantime, his leg was improving slowly, and he was getting about quite well. But something else was giving him far more concern now than the leg – his eyesight. He was beginning to have great difficulty in seeing on the easel what he had painted on the table. When he stepped back to judge the general effect, he could not see it with any clarity. A cataract was forming, but his eye specialist was not keen to operate until the cataract was fully developed, and it would be quite some months before surgery was possible. One eye was in better shape than the other, so it was hoped that the good one would not deteriorate further and enable him to keep working. The professional medical advice was that he should live his life on a much quieter note.

Regardless of this advice, he began arranging a major exhibition, perhaps the most important of his life. By the spring of 1969 he had completed various further commissions together with a large canvas of the new supertanker *Ardtaraig*, at Finnart, Loch Long painted for Lord Geddes.

Now he started to paint watercolours to help swell the collection of works he was gathering together for the coming exhibition. It was to be held at the Arun Art Centre, in Arundel, Sussex, and was to be a show which spanned his life's work as a professional artist. It was his own personal Jubilee and entitled "Fifty Years a Painter," and he was determined that the exhibition should make its mark before he went into hospital for the eye operation.

Muncaster had to take the main decisions for the framing and hanging, and to organise moving the pictures from Sutton to Arundel. The Art Centre was a tall, compact building with exhibition rooms on several floors, so apart from heaving heavy pictures in and out of the car, he was then helping to cart them up three flights of stairs. This was not quite what the doctor had ordered.

The show, which opened on 13 October 1969, attracted considerable publicity. The pressures increased. There was a private view, the opening speech, Press interviews and photo sessions, television and radio interviews; and correspondence by the mound. During the days of the exhibition came the shifting packs of people, many of whom wanted a word with the artist, often just to ask advice about their own technique of painting. On one occasion when I went along myself to see how things were going, I found a queue trailing down the street outside the Gallery. Inside, the mob of purchasers and interested visitors was such that it was really quite difficult to get a view of the pictures. Red spots went up so fast that the Gallery owners had to ask him to supply more works so that there would still be something for sale. He had to go back to the studio and sort out some sketches from the cupboard; no time for mounting or framing. These mostly went the way of the red spot, too.

It was an exciting time, and Muncaster's spirits were lifted high.

I had been working on the overnight news shift at Broadcasting House during a cold November 1969. Just after 9 a.m. I was free and decided to go down to Moorfields Eye Hospital to be there while the operation was being performed. There was no chance of seeing him beforehand, but at least I would be on the spot if there were any problems. But the operation had started a little before schedule, and I had a good hour to wait before the anaesthetist came in to report.

"I'm afraid we've had a bit of a time. He had cardiac arrest on the operating table and we had to give emergency resuscitation. Fortunately some heart specialists happened to be in the Hospital and we managed to call them to the theatre in time. I think he'll be all right. There's no reason why he shouldn't live quite actively for a number of years."

"And the eye?"

"We also think that will be fine; but it was a close thing. The surgeon had just one stitch to go when the heart stopped and he had to decide whether to lose the eye and save his life, or save the eye. In the event, both were saved."

I was suddenly moved. Prayers *had* been answered.

They had hoped to operate on the other eye the following week, but in the light of what had happened said that in no circumstances would he be put under another anaesthetic. Perhaps the other eye would not get worse.

So he came home, and once more to his bed. It was a shock to him to find that when the cataract was removed the focusing apparatus went, too, and he could see nothing out of the left eye but blurred light. It only occurred to him then that had they operated on his right eye at the same time he would suddenly have been totally blind. As it was, he experimented with contact lenses for the left eye, but it was several months before he found one which gave him good all round vision. Even this was only effective for about two hours a day. After that, mucus formed in the eye and no matter how often he cleaned the lens it made no difference.

"I now see life, as it were, through a basin of soapy water. Frequently I have double vision and, for instance, may see two spoons on the table, and am surprised to find that the one I try and pick up doesn't exist."

Meanwhile, the heart condition was also worsening. By 1971 he was spending long periods in bed and needed constant nursing. Yet still during the times when he was up and about, he was managing to explore another outlet. We worked together on a number of weekly series of "Thoughts for the Day," five minute meditative talks broadcast each morning on BBC Radio 4. He wrote and spoke the "Thought" and I helped by reading a piece of poetry or prose of his choice to supplement his word pictures. He was astonished and touched by the response to these broadcasts. He had hundreds of letters of appreciation and answered every one himself. Sometimes he was feeling so ill when a series was due that I had to go down to Sutton with a tape recorder and work with him in the moments he felt better enough to speak firmly. The producer's secretary even typed out his scripts for him in capital letters to help him see the words. People still speak to me of those broadcasts all these years later, so he must have got something through.

He had for quite some time been deeply interested in the subject of healing. This is less surprising, considering that he felt that painting could have a very definite therapeutic value. Every time he heard of someone who was ill or suffering in any way, he would add them to his private list for prayer. He used to sit in quiet prayer and meditation for an hour or so in the peace of his studio before he started work in the mornings. I can well remember hearing him slip quietly downstairs, perhaps as early as five o'clock, as I lay comfortably in bed. He never spoke of this outside the family as he stressed always that if anyone was miraculously better, he had no proof that his intercession had anything to do with it. He told me

above: *Southampton Castle* entering Durban: *oil*.
(By courtesy of the Union Castle Mail Steamship Co. Ltd.)

below: The artist at work on a waterfront at Littlehampton.

that when he sat in these periods of prayer, he worked through his list, imagining each person in full, brimming health, while at the same time surrounding them with a feeling of light and compassion.

There were certainly a number of extraordinary recoveries, but he would assert, "We do have to be very careful about all this, though, because who is to know who is really a healer? Maybe one day the true healers and the doctors will work together."

After his eye operation, he was advised by a specialist to spend a fortnight under intensive nursing to try to prevent the need for heart surgery. He responded quite well to treatment in King Edward VIIth Hospital in London, and just managed to avoid yet another operation. To recuperate, they went on a trip to South Africa in *Windsor Castle*. Soon after returning from this trip a clot of blood lodged in his lung and he was rushed to the King Edward VIIth Sanatorium at Midhurst. This was his thirteenth sojourn in hospital. At times he felt so wretched that he feared to go on.

But things did improve. After his return from Midhurst the doctors seemed to get his pill regime about right – at one point he was taking seventeen different pills a day – and on some days he was really quite perky. He managed to keep writing, too. These closing thoughts came from his pen just ten days before he died . . .

"To the outsider, it must seem that my life can give me little joy. Certainly, it has its frustrations. But I am seldom depressed, for my acceptance and awareness of there being a reason for all things keeps me reasonably buoyant.

"I painted my last picture in 1969. I was told I was painting in brighter colours. I did not realise then I was looking through a yellow fog and so had to paint things brighter to satisfy my colour sense. The same thing happened to Turner, and more recently to Matthew Smith. Although the artistic intellectuals will tell you that Turner's last period of uninterpretable subject matter was Turner at his best, I never approved of their assumption. This later Turner seemed to me so alien to all I admired in that great painter's works.

"Though I can't paint now, at least I can just see to write and am able to express something of what I feel and think. I can hardly see anything of our superb view, but I know it is there and I am thankful. I miss not being able to see flowers properly and cannot enjoy my wife's flower arrangements. I know that I am exceptionally fortunate in the love I receive from my family.

"I find that many of the things I like are the old and established things. I revere the great masters of the arts. I pay homage to culture and philosophy. I derive immense pleasure, or did when I could properly see them, from the vast stretches of nature unsullied by man-made noise, by chain saw, the bulldozer and pollution. I love beauty of every kind, and such simple beauty as nature provides. I admire those who meet suffering with fortitude. I welcome the qualities of humility, love and compassion. I welcome the qualities which shine from young people, but which never make the headlines. If only more would realise the joy it brings to the old and lonely to have a fresh young visitor.

"I get the feeling that many are searching for, and desiring a belief which will give them hope and purpose, which will teach them that death is not the end. At the moment it seems that God is a God of science and technology. The spiritual dimension doesn't seem to get much of a look in. Man can and does take credit for some amazing achievements, and the speed of discovery is extraordinary. In my own span of seventy years the advances have been enormous. Whereas I used to go to school by horse and trap, now they put men on the moon. Such achievements are beyond praise, but I fear that instead of probing space for peaceful purposes, man will develop a technology of space for the conduct of wars.

"I do not believe that the world will be destroyed. There may be great disasters, and continents may disappear (as it is said Atlantis disappeared when man became too clever); but we may need such disaster before we will acknowledge there is a law which is Divine and cannot be changed. There is the inescapable law of cause and effect. Just as we put pencil to paper, we cannot help but draw a portrait of ourselves. It would be as well for artists to remember this and study objectively what they have portrayed.

"What I see and say has been seen and said a million times already. The only difference is the way in which I have said it. This may be the only contribution anyone can make: the personal and individual one. This is even more important when the trend is to denude us of individuality and clothe us uniformly as state numbers.

"As to death, I do not fear it. I think of my own death mostly perhaps in terms of the nature of it – whether it will be peaceful or painful. I trust my own may be peaceful.

"I now see things much less clearly, yet in my mind the vision of the future is brilliant and crystal clear. I feel like Alice in Wonderland who looked through the little door on to a beautiful garden, but found herself too large to get through. As the flesh withers, the spirit surely lives on, and there are no barriers to its journeyings save for the barriers of one's own thoughts.

"Apart from my having no fear of death, I shall still welcome a helping hand to see me through. For it is said that just as each one of us has a guardian angel, so to each of us comes somebody to help us over the last stile. But once I am over, I know that a door will open on to a new loveliness and freshness of colour, form, and light, which is something far more beautiful than anything I have ever seen here or even imagined."

As the years went by, I suppose I matured somewhat, and I saw much about me of a new form of art which seemed completely divorced from Nature as I knew her and loved her, and I began to question my own approach. Was something wrong with me, or Nature, that other artists were painting her and all else in terms which made all objects they painted completely unrecognisable? Were my ideas about Nature and beauty just so much old hat? Ought not I, too, to become a little bit more with it; forget the Old Masters, tradition and all that, and direct my art into channels which were more materialistic and modern in concept?

All this led me into a period of rather painful heart-searching.

But the idea that art was ageless still persisted. I just could not resist natural beauty, and the more painters and musicians became, to my way of thinking, less and less attuned to Nature but at the same time were acclaimed by the critics as progressive, the greater revulsion I felt for their ugly interpretations. I could have followed this trend and lost my identity, but I didn't.

Instead, I turned again to Nature and continued to study, and eventually re-discovered just one or two of the simplest laws which Nature has to offer.

Not one single scientific invention could have come into being without the forces and resources of Nature. She is the mainstay of our existence, and I believe some contemplation of her from time to time can do us no harm. As an artist I have learned to appreciate some of her laws and beauties, and have long since come to regard her as the greatest visual manifestation on earth of the Divine.

INDEX